BEST CHOICES
IN THE NATION'S CAPITAL
WASHINGTON, D.C.

The District of Columbia, Alexandria, Arlington, Fairfax County, Montgomery County, and Prince George's County

By DANIEL WEBSTER HERLONG

PUBLISHED IN THE UNITED STATES OF AMERICA

Best Choices Staff:

Allan Diede — Publisher
Maryann Huk — Executive Editor
Sunie Barr Clark — Managing Editor

Field Staff:

Miles T. Dalton — Production Manager
Ellen Brown, Lisa Grayson — Interviewers

Contributing Writers:

Michael Dolan, Tom Hovis, Susan Kenney, Maurine Kenney Salvatore, Julie Dillingham and the 1st, 3rd, 4th and 7th Grades at the All Saints School in Manassas Virginia

Rita Haines — Fitness Consultant

Monongahela Publishing

Editorial Staff:
Barbara Barkley, Laurie Martin

Administration:
Patricia Dailey, Marcy Wasilko

Art Work:

Christopher Wrenn Herlong — Artist
Michael O. Cutruzzula, Paul Van Deusen — Cover layout and maps

Library of Congress Number 90-063830
ISBN Number: 1-877912-08-5 First Edition: 1991

Best Choice Series:

Best Choices on the Oregon Coast (not in print)
Best Choices in Portland
Best Choices in Southern California / Bay Area Edition
Best Choices in Northern California
Best Choices in Western Washington
Best Choices in Orange County
Best Choices in Arizona
Best Choices in Colorado
Best Choices in San Diego
Best Choices in Sacramento
Best Choices in the Tampa Bay Area
Best Choices in Central and Southeast Texas
Best Choices in the Seattle-Tacoma Area
Best Choices in Eastern Washington
Best Choices in New Mexico
Best Choices in Alaska
Best Choices in Idaho
Best Choices in Los Angeles
Best Choices on the California Coast
Best Choices in St. Louis
Best Choices in Atlanta
Best Choices in Utah
Best Choices in Ohio
Best Choices in Pittsburgh and Western Pennsylvania
Best Choices Along the Great Lakes
    Vol. 1, Lake Erie and Lake Ontario
Best Choices in Eastern Pennsylvania
Best Choices in the Nation's Capital (Washington, D.C.)

For additional copies, write or call:
Monongahela Publishing
541 Fifth Avenue
McKeesport, PA 15132
1-800-777-9930

This book is dedicated to my Grandfather, Raymond Gordon Clark, Sr. As a native of the Nation's Capital, he has witnessed much of its changes and development during his ninety-five years. His support has been a very important part of this project. It is also dedicated to the good people of the Greater Metropolitan Area, whose efforts and support made it all worthwhile.

Acknowledgements

I wish to acknowledge the tremendous teamwork of the staffs of Best Choices, Monongahela Publishing and Regal Direct Publishing. Special thanks to Sunie Clark. Without her dedication and sleepless nights, this project could not have been a success. Many have contributed and all have my heartfelt appreciation.

DISCLAIMER

Not all, but many of the businesses featured in "Best Choices" have subscribed to the project in advance of publication. Their participation in promoting this book includes acquiring copies of this publication for their own business purposes. This subscription was not mandatory for inclusion, and promotional consideration alone is not enough for selection as a "Best Choice." Most of these "Best Choices" were recommended by other "Best Choices," including those in the same category of business. All "Best Choices" were personally visited by one of our Travel Writers, and our report on each one is based on first-hand experience.

FOREWORD

During the last 200 years, America's Hometown has developed into a sophisticated "Capital City" that radiates power and might. It is a city that belongs to all the citizens of the United States and it is shared with all those who visit from foreign lands. Washington, D.C. is a city to be taken seriously as the seat of a major world government. But also a place to be enjoyed--rich with culture, history and entertainment. As you peruse the selections and read the stories, realize that a complete listing of all the Best Choices in the Nation's Capital would be an impossible task, but those listed are some of the best of the best. Things change, people come and go--so the information in this book is in a constant state of flux. Every effort was made, at the time of printing, to assure quality and accuracy, but if you, the reader, find wrong information, have suggestions about how we can make the book better, or know of Best Choices we should include, please drop us a line.

Meanwhile, be our guest and enjoy the terrific Best Choice opportunities for inspiration, learning, dining, accommodations, shopping and fun.

TABLE OF CONTENTS

Germantown
Middlebrook
Mt. Zion
Brookeville
117
Old Germantown
118
107
Redland
Olney
Gaithersburg
MONTGOMERY
CO.
Dawsonville
Quince
Orchard
Norbeck
28
Sugarland
Darnestown
355
Hunting Hill
Layhill
Aspen Hill
Seneca
River
Travilah
Rockville
586
Glenmont
189
270
Shady Oak
190
Potomac
97
846
38
36
34,35
31
Dranesville
Great Falls
495
355
33
185
228
Colvin Run
Cropley
40
39
Bethesda
Chevy
Chase
41
Reston
267
TOLL
7
193
14
13
3
4
5
602
7,8
267
9,12
McLean
Tysons Corner
11
WASHIN
FAIRFAX
CO.
123
10
665
Vienna
495
20
24
25
Navy
Oakton
19
22
23
66
9,18
Falls Church
17
ARLINGTON
CO.
Pender
15
16
66
29
Seven
Corners
Merrifield
50
50
14
Fairfax
8
7
Baileys
Crossroads
395
244
6
6
4
5
Annandale
236
Fairfax
Station
Alexandria
3
Clifton
Burke
495
2
95
2
3
1
Springfield 1,4,58
123
57
Franconia
Groveton
Newington
56
Hybla Valley
Potomac
River

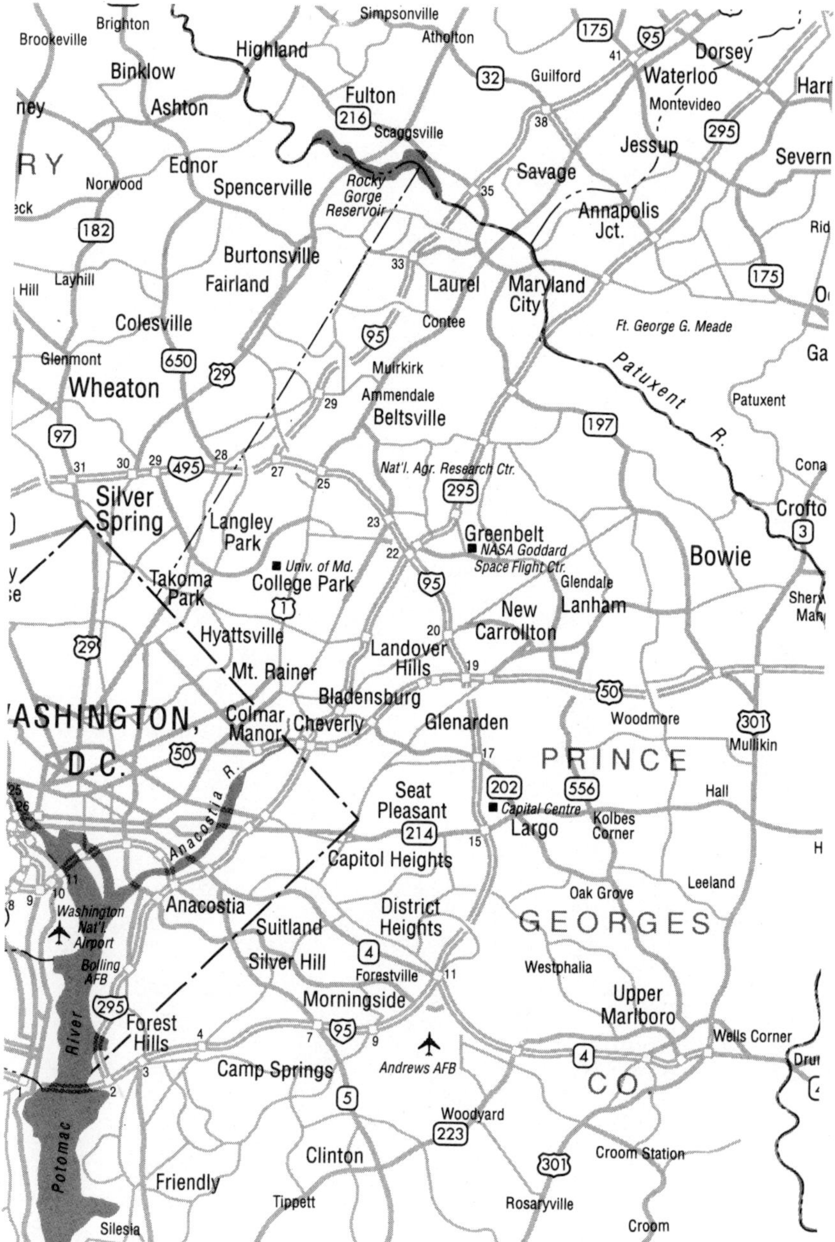

Simpsonville
Brighton
Brookeville
Atholton
175
95
Highland
Dorsey
Binklow
41
32
Guilford
Waterloo
Ashton
Fulton
Montevideo
216
Scaggsville
38
295
Jessup
Severn
Ednor
Savage
Norwood
Spencerville
Rocky Gorge Reservoir
35
Annapolis Jct.
182
Burtonsville
33
175
Layhill
Fairland
Laurel
Maryland City
Colesville
Contee
Ft. George G. Meade
95
Glenmont
650
Muirkirk
Patuxent R.
Wheaton
29
Ammendale
Patuxent
29
Beltsville
97
197
31
30
29
495
28
27
Nat'l. Agr. Research Ctr.
25
Silver Spring
295
Langley Park
23
Greenbelt
NASA Goddard Space Flight Ctr.
3
22
Univ. of Md.
Bowie
Takoma Park
College Park
95
Glendale
1
New Carrollton
Lanham
Hyattsville
20
29
Landover Hills
Mt. Rainer
19
Bladensburg
50
Colmar Manor
Cheverly
Glenarden
Woodmore
301
Mullikin
50
D.C.
17
PRINCE
Anacostia R.
202
556
Seat Pleasant
Hall
Capital Centre
25
26
Kolbes Corner
214
Largo
15
Capitol Heights
Leeland
11
Oak Grove
10
9
8
Washington Nat'l. Airport
Anacostia
District Heights
Suitland
GEORGES
Silver Hill
4
Bolling AFB
Westphalia
Forestville
11
Upper Marlboro
295
Morningside
Forest Hills
River
4
7
95
9
Wells Corner
Andrews AFB
4
3
Camp Springs
CO.
1
2
5
Woodyard
223
Clinton
Potomac
301
Croom Station
Friendly
Tippett
Rosaryville
Silesia
Croom

BITS AND TIPS FOR TRAVELERS

It is said that Pierre L'Enfant became angered and left the newly developing Federal City to fend for itself. One of his associates finished a great deal of the work without benefit of plans. Another interesting facet of the story is that the bill for planning the city amounted to $95,000! It seems that eight years later he accepted $2,500 from Congress. He died in poverty in 1825.

Thomas Jefferson and John Adams died on the same day, 50 years after they signed the Declaration of Independence.

The oldest house in Washington, D.C. was built in 1765 and it still stands on its original ground at 3051 M Street, N.W. (202) 426-6851).

It was 1968 before District of Columbia residents were allowed to vote in a presidential election.

In 1896, the first automobile was driven down Pennsylvania Avenue.

Georgetown University was founded in 1789. It was the first university in Washington and the first Catholic University in the United States.

Julia Ward Howe wrote "The Battle Hymn of the Republic" while at the Willard Hotel. When Abraham Lincoln heard it played, he wept. No one agonized more over the War Between the States than he.

area trivia

1. Who was the first president to be inaugurated in Washington, D.C.?
2. What was the name of the woman presidential candidate who opened her campaign in Laurel, MD.?
3. The Bill of Rights were taken from a list written by a Virginia citizen. Name the citizen.
4. What was the original name of Rockville, MD?
5. Which Potomac River Bridge is the oldest in D.C.?

Answers:
1. Thomas Jefferson.
2. Belva Ann Lockwood, in the year 1884.
3. George Mason.
4. Williamsburg.
5. Chain Bridge.

tips

If you are from out of town, it could be very beneficial to write your Congressman or Senator approximately five months prior to your visit. You might be pleasantly surprised to get some special VIP passes to such attractions as the Capitol, White House, FBI Building, Kennedy Center or the House or Senate. Your Representative's address is: US House of Representatives, Washington, DC, 20515 and the Senator's is US Senate, Washington, DC, 20510.

Visitors from other countries can benifit by contacting the International Visitors Information Service, 733 15th St.,NW; Tel: (202) 347-0101. This is a volunteer organization that can help visitors in their native tongue.

The Washington Post newspaper has a Friday center section that will give you current information concerning times and dates of local happinings. Washington DC also has the "Where" Magazine that can be most useful and a "GO Nation's Capitol" Magazine that is small but a good source of current events.

The Ticket Place often has half-price day-of-show tickets. call TICKETS Hrs: Tue. - Fri. 12 Noon -Sat. 11a.m. -5 p.m.

The Washington, DC, Convention and Visitors Association, 1212 New York Ave. NW, Sixth Floor, Washington , DC, 20004; Tel: (202) 789-7000. They are here to assist.

The Washington Information Center, on Pennsylvania Ave. between 14th and 15th Sts.; Tel: (202) 789-7000

The Travelers Aid Society, 1015 12th St. NW; (202) 347-0101. These people will help if you have a problem.

Known throughout Washington by its trademark green-and-orange trolley, **OLD TOWN TROLLEY TOURS** may begin at any one of 17 locations. A fully narrated, 90-minute tour of Washington includes Capitol Hill, Georgetown, and the Washington National Cathedral. Guests may choose to stay aboard for the entire tour, or disembark at any of 12 stops and reboard at a choice of 20-minute intervals. A tour of Alexandria includes 17 points of interest. Open daily, 9:00 a.m. - 6:00 p.m. (202) 269-3021

Authorized by the National Park Service and offering the only mobile tour of Arlington National Cemetery, **TOURMOBILE SIGHTSEEING** is one of the most convenient ways to see Washington. A fully narrated tour will take you to over 300 points of interest with stops at 18 major attractions, including The White House, Kennedy Center, Arlington National Cemetery, and the Vietnam Veterans Memorial. Shuttles run 20 minutes apart, and passengers are free to depart at any stop and reboard later at no extra charge. Tickets may be purchased at any of the stops. Tourmobiles exclusive tour of Arlington National Cemetery includes the Kennedy Gravesites, the Robert E. Lee Memorial, and the Changing of the Guard at the Tomb of the Unknowns. In addition to the Washington and Arlington tours, Tourmobile offers narrated tours to Mount Vernon and the Frederick Douglass Historic Site. Tours daily. (202) 554-7950

local phone numbers to have on hand...

Police, Ambulance, Fire	911
TY/TDD	(202) 727-9334
Emergency	8DC-HELP or 832-4357
All Night Drugstore	(202) 785-1466
	(202) 628-0720
D.C. Hotline	(202) 223-2255
Montgomery County Hotline	(301) 738-2255
Northern Virginia Hotline	(703) 527-4077
Washington, D.C. C.O.C	(202) 347-7201
Convention & Visitors Center	(202) 789-7000
Daily Happenings On Tape	(202) 737-8866
Montgomery County C. O.C	(301) 424-6000
Prince George's County C.O.C	(301) 731-5000
Visitors' Bureau	(301) 957-8687
Alexandria, VA C.O.C	(703) 549-1000
Arlington, VA C.O.C	(703) 525-2400
Fairfax, VA C.O.C	(703) 749-0400
Falls Church, VA Answer Line	(703) 241-5130
International Visitors	(202) 763-6540
Time	(202) 844-1111
Weather	(202) 936-1212

metro memos metro memos metro memos

(202) 637-7000 tdd: (202) 638-3780

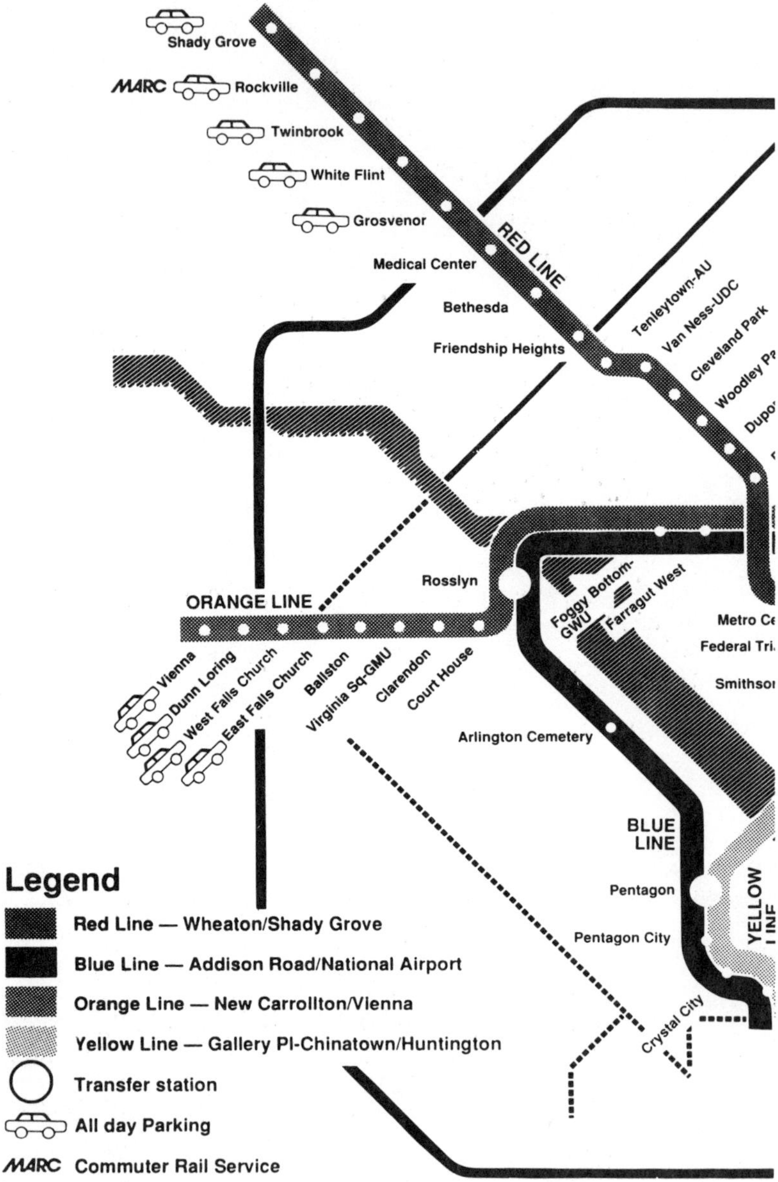
Shady Grove
MARC
Rockville
Twinbrook
White Flint
Grosvenor
Medical Center
Bethesda
Friendship Heights
RED LINE
Tenleytown-AU
Van Ness-UDC
Cleveland Park
ORANGE LINE
Rosslyn
Foggy Bottom-GWU
Farragut West
Vienna
Dunn Loring
West Falls Church
East Falls Church
Ballston
Virginia Sq-GMU
Clarendon
Court House
Arlington Cemetery
BLUE LINE
Pentagon
Pentagon City
YELLOW
Crystal City
Legend
Red Line — Wheaton/Shady Grove
Blue Line — Addison Road/National Airport
Orange Line — New Carrollton/Vienna
Yellow Line — Gallery Pl-Chinatown/Huntington
Transfer station
All day Parking
MARC Commuter Rail Service

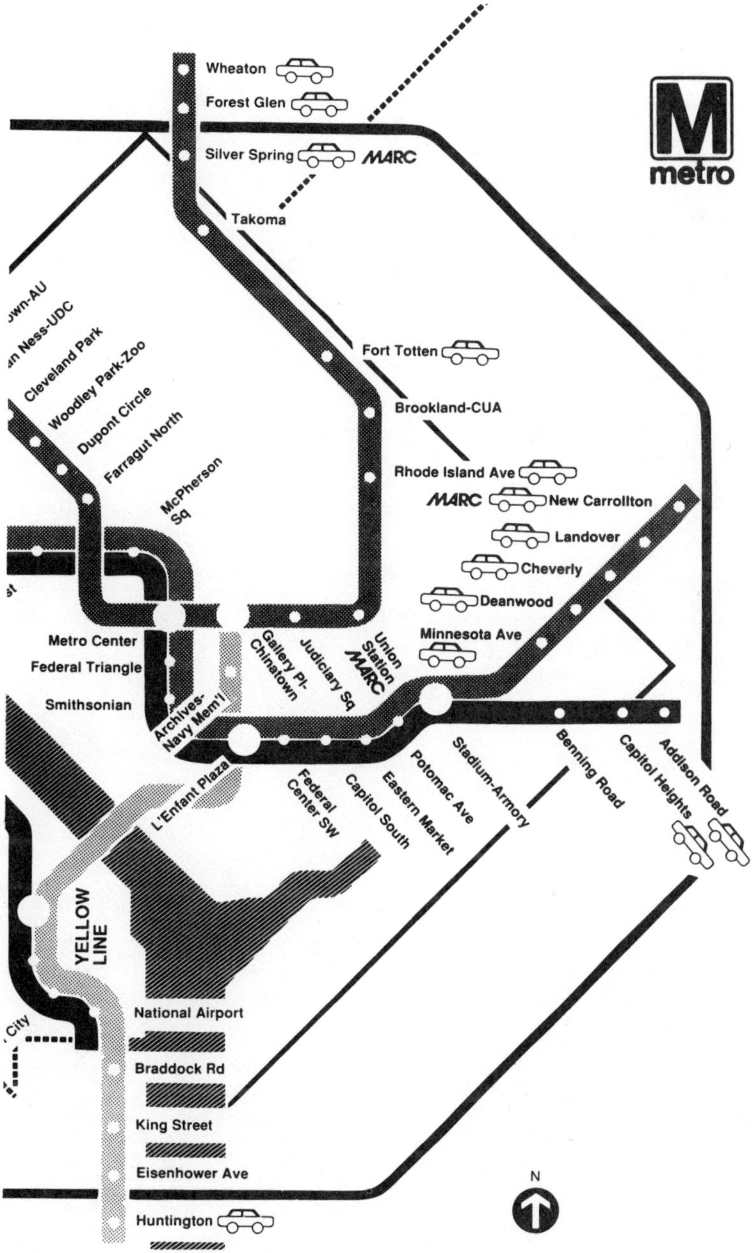

Wheaton
Forest Glen
Silver Spring
MARC
Takoma
metro
Fort Totten
Brookland-CUA
Rhode Island Ave
MARC
New Carrollton
Landover
Cheverly
Deanwood
Minnesota Ave
Cleveland Park
Woodley Park-Zoo
Dupont Circle
Farragut North
McPherson Sq
Metro Center
Federal Triangle
Smithsonian
Archives-Navy Mem'l
Gallery Pl-Chinatown
Judiciary Sq
Union Station
MARC
L'Enfant Plaza
Federal Center SW
Capitol South
Eastern Market
Potomac Ave
Stadium-Armory
Benning Road
Capitol Heights
Addison Road
YELLOW LINE
National Airport
Braddock Rd
King Street
Eisenhower Ave
Huntington
N

MARVELOUS METRO

Mass transit has definitely come a long, long way in this capital city. From buggies, trolleys, buses,and trains to more and more taxis, the city can be proud of its progress. And now, the Marvelous Metro has appeared on the scene! Metrobus and Metrorail with their 1,500 buses and four subway lines complement, meet, and intersect to serve the entire Metropolitan area. Street signs in downtown Washington point the way to sleek, modern, bronze-colored columns with a large "M" at the top, marking the spot where one can enter the world of Metro Magic. In outlying areas, the same "M" declares its presence as a vital sign of the area's growth and development.

Washington's subway system is admired and enjoyed by all who use it--especially those who have experienced other systems. It's safe, clean, quiet, clearly marked, well-lighted and has cordial attendants on duty until closing time. It may not always go exactly where you want it to go, but it comes close! Metrobus dovetails with Metrorail to affect a thoroughly capable job of people-moving.

To entice drivers out of cars, there is a reasonable fee for parking but spaces are limited. If you leave the lot before 3 p.m. or after 10 p.m., it's free, but no overnight parking is allowed, ever. Bicycle racks and lockers are available and passes may be obtained to take bikes on the Metro in the evenings, on weekends, and holidays. Up to two children under five are allowed to ride free with a paying adult.

Time schedules are really unnecessary. There is usually a short wait of six to fifteen minutes during non-rush hours, decreasing to three to six minutes during the morning and evening rush. No eating, smoking, drinking or loud noise is tolerated. The comfort of the passengers is protected by law.

Red, yellow, blue, orange, and before long, green are the guiding colors from point to point, and they are clearly marked on the "M" stanchion outside each station and on each train. The destination is also on the front and side of each car, but it is always the name of the very last stop. The secret of getting on the train going in the right direction is to check the columns and follow the arrows. Under the name of your location are those that are to come. It is easy to double check when on the train, also. A large, color-coded map is displayed prominently and the driver announces both destination and color as the train leaves each station. As announces both destination and color as the train leaves each station. As it pulls into the next, the name of that stop will be announced, as well as which doors will open--which is helpful, since landing platforms are located on different sides at different stations.

Intersecting colors warn of bilevel stations, which are key transfer centers from one line to another. They are not too complicated due to clear, concise signs. Check the signs. Ask if in doubt. The attendants who are there understand the problem and are kind and compassionate.

ecard machines are often crowded and sometimes out of order. After checking the list on the attendant's booth to find the fare to your destination (note the higher fare if traveling during rush hours), be sure to put in an amount that will cover the entire round trip. Or invest in a larger sum (up to $30.00), save the card and be able to hop on the train any time.

Only a few stations have machines that will handle ten and twenty dollar bills, so it's important to have ones and fives. Bills must be smooth, especially all corners, or the machine will continue to reject them.

Transfers can save money traveling from Metrorail to Metrobus but, strangely enough, it doesn't work the other way around. Be sure to get the transfer when entering the system or the opportunity is lost. There are Addfare machines inside the faregates, in case the card turns up with too fare to get out. Just insert the card, add the required amount, and the card will be returned, so you can proceed. On Metrobus, ask for a transfer to other buses as you board. And, always remember, bus drivers do not carry change, so be prepared, have your own.

The base fare has been increased, but it's nominal, and there are ingenious ways to save. Metro has devised nine different kinds of Flash Passes at bargain rates which can be purchased every two weeks from ten Metro sales offices and some 400 independent outlets. Senior Citizens and people with disabilities can get Metro ID cards that will entitle them to reduced fares. The bargain of the moment, however, is the Family/Tourist Pass. For a special price, four family members, or friends, can ride the Metro System for one entire day of a weekend or any holiday other than July 4, all day, for one price! There are informative maps, cards and folders available at the attendants' desk in each Metro station. Look them over and take what you need or want, before you embark on the Metro adventure.

Alexandria has a DASH system which operates each day. Specific information may be obtained by calling (703) 370-3274. The Fairfax CUE system operates on four routes. Call (703) 385-7859. To find out about the Fairfax Connector routes, call (703) 339-7200. In Prince William County, the number to call is (703) 494-9166. And, if you want to ride Amtrak, dial (202) 484-7540.

For information about routes, fares and/or advice for the entire Metro system in the Greater Metropolitan Area, you may call (202) 637-7000, TTY (202) 638-3780, between 6:30 a.m. and 11:30 p.m. The "M" is the way to go--fast, easy, inexpensive and dependable--mobility IS Metro!

CH

SECTION ONE: WASHINGTON D.C.

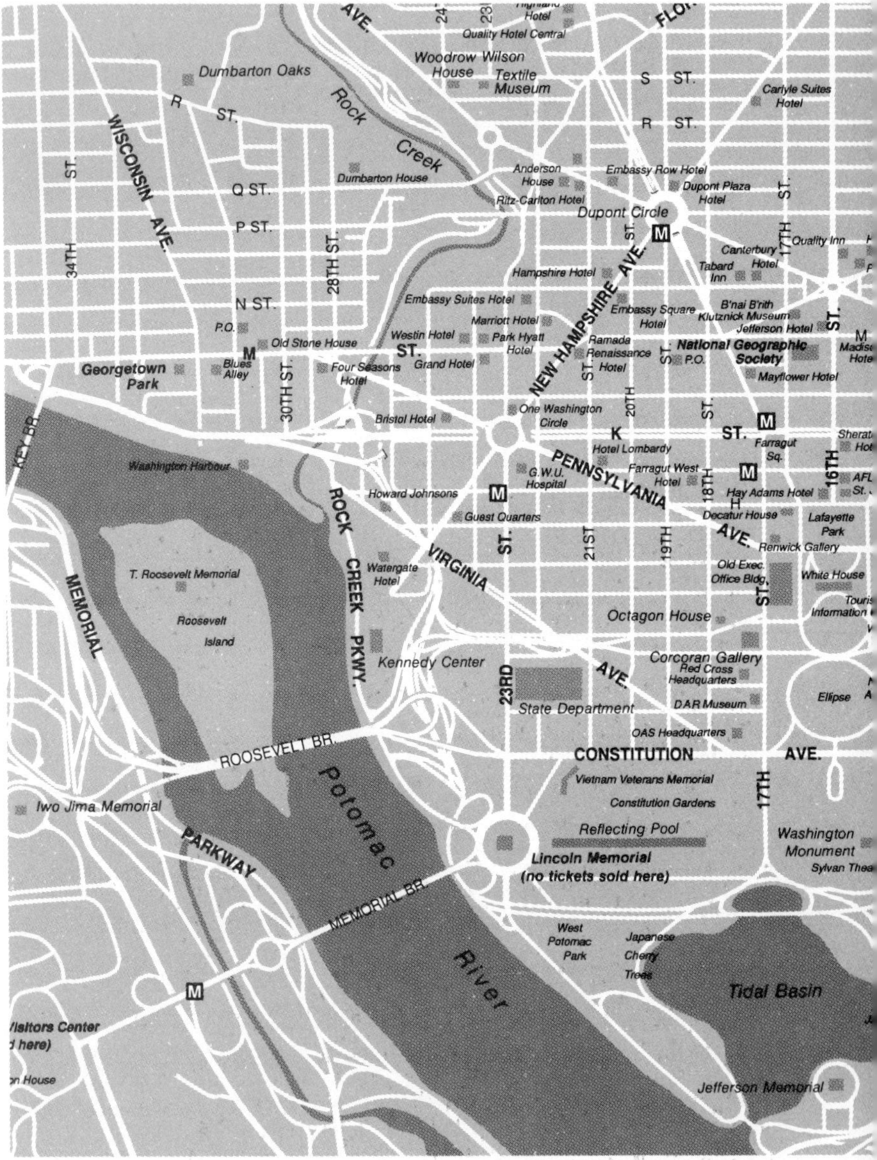

washington d.c.

DISTRICT OF COLUMBIA: A HISTORY

Fly into Washington, D.C. at night, and you'll be certain you're approaching a fantasy land. Approach by train, and you'll gasp with pleasure, and perhaps pride, as you walk out the door of Union Station and catch the first impact of this capital city. Drive in from the South, and you'll be treated to an entrance by bridges which affords a panorama of familiar, famous monuments as it carries you over the Potomac into the heart of the city. Drive in from any other angle and you'll be startled to find yourself being drawn straight into the imposing sight of the Capitol dome itself!

There is no way to approach this powerful city unmoved. Whether a casual visitor, or a serious one; a foreign guest, a native, born and bred under this flag; or an adoptive son or daughter; each visitor to Washington has his or her own background and story. But all share in the pain and the joy of this nation's history. It was seven years after the forefathers declared this country to be fully free, when a fledgling Congress passed the Residency Act on July 19, 1790 and declared Washington, D.C. the official capital of the United States of America.

This sleepy, country swampland had been singled out by a compromise between Northern and Southern leaders to be groomed and developed into the polished and shining star it has become. Washington is the dream and vision of Pierre L'Enfant, the man George Washington designated to be the official designer and planner of the city of the future. He saw the seat of government as being a city of the people; a clean, clear, orderly setting in which to properly showcase a most noble venture.

This city is your city! It's my city! It belongs to all of us once we're here, and for as long as we want it to be. This city was born out of the extraordinary faith of ordinary people. Those people sincerely believed that the good of all was important enough to outweigh the position of one; that the majority should be able to set the pace for all, and that this nation, under God, had the ability, wisdom and faith in one another to govern itself without the interference of nations outside its borders. It was a radical position at the time -- we called it Democracy. The world watched and waited for us to prove ourselves. And so we did! And so everyone comes to see. And everyone is welcome!

Now, as Americans, preparing to enter our third century, we're celebrating over 200 years of successfully living a dream. There are Government Bicentennial plans being developed for the entire decade of the 1990s! When you come to share in your inheritance, or, if you are fortunate enough to live here, be on the lookout for current announcements in the newspapers and magazines.

Various neighborhood museums will have special showings and demonstrations. Call (202) 387-2151 and (202) 673-4034 for particulars. The July Fourth celebration in Washington, D.C. is unparalleled and is always worth the effort of getting there and waiting. Call early for details (202) 619-7222. In September, an International affair will take place. Call (202) 789-7000 for pertinent information concerning this particular occasion and others to be planned later in 1991 and 1992.

Let this be the time to plan a trip to the National Archives (Constitution Ave. between 7th and 9th N.W. (202) 501-5000). Here, you will see the three documents that support the very existence of this country, who we are as Americans, and which give us the freedom to express ourselves and our faith. These documents are The Declaration of Independence, The Constitution of the United States and The Bill of Rights. Let the children see, lest we forget!

After you have visited all of the statues, monuments, parks and fountains that you need to see at this time, take a closer look at this Hometown, U.S.A. See the people who are the Nation's neighbors. Take time to ride the Metro and watch. Get off at a stop or two to look around. Take a taxi ride to Haines Point to see the larger-than-life sculpture Awakening -- it's impressive! On your way, watch the people on both sides of the road. Many will be native Washingtonians. Stroll around the National Zoo or up Pennsylvania, Constitution, or Connecticut Avenue. You'll find some neighbors. Try to really SEE the people who live here. Notice the mix from the melting pot. Rejoice in it!

This country took shape out of a potpourri of races, creeds and colors, sizes and persuasions; out of dreams of riches, power and justice, out of hope, love and, above all faith. Faith that mixing and matching, stirring and sharing, loving and coping, living and dying will bring forth new dreams, new beginnings and new faith. It is, indeed, imperative that these shall not perish from the earth.

Let us each welcome one another! The Government Bicentennial begins!

THE CAPITOL

Since 1800, the United States Capitol Building has dominated the Washington skyline. Then it was just a fraction of the size that it is today, but as changes in taste, a succession of architects, a tragic fire, and a growing Congressional population brought about several changes in the building's original plans. The Capitol Building has endured all of these changes and setbacks, and today, more than 1.3 million people pass through its doors each year, making the Capitol Building the most visited site in Washington.

The idea for the Capitol Building was set in place by Pierre L'Enfant, the city's original planner. He envisioned the Capitol Building as a grand monument to democracy, sitting atop Jenkins Hill where it would be seen by everyone in the city. Construction on the Capitol Building began in 1793, when George Washington himself laid the cornerstone. The original plans for the building were designed by a West Indian physician, Dr. William Thorton. His plan called for a modest dome across a cubical central section to be flanked by the House and Senate wings. Congress moved into the North Wing in 1800, but unfortunately, disputes between Thorton and those who wanted to improve his plan resulted in his dismissal. In 1803, Benjamin Henry Latrobe was appointed surveyor of public buildings, and under him, the House wing was completed and linked to the North wing.

It seemed as though the Capitol was finally finished, but in 1812, The British invaded Washington and set fire to it . After the war, Latrobe rebuilt the wings, but was replaced in 1819 by Charles Bulfinch, who built a larger dome than any of the other builders had imagined. In the 1850s, Thomas Walter built new wings with larger chambers for the House and Senate and replaced the dome, adding the massive drum encircled with pilasters and columns. Finally, in 1863, the Capitol building as we know it today, was finished.

A tour of the Capitol Building is an excellent way to reaquaint yourself with United States history, and with the legislative process. Constantino Bumidi's impressive murals and frescoes, the handsomely adorned dome ceiling, and Statuary Hall, with its statues commemorating some of the country's most important citizens, all celebrate the glorious history of the United States. When Congress is in session, you will visit the House and Senate chambers to witness the legislative process. You will also visit the nearby House and Senate office buildings, where you may find a Congress person who is willing to participate in a picture taking session.

The history of the Capitol Building is as rich and as varied as the history of this nation. The most important business in the United States is conducted here, and it is a storehouse for some of the country's most cherished history and artwork. If you only have time to tour one building during your stay in Washington, you would be wise to make it the Capitol Building.

THE WHITE HOUSE AND LAFAYETTE PARK

In 1797, George Washington saw the front portico of the White House (McPherson Square Metro stop, 1600 Pennsylvania Ave., N.W.) just the way we see it today. The oldest public building in Washington has a long history that includes being burned by the British in the War of 1812. Recent, extensive restoration has brought back the splendor and simple elegance originally intended for the "President's Palace."

George Washington as first President had a lot to say about the design and construction of Washington, D.C. and the First Residence, but he never lived to move in. John Adams and his wife were the first residents. They began the tradition of each new President making changes to suit his family's personal taste. It was John Quincy Adams that planted what is now the oldest surviving tree on the White House Grounds. President James Garfield used the East Room for his son's bicycle races. President Lincoln never slept at the White House during the hottest of summer days, but would retire instead to the Soldiers Home north of the city.

Some of the changes can be seen along with presidential memorabilia during a self-guided tour of seven of the 132 rooms. During the summer months at 8:00 a.m., free tickets can be obtained at a booth on the South side of the White House.From September through May, they are not required. Since the White House is one of the most popular attractions in the city for visitors and local residents alike, it pays to get in line early for the 10:00 a.m. opening. The number of tickets available is limited. The ticket booth remains open until noon, Tuesday through Saturday. Parking is better on Saturday when staff parking is available to the public (202) 456-2200.

Directly across Pennsylvania Avenue from the north entrance of the White House is Lafayette Park,named for the Marquis Marie Jean Paul Roch Yves Gilbert Motier de Lafayette, who was known to the American Continental Army Officers as Gilbert. It was the Presidents' front lawn, but in 1824,Thomas Jefferson thought it better and more appropriate to be a public park. Revolutionary War heros are prominently displayed, one in each of the four corners: The Marquis de Lafayette, Major General Comte Jean de Rochambeau and Brigadier General Thaddeus Kosciuszko and Baron von Stuben. In the center is a statue by Clark Mills of Andrew Jackson on horseback, an exact replica of Jackson's statue standing in Jackson Square New Orleans. It was the capital's first equestrian statue.

THE MALL

Looking at the Mall today, it is difficult to imagine that at one time, this beautiful stretch of ground, lined with memorials and museums, was an embarrassment to the nation's capital.

In Pierre L'Enfant's plan of 1791, the two-mile stretch of land from the Capitol to the Lincoln Memorial was reserved to visually connect the Capitol Building to the Potomac River. His plan called for the main avenue of the mall to be tree lined, with a canal, and flanked with museums, shops and cultural centers.

Unfortunately for the city, L'Enfant lost his job after one year, and the mall continued to remain vacant, except for some scattered shacks. During a renovation of the city in the 1870s, the mall was completely ignored; the Washington Monument remained unfinished, at about one-quarter of its completed height, with railroad tracks and a depot located nearby.

Conditions at the mall remained similar for the rest of the 1800s -- unkempt and damp. In 1900, the MacMillan Commission, under the direction of Sen. James MacMillan of Michigan, drained the land and undertook the task of landscaping the property. The railroad was relocated to Union Station and the Botanic Gardens was moved from the center of the mall to its edge.

THE SMITHSONIAN INSTITUTION

Take time to visit to one of the Smithsonian's 13 museums and galleries and you're likely to find just about anything from fabulous jewels and masterpiece art, to the air and space technology that made the U.S. a world leader in flight technology.

The Smithsonian began with an odd and unexpected bequest of 105 bags of gold sovereigns donated by an Englishman, James Smithson, who never set foot in America. Smithson left his fortune to his nephew with the desire that, if his nephew should die without heirs, the money would go to Washington, D.C. for the establishment of an institution "for the increase and diffusion of knowledge."

Congress debated for over eight years whether it was legal and correct to accept this unusual legacy of 100,000 gold sovereigns before constructing The Smithsonian Institution.

Today, The Smithsonian stands as the premier cataloguer of this nation's artifacts with well over 37 million pieces in its total collection, as well as being an extraordinary research and education facility. James Smithson's wish has grown beyond his wildest dreams and has meant a wealth of knowledge for the American people for nearly a century and a half.

The Smithsonian Institution Building

The Smithsonian's first home, sometimes affectionately referred to as "The Castle", was built in 1855, after the design made by James Renswick Jr. The facility is a 12th century Italian Romanesque castle, turreted with nine towers in several distinct designs. It was in the main tower of The Castle that President Abraham Lincoln stood to observe U.S. Army signal corpsmen practice lantern drills during the Civil War.

The facility originally contained laboratories, a lecture hall, an art gallery, and a science museum, in addition to office space. Some scientists had living space in The Castle and the institution's first secretary, Joseph Henry, moved his entire family into the facility, where he conducted research on electricity and magnetism, leading to such amazing developments as the telegraph. Henry also organized the world's first group of weather forecasters, leading to the eventual formation of the U.S. Weather Bureau.

The Castle, recently renovated in 1989, now serves as the Smithsonian's Information Center, offering. audio-visual aids, printed information, and scale models of the museums.

National Air and Space Museum

The Smithsonian's largest museum, the National Air and Space Museum, receives the greatest number of visitors each year.

The Air and Space Museum boasts 23 exhibition areas that trace the history of aviation from the Wright Brothers' historical flight in Kitty Hawk, N.C. to modern-day space and air travel.

The **Milestones of Flight** gallery is the one that attracts and awes many of its visitors, since it displays the actual aircraft that made history. In it are the Langley Aerodrome #5, the aircraft, designed by Samuel Langley, that made an unmanned flight in 1896; the Wright Brothers airplane; and Charles Lindbergh's "The Spirit of St. Louis."

Artifacts of space flight from moon rocks to space travel equipment are on hand to give guests a first-hand look at how some of the most amazing scientific achievements of the 20th century were accomplished.

Arts and Industries Building

Restored in 1976, this 109-year-old facility now has the feeling and energy of the 1876 Centennial Exhibition.

Containing the nearly 60 trainloads of items from the Exhibition, the museum also has wings dedicated to 18th century artifacts and industrial exhibits such as the original telegraph and early printing machinery.

National Museum of American History

The impressive array of American historical artifacts at the National Museum of American History is guaranteed to bring out the patriot in everyone that views them.

The first floor of the museum is dedicated to science and technology; the second floor is dedicated to social and cultural history; and the third floor to national collections.

The hallmark of the museum is the American flag that inspired Francis Scott Key to write the "Star Spangled Banner." For preservation purposes, the flag is only put on public display for two minutes every half hour.

A special display is a recreation of rooms in the White House as decorated by various 20th century presidents. Included in the display are First Ladies' inaugural ball gowns china, and other presidential artifacts.

National Museum of Natural History

The macrocosm of earth and man is displayed in the microcosm of the National Museum of Natural History. Since opening in 1911, the museum has amassed an astounding 118 million pieces including fossils, gems, meteorites, animals, and displays from around the world.

The facility itself centers on a rotunda that is highlighted by a 13-foot-high, mounted African elephant. Separate galleries focus on ancient plants, trees, marine life, dinosaurs, and anthropology.

National Gallery of Art

Chartered by Congress in 1937, the National Gallery of Art was the brainchild of Andrew W. Mellon, Pittsburgh banking and steel magnate.

Mellon, a Secretary of the Treasury in the 1920s, began collecting art for a national art gallery and encouraged his peers to do likewise. What sets the National Gallery apart from other museums is that although the museum operates on Federal government funding, all of its works have been purchased from private funds.

There are two buildings that comprise the National Gallery. The West Building has an awe-inspiring collection of 19th century art from all over the world. Some of the masters represented are Leonardo di Vinci, Rembrant, Van Gogh, Monet, Eakin, and Whistler, along with a host of others

The East Building is the newer of the two and contains the Smithsonian's comprehensive collection of 20th century art. Featured artists include in Picasso, Matisse, and Pollock.

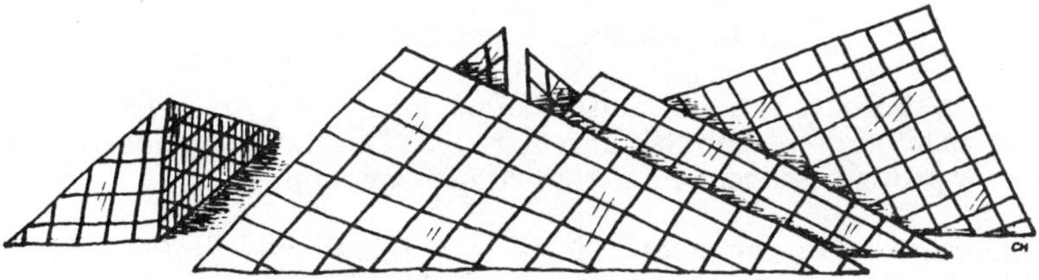

Hirshhorn Museum and Sculpture Garden

Donated by collector Joseph Hirshhorn in 1966, the Hirshhorn Museum boasts a wonderful collection of modern art. Masterpiece sculptures scattered throughout the plaza and courtyard beckon visitors inside the doughnut-shaped building where they will find works by such legends as Rodin, Picasso, Degas, Matisse, and more. Though most of the works are modern in nature, Mr. Hirshhorn managed to acquire a significant collection of works by John Singer Sargent and Thomas Eakins.

Freer Gallery of Art

A fabulous collection of Asian art as well as an encompassing collection of works by James Abbott McNeill Whistler is displayed at the Freer Gallery of Art. The collection is a donation from Charles Lang Freer, who was an avid fan of Whistler's work and later grew to be friends with him.

Whistler guided Freer in his acquisitions of Asian treasures; as a result, the collection is varied and impressive, and includes paintings, ceramics and bronze pieces.

The Whistler collection at the Freer Gallery number well over 1,000, and includes his oils, pastels, watercolors, and prints. Anyone visiting the Freer Gallery should not miss the Peacock Room, named for the peacocks Whistler painted for a room he designed for an English businessman called "Harmony in Blue and Gold."

The **Arthur M Sackler Gallery** can be reached by going through a underground passage from the Freer Gallery where displays of Chinese artworks in lacquer, metal, bronze, paint, and jade can be found.

The National Museum of African Art

This is the only national museum that focuses on the collection, study, and exhibition of sub-Saharan Africa. This building, located mostly below ground, is circular and topped with six copper domes.

There are two permanent collections in this four-year-old facility. The first is an overview of African art including its materials, styles, and cultures; the other collection is of Royal Benin art, which are sculptures made between the 16th and 19th centuries by the lost-wax casting method. The remainder of the gallery hosts traveling exhibitions.

Renwick Gallery

The collection at the Renwick Gallery, once the controversial Corcoran Gallery - home of a sculpture that had to be viewed by men and women at separate times - focuses on decorative arts and crafts. Many temporary exhibits highlights the permanent collection. The Grand Salon and Octagon Rooms are decorated in furnishings of the mid-to late 1800s.

National Portrait Gallery

The Hall of Presidents is the highlight of this gallery, which focuses on portraits of men and women who have influenced history.

The Hall of Presidents shares the second floor of the gallery with the Gilbert Stuart portraits of George and Martha Washington. There are also two galleries of historical governmental leaders, as well as of those who were outstanding in the military, law, literature, and the arts. There are also halls devoted to explorers, scientists, and inventors, and the Meserve Gallery exhibits an extensive collection of photographs by Mathew Brady.

Anacostia Museum

Dedicated to African-American heritage and culture, the Anacostia Museum was an experiment in which the Smithsonian attempted to bring the museum to the people, rather than making the people come to the museum.

Located in historic Anacostia, the museum covers such subjects as the Harlem Renaissance, the Middle Passage, black churches, and black aviators.

In addition to exhibits, a research library on the museum grounds is dedicated to African art, history, and culture, and is open for study.

National Zoological Park

Now in its second century, the National Zoo is leading the world in zoo development by becoming the world's first BioPark and creating natural environments based on the interdependence of life systems.

In addition to the famous pandas, visitors to the zoo can literally see hundreds of animals, along with nature art and beautiful, brilliant flowers

Those interested in becoming Resident Associates of the Smithsonian may write to: Smithsonian Institution, Dept. 0052, Washington, D.C., 20073-0052. Members are afforded a considerable discount on all Smithsonian activities.

THE C & O CANAL

In the 1830's, long before the railroad was considered a viable mode of transportation in this country, a grand scheme of a canal, linking Virginia's Chesapeake and the state of Ohio was a bold idea. After 20 years of digging and building locks, a portion of the proposed system was completed. At 184 miles long, with 74 locks, 11 stone aqueducts and seven dams, the system allowed for a difference in elevation of 600-feet and was testimony to America's engineering prowess and human endurance. It connected Washington, D.C. to Cumberland, Maryland and for a few short years it was the most reasonable way to ship goods North and South. Coal, grain, lumber and furs were some of the cargo transported on barges pulled by horses or mules. The mule became the favorite of barge captains because,unlike a horse, a mule will quit short of exhaustion. The canal became a way of life for entire families who were living on the barges. Then the trains came, and since they were faster and eventually cheaper, the canal was phased out and never really made a profit for the people who dug it.

Wednesday through Sunday during the summer, and a slightly reduced schedule for spring and fall, you can relive history as you cruise on one of two C & O Canal boat trips. If you begin your trip at Great Falls, five or six rangers from the National Park Service and volunteers dressed in period clothes begin to prepare the Canal Clipper for the journey. Using thick ropes, the crew guides the boat into Lock 20. Quickly, gates are secured, paddles are opened, and the Clipper creeps higher and higher. When the old vessel meets the level of the upper canal, the forward gates open, the mules are hitched, and the adventure begins,

Scraggly "Captain Gus" enthusiastically shares his knowledge about the building of the canal, its triumphs, mechanics, and catastrophes. The clip-clop of the distant mules is barely audible as the boat glides on the peaceful waters. The mule skinners are kept busy diverting Ellie the mule's attention from the tasty bushes on the side of the towpath and keeping it focused ahead.

Lock 21 draws close. The mules are turned and rehitched. Bound for home, Captain Gus conducts a 19th century sing-a-long while the crew accompanies the passengers with washboard and dulcimer. It is thrilling to slip into the past, if only for an hour or two.

After the cruise you are free to explore the towpath and observe the moods of the Potomac River.

The C & O Canal National Historical Park is 184.5 miles of nature blended with history. It is an excellent for hiking and biking. For more information about a variety of recreational opportunities available, write:Superintendent, C & O Canal National Historical Park, Box 4,Sharpsburg, MD, 21782. Tel: (301) 739-4200

Departure points of The National Park Service C & O Canal Barge tours are:

Foundry Mall
National Historical Park
1055 Thomas Jefferson Street
Washington, DC 20007
(202) 472-4376

Great Falls Tavern
11710 MacArthur Blvd.
Potomac, MD 20854
(301) 299-2026

MONUMENTS & MEMORIALS

One of the most exciting things about Washington, D.C. is the backdrop it provides as testimony to our country's greatest achievers. Parks, monuments, memorials, and statues of all kinds remind us of those who have labored, lived, and died for the good of all.

Arlington National Cemetery

Arlington National Cemetery (Arlington Cemetery Metro stop, in Va. across the Memorial Bridge from the Lincoln Memorial) is the largest resting place for the honored dead of our Nation. Once the magnificent estate of Gen. and Mrs. Robert E. Lee, it was confiscated and occupied by Federal soldiers during the Civil War. As a testament to our own mortality, veterans of all of the country's wars sleep together with statesmen, leaders and those closest to them. Pierre Charles L'Enfant is buried here, overlooking the city which he planned. The grave of John F. Kennedy is highlighted by the eternal flame which burns as a constant reminder of his assassination in 1963. The ceremonial changing of the guard at the Tomb of the Unknown Soldier is an impressive and moving experience. It takes place every hour on the hour. Open 8 a.m.- 5 p.m. daily; Until 7 p.m. April - September. (703) 692-0931.

Arlington House

High on the hill above Arlington National Cemetery is Arlington House (Custis-Lee Mansion--Arlington Cemetery Metro stop, on the Arlington National Cemetery grounds). It is a memorial to General Robert E. Lee and was built about 1802 by George Washington Parke Custis, the grandson of Martha Washington. In 1864 when Mrs. Lee failed to appear in person to pay the taxes, the entire 200 acre estate was then confiscated by the Federal Government. Open 9:30 a.m. - 4:30 p.m. (703) 557-0613.

The Jefferson Memorial

South of the Mall, surrounded by Japanese cherry trees at the Potomac river's Tidal Basin, is the Jefferson Memorial (six blocks from the Smithsonian Metro Stop at the South end of 15th St. S.W.), one of the newer historical monuments in the city. Born of controversy while the country was in the middle of World War II, this Pantheon-like structure characterizes the life and achievements of Thomas Jefferson. Designing the building, John Russell Pope incorporated Jefferson's designs of the University of Virginia's rotunda and his home, Monticello,near Charlottesville, Virginia. A Magnificent nineteen foot bronze statue by sculptor Rudolph Evens stands in the center. With quotations from Jefferson's Declaration of Independence and Virginia Statute of Religious Freedom, they serve as a reminder that Jefferson's words were larger than life. (202) 426-6821.

Lincoln Memorial

West of the Mall at the foot of the Memorial Bridge, a long shimmering pool reflects the Lincoln Memorial (Foggy Bottom Metro stop, 23rd St. between Constitution and Independence Aves. N.W.) stands with dignity and strength. A man of 6'4" in life, he would stand 28' if his sculpted form chose to stand. A tribute to Abraham Lincoln as he looked during the war-torn years of the Civil War, Daniel Chester French's marble statue reflects the somber, soul-searching man who put an end to enslavement in the United States. Engraved in the walls are the Gettysburg Address, the Second Inaugural address, and the dedication quote, "In this temple as in the hearts of the people for whom he saved the nation, the memory of Abraham Lincoln is enshrined Forever". It was here that Martin Luther King proclaimed the immortal words "I have a dream" (202) 426-6895.

Marine Corps War Memorial

Dedicated to all Marines who have died defending the United States, the Marine Corp War Memorial (Rosslyn Metro stop, In Va., off of Route 50, adjacent to Arlington National Cemetery) is better known as the Iwo Jima Memorial. It depicts the five marines and the sailor who raised the

U.S. flag on Mt. Suribachi after one of the bloodiest battles in the Pacific during World War II. Horace W. Peaslee designed this, the largest bronze statue ever cast, after Joseph Rosenthal's Pulitzer-winning photograph. Etched in Swedish Granite, the base of the statue contains the names and dates of Marine Corps military engagements that have occured over the past two hundred years. (703) 285-2600.

U.S. Navy Memorial

"In honor of those who served to forge the heritage of the United States Navy. In tribute to those who perished to provide peace and security for our maritime nation. In gratitude to those now serving" is the dedication inscription at the U.S. Navy Memorial (Archives Metro stop, between 7th and 9th Sts. on Pennsylvania Ave. N.W.). It includes an open-air amphitheater that seats 5,000 for summer, military band concerts free of charge.The Lone Sailor ponders the world on the two masted memorial and its sea of granite. A lighted water wall with cascading overflow surrounds a map, 100 feet in diameter, depicting the world with Washington, D.C. as the center.

Vietnam Memorial

Just a short walk down the steps from the Lincoln Memorial is a simple, polished, V-shaped, black granite wall, spanning 500 feet dedicated to Vietnam Conflict. The powerful, emotionally-inspiring Vietnam Memorial (Foggy Bottom Metro stop, on 23ed St. N.W.) is a personal tribute to each of those lost in the defense of South Vietnam. 58,156 names are etched in the granite. Each year, they are read, touched by millions of friends, relatives and ordinary visitors, some of whom leave mementos such as flags, flowers and letters. In 1981, over 1,400 designs were submitted for the Vietnam Memorial. The one chosen was submitted by Yale University student, Maya Lin.

the nation's capital

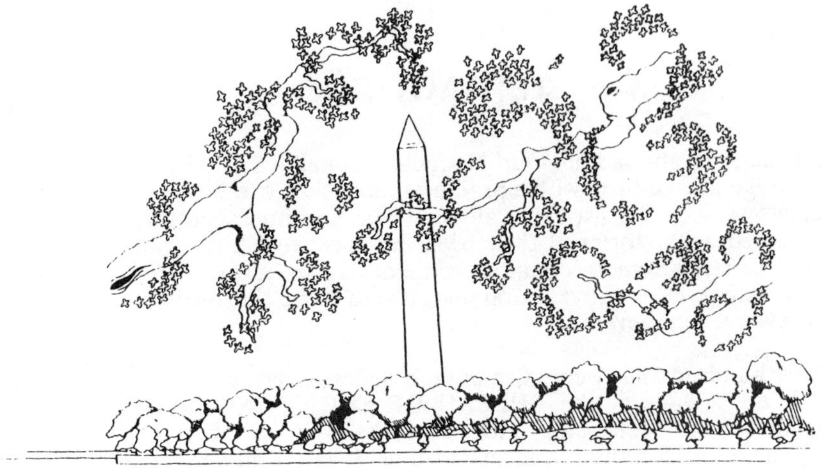

The Washington Monument

At the center of the Mall, the Washington Monument (Smithsonian Metro stop, West Mall, south of Constitution Ave. N.W.), no longer the tallest structure in the world, remains, nonetheless, the dominant monument on the Washington skyline. Its obelisk form stretches exactly 555 feet 5 1/8 inches skyward and stands on a 55 square foot base. The designer, Robert Mills, had in mind a grander, colonnade structure, bu there were fifty one years of delays, including a block of marble donated by Pope Pius IX which was stolen by the Know Nothing Party; proportion changes by the U.S. Army Corps of Engineers, and the Civil War. In 1884, the completed monument of white Maryland marble weighed 81,120 tons, with 898 spiraled steps ascending to the 3,300 pound capstone. It was actually raised another 1/2000 of an inch on August 31, 1886 during a seismic disturbance. Today the base includes a ring of fifty American flags and, the top offers four of the most remarkable scenic views of our Nation's Capital. The elevator, once only for women and children, now takes everyone to the top in a scant 70 seconds. For the energetic and strong of heart, at 10 a.m. and 2 p.m., on Saturday and Sunday only, there is the option of walking down the steps to see the 192 memorial stones. You may not have to wait in line if you arrive on time and tell the ranger you want to climb. You can call (202) 426-6841 for walk-down reservations. Open April to Labor Day, 9 a.m. to midnight and 9 a.m.- 5 p.m. September through March. (202) 426-6839.

ATTRACTIONS

Attractions abound in Our Nation's Capital! The city is rich in its heritage and culture, with a proliferation of things to do, places to go and sights to see. To list them all would be an impossible task. We have featured, with stories of their own, the ones we felt most important to our readers. Some are famous while others are just developing. All are interesting, informative, intriguing places to be thoroughly enjoyed and forever remembered.

One hundred and twenty five million dollars a day, twenty billion a year, roll off presses at the **BUREAU OF ENGRAVING AND PRINTING** (Smithsonian Metro stop, 14th and C Sts. S.W.) and it can be witnessed by taking a 25 minute self guided tour. It takes minutes to print a one dollar bill but it only lasts 18 months. Money is always fascinating, so line up early to see the inking, stacking and cutting of U.S. currency. Open Mon - Fri 9 a.m.- 2 p.m. Get there before noon. (202) 447-1391.

Situated in historic Georgetown and lovingly restored and maintained by the Colonial Dames of America, **DUMBARTON HOUSE** (2715 Q Street NW) brings American history to life. When you stroll through the eight rooms that are open to visitors, you will be struck by the beautifully restored 19th century American and English antiques. A walk through the house reveals special displays, such as a coat worn by Martha Washington, a handmade quilt crafted by one of Georgtown's early residents, and furniture created by some well known American artisans. Open Monday through Saturday, by appointment. (202) 337-2288.

At the highest point above Georgetown, is the grand **DUMBARTON OAKS** estate (1703 32nd St., N.W.). Take a step back in time and place and wander around 16 acres of gardens, a lovely house built in 1801 and a Pre-Colombian ancient artifact museum. At times, there's a chance to see a concert in the music room; call and check. The museum is the work of Mr. Robert Woods Bliss, former U.S. Ambassador to Sweden and Argentina, who purchased the estate in 1920. The estate gets it's name from the Rock of Dumbarton in Scotland and is known for the 1944 multi-power conference that forged the United Nations. Open 2-5 p.m., gardens only, except holidays. (202) 338-8278.

Controversial for it's cost and appearance, the J. Edgar Hoover Building houses the administration and crime fighting laboratories of **THE FEDERAL BUREAU OF INVESTIGATION** (Federal Triangle,

Archives or Gallery Place Metro stops, Pennsylvania Ave. between 9th and 10th Sts., N.W.). Generally thought to be less than beautiful, The F.B.I. Building, as it's most often called, looks like a fortress representing the strength and security we have come to expect from Federal Agents. Children and adults enjoy tours through the building to see relics of former, solved crimes and memorabilia of on-going investigations. At the tour's end, behind bullet proof glass, F.B.I. Agents demonstrate their expertise with firearms. Open Mon.- Fri. 9 a.m. - 4:15 p.m. We recommend calling (202) 324-3447 for a reservation. Closed on holidays.

Shakespearean delight in an Elizabethan world can be enjoyed at the **FOLGER SHAKESPEARE LIBRARY AND THEATER** (Capitol South Metro stop, 201 E. Capitol St., S.E.). Outside is the statue of Puck, inside is a library, available only to special scholars, that has the world's largest collection of Shakespearian literature. A gift of former, Standard Oil Chairman, Henry Clay Folger, the Grecian Art-Deco building boasts a grand Elizabethan Hall, a full scale, in-yard, Elizabethan theater, and museum exhibits that include a scale model of the famous Globe Playhouse. Theater and musical performances are worth inquiring about, as are the poetry reading and lecture series. There are no scheduled tours, but, special tours are available with advance reservations. Mon. - Sat. 11 a.m. - 1 p.m. Open daily 10 a.m.- 4 p.m., April 15 through Labor Day. Then, it's open Mon.- Sat. 10 a.m.- 4 p.m., for the remainder of the year. It's closed on holidays. Library (202) 544-7077, theater (202) 544-4000.

The site of a momentous occasion in American history -- the assassination of President Abraham Lincoln by John Wilkes Booth -- **FORD'S THEATER**, (511 Tenth St. NW) is now open for public inspection.

Lincoln was shot April 14, 1865 while watching the comedic play, "Our American Cousin." After shooting the president, Booth lept onto the stage shouting "Sic semper tyrannis! (Thus always to tyrants), breaking his leg in the process. Booth escaped, but was fatally shot just 11 days after Lincoln passed away.

The theater was bought by the government soon after the assassination; it served as the site of the Army Medical Museum and general office space. In the 1960s the facility was restored. Box Seven, where Lincoln received his mortal wound, is furnished with reproductions of the furniture, including Lincoln's indispensable rocking chair. Guests may also view the Derringer used as the murder weapon, the flag covering Lincolon's coffin, and some of his personal effects.

A few blocks from the **IMMACULATE CONCEPTION SHRINE ATt THE FRANCISCAN MONASTERY** (Brookland-CUA Metro stop, 140 Quincy St., N.E.), you will find forty-four acres of the most delightful gardens and peaceful walkways through an abundance of flowering shrubs and trees. Along the pathways, there are authentic reproductions of the shrines of the Holy Land and a representation of the ancient catacombs used by early Christians to escape persecution. Thirty minute tours leave every hour except Noon 9 a.m. - 4 p.m.. Sun. 1 p.m. - 4 p.m.. Open Mon.- Sat. 8:30 a.m.- 4 p.m., Sun. 1-4 p.m.; Masses at 6:30, 7 and 8 a.m. Mon.- Sat.; 6 a.m., 9 a.m. on Sun. and Holy Days with Benediction at 3:30 p.m. (202) 526-6800.

Facing the holy city of Mecca, the **ISLAMIC CENTER** (2551 Massachusetts Ave., N.W.) welcomes visitors of all faiths. Women must be covered--head, arms and legs. Shoes must be removed before entering the mosque's rich interior where you will find layers of beautiful Persian carpets, walls covered with Turkish tile and grand Egyptian chandeliers.

Five times a day you may experience the faithful being called to prayer by a muezzin, high above, in the 160 ft. minaret. Guided tours Sun.-Thurs. 10 a.m. - 5 p.m., Services held 1-2 p.m. on Fridays. (202) 332-8343.

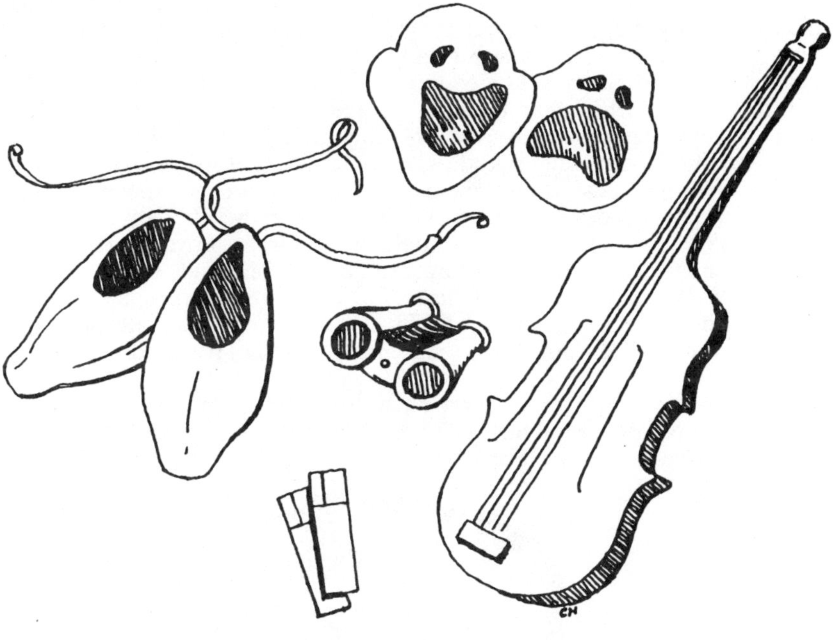

Serving as both a cultural center for the United States and as a memorial to the late President John F. Kennedy, **THE JOHN F. KENNEDY CENTER FOR THE PERFORMING ARTS** (Foggy Bottom Metro stop, southern end of New Hampshire Avenue, NW) is a must-see for anyone visiting Washington, D.C. Whether you choose to take a self-guided tour of the complex, or a more comprehensive 50-minute guided tour, you are sure to learn something about the artistic history of this nation.

Plans for a national cultural center began with President Dwight D. Eisenhower's 1958 approval of legisation that designated 17 acres in Washington's Foggy Bottom neighborhood for the purpose. President Kennedy, famous for his patronage of the arts, was very much involved in the project. Following his assassination, President Johnson signed a bill that, among other things, gave the center its name. Opened in 1971, KENNEDY CENTER houses two theaters, an opera house, a concert hall and The American Film Institute, making it one of the premier art centers in the United States.

A tour of the Center reveals much more than just theaters. For instance, in the **HALL OF NATIONS**, you will view the flags of every nation recognized by the United States. This hall stands as a reminder of the fact that the Center would never had been possible without the generous contributions of many other countries. You will also want to see the Israeli Lounge which has been decorated with 40 painted and gilded panels depicting musical instruments mentioned in the Bible, as well as the African Rooms decorated with beautiful tapestries from various African nations. Also impressive is the Hall of States, in which the flags of all 50 states have been hung in the order in which they joined the Union. The size of two football fields, The Grand Foyer is the site of many free concerts and performances. You will be struck by the notable works of art that are found here, including a sculpture by Barbara Hepworth, several tapestries by Henri Matisse, and an albaster vase dating from 2600 B.C. that was found in an Egyptian pyramid.

Spectacular theaters and concert halls, magnificent displays of artwork, and an overall sense of history are sure make a visit to the John F. Kennedy Center for the Performing Arts one of the highlights of your Washington vacation.

A Tribute of American Catholics to Mary, the Blessed Mother, Patroness of the United States, the **NATIONAL SHRINE OF THE**

IMMACULATE CONCEPTION (4th Street and Michigan Avenue) is the country's largest Catholic Church. While contemporary in style, the architects of The Shrine were obviously influenced by Romanesque and Byzantine design. In tribute to the large numbers of Catholics who immigrated to the United States from other countries, the Shrine contains 57 ethnic chapels, and services are celebrated in many languages in the Roman and Eastern rites. Two thousand worshippers are accommodated by the Upper Church, while the Crypt Church, designed in the style of the early catacombs, and the ethnic chapels are used in more intimate ceremonies. The domes and vaults of the church are adorned with an impressive collection of mosaics depicting such miraculous events as the Descent of the Holy Spirit, Creation, and the Assumption of the Blessed Virgin. If you plan your visit well, you may be able to attend one of the frequently given concerts on the Shrine's two pipe organs and the Choir of the National Shrine, or hear a weekly recital of the 56-bell Knights' Tower Carillon. Services and tours daily. (202) 526-8300

Presented to the American people by the citizens of the Netherlands as a token of their appreciation for aid received during and after World War II, **THE NETHERLANDS CARILLION** (intersection of Route 50 and Fort Meyers Drive, Arlington Va) is dedicated to the principles of freedom, justice, and democracy. The carillon contains 49 bells cast from a bronze alloy, and its total weight is 61,403 pounds. Each bell carries an emblem signifying a group of Dutch society and a verse composed by Dutch poet Ben Van Eysselsteijn. Designed by Joost W. C. Boks, a leading Dutch architect, The Netherlands Carillon tower is about 127 feet high, 25 feet deep, and 36 feet wide. Situated on a large quartzite plaza enclosed by a lava stone wall, and guarded by two bronze lions designed by Dutch Sculptor Paul Koning, the carillon is truly a majestic sight. The carillion is played by a trained carillonneur or, it may be operated by an automatic electronic system. Carillion concerts presented Saturdays and national holidays from April through August. (202) 285-2598

The gold-leafing ceiling alone makes a trip to **UNION STATION** (Union Station Metro stop, 50 Massachusetts Avenue, NE) worth the time. Designed by architect Daniel Burnham, the Beaux Arts building was inspired by the triumphal arches and baths of Rome. Neglected for many years, Union Station has recently been restored to its former splendor. This grand building is now the home of upscale restaurants, over 100 well-known national and specialty retailers.

Visit the **U.S. BOTANIC GARDENS** (Federal Center Metro stop, at Maryland Ave. and 1st., S.W., Inbetween the Air and Space Museum and the Capital. In 1842 an expidition returned to the U.S. with many exotic plants from the South Seas and they created such excitement that the Botanic Garden was created from the Old Patent Office Building. The gardens are now one of the most interesting .gardens in the country. (202) 225-8333.

Standing majestically on Mount Saint Alban is the world's sixth largest cathedral, the **WASHINGTON NATIONAL CATHEDRAL** (at Massachusetts and Wisconsin Avenues). Recently completed in 1990, the Cathedral is the final resting place for many notable Americans, including Woodrow Wilson, and possesses a beautiful series of stain-glass windows depicting scenes from American history. The Cathedral boasts an impressive Gothic design, and its Gloria in Excelsis Tower is 676 feet above sea level, making it the highest point in Washington. Officially known as the Cathedral of Saint Peter and Saint Paul, it is Episcopal in domination; but unlike other parish churches, it has no congregation of its own, and was built for national purposes as "a house of prayer for all people." Each year, thousands of Christians of every persuasion attend services here, and the leaders of many Christian denominations have stood at its pulpit. Throughout the year, The Washington National Cathedral is host to some of the world's finest religious music, with concerts presented by its Cathedral Choir of Men and Boys, the Washington and Cathedral Choral Societies, and members of the National Symphony Orchestra. Open daily, sunrise to sunset, with tours from 10:00 a.m. to 3:15 p.m, and services weekdays at 7:30 a.m., noon, and 4:00 p.m; and Sunday at 8:00 a.m., 9:30 a.m,., 11:00 a.m., and 4:00 p.m. (202) 537-6200

HISTORICAL SITES

It was at **BLAIR HOUSE** that Robert E. Lee refused to accept the command of union forces. Now Blair house is used to house visiting dignataries. During the massive restoration of the White House during the Truman Administration the president uesed it as a temporary White House.

One of the United States greatest abolitionists, Frederick Douglass, who never attended school, was completely self taught and became a tireless defender of freedom. In tribute to this great man, the **FREDERICK**

DOUGLASS NATIONAL HISTORIC SITE (Potomac Station Metro Stop, 1411 W Street SE) was established at Cedar Hill, the house where Douglass spent his last years. With nearly 90-percent of the original possessions that belonged to Douglass and his family members on display, this 21-room Victorian home is a rarity among historic sites. A highlight of the tour is the Growlery, a small building away from the main house, that Douglass used when he wanted to be alone to think and work in peace. Artifacts that document Douglass' life as a slave, abolitionist, civil rights leader, and statesman, together with two films, tell the story of this man who was born a slave and became a spokesman for his people. Open daily, 9:00 a.m. - 5:00 p.m., with tours conducted every half hour. (202) 426-5960

Beautifully situated on the banks of the Potomac River, George Washington's family estate, **MOUNT VERNON** (Southern terminus of the George Washington Parkway) gives visitors a glimpse of the private man who was the nation's first president. The house was erected in 1743 by Lawrence Washington, the President's half -brother, and it remained in the Washington family until 1860, when it was purchased by The Mount Vernon Ladies Association. The Association's technicians have beautifully restored the home, and scattered throughout it are period furnishings and artifacts from Washington's life. The formal gardens have been restored as well, and a large greenhouse provides the conventional and exotic flowers and plants popular with the Washington family. A tour through the outbuildings, gardens, and slave quarters gives visitors valuable insight into Colonial plantation life. Open daily, March to October, 9:00 a.m. -5:00 p.m.; and November to February, 9:00 a.m. - 4:00 p.m. 780-2000.

The home of all the important documents , including the Declaration of independence, The Constitution and the Bill of Rights is **NATIONSAL ARCHIVES** (7th and 9th Sts., N.W.)The bronze entrance doors fron Constitution Avenue are six and a half tons each.(202) 523-3000.

After leading the United States in World War I, President Woodrow Wilson retired to this townhouse in Dupont Circle that is today designated **WOODROW WILSON** House (Dupont Circle Metro Stop, 2340 S Street, NW), a National Historic Landmark. Over 90-percent of the items on display actually belonged to the Wilson's during their retirement. Wilson, who lived here from 1921 until 1924, was the only president to live in Washington after his retirement. It was in this unassuming house that the Wilsons entertained distinguished guests, including David Lloyd George and Georges Clemeneau. All of the Wilson's furniture, private possessions, and presidential momentos that are on display have made Woodrow Wilson House a time capsule of the 28th President's era. Open Tuesday - Saturday, 10:00 a.m. - 4:00 p.m.; Sunday, Noon - 4:00 p.m. (202) 387-4062

MUSEUMS

THE ARMED FORCES MEDICAL MUSEUM (14th and Dahlia Sts. at Walter Reed Army Center

They have the leg bone ofMajor General Daniel Sickles who had it blown off during the battle of Gettysburg. Representative Daniel Sickles shot to death the son of Francis Scott Key in a dispute over Sickles' wife. Open: Mon. - Fri. 9:30p.m. - 4:30 p.m., Sat. 11:30a.m. - 4:30 p.m.

Founded on the philosophy that children learn best by doing, **THE CAPITAL CHILDREN'S MUSEUM** (Union Station Metro stop, 800 3rd Street) does a truly excellent job of introducing young people to the arts, sciences, and humanities. Unlike typical museums, which most children find boring, The Capital Children's Museum is a "hands on" museum, and allows children to touch, and even play with, the exhibits. Your child may be given the chance to make a paper flower or tortilla in the International Hall, or explore career choices by sliding down a fire pole or driving a city bus. Other exhibits include the Communication Exhibit, which traces the history of communication from the dawn of civilization to the computer age; and the Sound and Silence exhibit, which, among other things, presents the experience of the hearing impaired in more than 30 hands-on experiences. Because it is geared specifically to children, The Capital Children's Museum provides parent's with the opportunity to introduce their children to museums in a fun and imaginative way. Open daily, 10:00 a.m. - 5:00 p.m. (202) 543-8600

Possessing the most impressive array of Russian decorative arts outside of the Soviet Union, the **HILLWOOD MUSEUM** (4155 Linean Avenue, NW) is one of Washington's most unique galleries. The Museum's collection of Russian decorative arts was donated by the estate of the late cereal heiress, Marjorie Merriweather Post, and includes porcelain, glass, silver, and rare paintings. Hillwood Museum's most treasured possessions include a diamond wedding crown worn by three czarinas, two jewel-encrusted Faberge Easter eggs, and a gold chalice inlaid with diamonds and other precious gems that once belonged to Catherine the Great. Outside, you will find an exquisite garden that houses an authentic Russian summer house, called a dacha, and an Indian Building that features a large collection of American Indian artifacts. Open daily except Sunday and Tuesday, March - January. Advance reservations are required for admission to the museum, but not the grounds. (202) 686-5807

Once restricted to the home and not recognized as historically significant, the works of women artists are finally given the respect they so richly deserve at the **NATIONAL MUSEUM OF WOMEN IN THE ARTS** (Metro Center Metro Stop, 1250 New York Avenue, NW). Opened in 1987, this is the only museum in the world dedicated to the work of women artist. The museum possesses an impressive collection of 700 works, representing the achievement of 300 women from 28 different countries. The collection is displayed in such a way that it accurately chronicles the political and social conditions that women have faced, and the way their art was treated. Works by Mary Cassatt, Lilla Cabot Perry, Louise Nevelson, Georgia O'Keefe, and Helen Frankenthaler are indicative of the excellence of the Museum's collection. In addition to the galleries, the museum houses a Library and Research Center dedicated to promoting the study of women in the arts. The facility contains thousands of books and periodicals, as well as resource files on over 10,000 artists from all periods and countries. Open Tuesday - Sunday, tours arranged in advance. (202) 783-5000

Two very elegant Victorian houses in picturesque Dupont Circle are home to **THE TEXTILE MUSEUM** (Dupont Circle Metro stop, 2320 S Street, NW), the only museum in the world dedicated to the study and preservation of handmade textiles. Working from an extensive collection of 12,000 woven pieces, the Textile Museum mounts three to four major exhibits each year. In the past, these exhibits have included an extraordinary display of pre-Columbian textiles from Peru, Spain and Africa. An impressive array of Oriental Carpets dating from the 15th to 19th century reflect a tremendous amount of diversity within the Islamic world. A guided tour through these, and other exhibits is an excellent way to become more familiar with textile arts throughout the world. An Arts Library is divided into sections on fine arts, decorative arts, techniques and textile processes. Open Tuesday - Saturday, 10:00 a.m. - 5:00 p.m.; Sunday 1:00 p.m. - 5:00 p.m. (202) 667-0441

Located in the historic Washington Navy Yard, **THE U.S. NAVY MEMORIAL MUSEUM** (Eastern Market Metro stop, The Washington Navy Yard, 9th and M streets, building 76) stands as a tribute to the United States' Navy's glorious past and promising future. Housed in what was once the Breech Mechanism Shop of the old Gun Factory, the museum has on display artifacts, models, documents, and fine art that chronicle the history of the U.S. Navy from the Revolution to the present. While wartime heroes and battles are commemorated here, the museum also remembers the Navy's peacetime contributions in exploration, navigation, and humanitarian services. The Navy Museum holds many surprises, and you may have the opportunity to climb aboard guns, walk a gun deck, or examine a Japanese Kamikaze plane. Through an examination of tools, equipment, and other naval artifacts, you will be able to gain a better understanding of naval customs and way of life. Summer hours are Monday - Friday, 9:00 a.m. to 5:00 p.m.; weekends and holidays, 10:00 a.m. - 5:00 p.m.. Fall and Winter hours are Monday - Friday 9:00 a.m. - 4:00 p.m.

A favorite among children and adults alike, and one of the most unique and charming museums found in Washington, **THE WASHINGTON DOLL HOUSE AND TOY MUSEUM** (Friendship Heights Metro stop, 5236 44th Street, NW.) houses an impressive collection of Victorian and other toys of all sorts. Founder and dolls' house historian Flora Gill Jacobs has brought together an interesting and well-researched array of doll houses, dolls, antique games and other toys. While the focus is on toys, The Washington Doll House and Toy Museum is not a frivolous endeavor, since the dolls' houses of the past comprise a study of architecture of the past. There is a heavy emphasis on American toys, with pieces by such American manufacturers as Bliss, Reed, Crandall, and McLouglin making up a large part of the collection; but other countries are also represented. The collection itself is very large, so only a fraction of it is on permanent display, with the remainder reserved for special or seasonal exhibits. After a tour of the museum, you may want to stop at the gift shop, which features pieces on consignment, doll houses, furniture, accessories, and building supplies. Open Tuesday - Saturday, 10:00 a.m. - 5:00 p.m.; Sunday, noon - 5:00 p.m. 244-0024

GALLERIES

With a five block walk south on 17th street from the Farragut West Metro stop, you will find the oldest art gallery in Washington, the **CORCORAN GALLERY OF ART** (17th St. and New York Ave., N.W. (202) 638-3211). Here you can see the George Washington portrait that is found on every one dollar bill. The emphasis is on American Art, but other events and exhibits will also hold your interest. Admission is free due to a special grant from Mobil Oil and the Armand Hammer Foundation. William Wilson. Corcoran, The founder, told his grandchildren that "The most valuable bequest I can make to you is a good name" Free, thirty minute tour start at 12:30 p.m. Tue. - Sun. and 7:30 p.m. on Thursdays.

Built on the extensive personal collection of Duncan and Marjorie Phillip, **THE PHILLIPS COLLECTION** (Dupont Circle Metro Stop, 1600 21st Street, NW) was the nation's first permanent collection of modern art. Since it opened in 1921, the collection has amassed over 2500 works of art. Cezanne, Bonnard, Braque, Daumier, Dove, El Greco, Manet, Matisse, O'Keefe, and Picasso are all represented here. The Phillips Collection is perhaps most famous for its collection of 19th and 20th American Modernist and French paintings, including Renoir's "Luncheon of the Boating Party", and Van Gogh's "Entrance to the Public Gardens at Arles". In addition to the galleries permanent collection, it is often host to temporary exhibitions, that in the past included "The Color Abstractions" and "Georges Braque: The Late Paintings" Free Gallery Talks are held on the first and third

EVENTS

Speeches and concerts are held throughout Washington in celebration of the January 21st **BIRTHDAY OF MARTIN LUTHER KING J.R,,** perhaps the United States' most important civil rights leader.

Parades, fireworks, and traditional dragon dancers mark **THE CHINESE NEW YEAR** in Washington's Chinatown district during the final week of January.

February is **BLACK HISTORY MONTH**, which is celebrated throughout the city with special events, musem exhibits, and other cultural programs.

A Wreath-laying ceremon and a reading of the Gettysburg Address at the Lincoln Memorial marks the **BIRTHDAY OF PRESIDENT ABRAHAM LINCOLN** on February 12.

Celebrate **GEORGE WASHINGTON'S BIRTHDAY** by attending a free open house at Mount Vernon, or a wreath-laying ceremony at the Washington Monument on February 18.

The U.S. Botanic Gardens is the site of an **EASTER SHOW**, March through mid-April.

Constitution Avenue hosts the **SAINT PATRICK'S DAY PARADE** on March 17th.

Fashion shows, parades, and a Japanese Lantern Lighting Ceremony highlight **THE CHERRY BLOSSOM FESTIVAL**, March 31 through April 7.

A Washington Tradition, **THE WHITE HOUSE EASTER EGG ROLL** is held the Monday after Easter on the White House Lawn.

Washingtonians celebrate **THOMAS JEFFERSON'S BIRTHDAY** with military drills and a wreath laying ceremony at The Jefferson Memorial on April 13.

The beginning of spring is marked with **THE WHITE HOUSE SPRING GARDEN TOUR**, in mid-April.

The Folger Shakespear Library markes **WILLIAM SHAKESPEARS BIRTHDAY** on April 20 with plays, music and children's events.

Cultural displays, crafts, and workshops are the featured at **THE ASIAN PACIFIC AMERICAN HERITAGE FESTIVAL** in early May.

Celebrate **MEMORIAL DAY** on the west lawn of the Capitol Building with a concert by the National Symphony, and wreath layings at The Arlington National Cemetary or the Vietnam Memorial.

The British Ambassador and his wife hold a **GARDEN PARTY AT THE BRITISH EMBASSY** in late May or early June in celebration of the Queen's birthday.

Reservations are required three weeks in advance for **THE MARINE BARRACKS PARADES** held Friday Evenings from mid-May until late August at the Marine Barracks on 8th and I Streets.

The Capitol west steps or the Sylvan Theater on the grounds of the Washington Monument are sites for MILITARY BAND CONCERTS on Monday, Tuesday , and Wednesday evenings through out the summer.

Parades are held every Tuesday evening, June through August, at the **IWO JIMA MEMORIAL.**

the nation's capital

Musical and visual presentations about today's Navy mark the **NAVY SUMMER CEREMONIES,** held Thursday evening's during the summer at the Navy Memorial.

SUNDAY POLO MATCHES are held on the Lincoln Memorial Field June through July and September through October.

Dancing under the stars is a treat at the Sylvan Theater on the grounds of the Washington Monument during the **BIG BAND AND JAZZ COMBO SERIES,** held Wednesday evenings, June through August.

Washington goes all out for the **FOURTH OF JULY** with a parade down Constitution Avenue, and a concert and fireworks on the grounds of the National Monument.

Freedom Plaza (14th Street and Pennsylvania Avenue, NW) is the setting for **DC FREE JAZZ CONCERT** on July fourth.

President's Park (15th Street and Constitution Avenue) hosts the **CARRIBEAN SUMMER IN THE PARK** during July.

Hear the U.S. Army Band presents **CONCERT: 1812 OVERTURE** at the Sylvan Theater on August 20th.

The Capitol west lawn hosts the **LABOR DAY CONCERT** presented by the National Symphony.

The **NATIONAL FRISBEE FESTIVAL** is held the Saturday of Labor Day Weekend on the grounds of the Washington Monument.

An international celebration with music, food, and gifts marks **ADAMS MORGAN'S DAY** in mid-September.

Columbus Fountain in front of Union Station is the setting for the **COLUMBUS DAY CELEBRATION,** a festival of Italian cultural exhibits, speeches, and a military band concert.

A second **WHITE HOUSE GARDEN TOUR** is held in Mid October.

The District of Columbia Armory is the site of the popular **CHRISTMAS CRAFT SHOW** at the beginning of November.

Tours of Woodrow Wilson House mark Washington's **ARMISTICE DAY CELEBRATION,** held November 11 through November 25.

Wreath-layings and military bands are the highlights of **VETERAN'S DAY CEREMONIES** at Arlington National Cemetary and the Vietnam Veterans Memorial.

Free holiday programs are featured at the **KENNEDY CENTER HOLIDAY FESTIVAL,** .held the throughout the month of December.

The **LIGHTING OF THE NATIONAL CHRISTMAS TREE** takes place on the Ellipse in mid-December.

The **WHITE HOUSE CANDLELIGHT TOUR** is usually held three evenings during the holiday season.

The Old Post Office Pavilion celebrates **NEW YEARS EVE** live entertainment, and a giant "Love" stamp that descends at midnight.

WASHINGTON BICENTENNIAL CELEBRATION

Washington turns 100 years old in 1991, and a whole series of special events have been slated to celebrate this auspicious event. The following is only a tentative listing of those events, so please call (202) 789-7000 to confirm the date and time before deciding to attend any one of them.

An exhibition titled **WASHINGTON BEYOND THE MONUMENTS** will be held at the National Archives, January through the Fall.

WASHINGTON, D. C INTERNATIONAL FILM FESTIVAL, will be held in late April. No location has, as yet, been announced.

A program on **WASHINGTON, D.C. AND PEIRRE L'ENFANT** will be held at International Monetary Fund Visitors Center, May 15 through July 5.

Fords Theater will stage a **GRAND REOPENING** on September 4.

THE GRAND BICENTENNIAL PARADE will march down Pennsylvania Avenue on September 7.

NORTH WEST

ADAMS MORGAN

Often compared to Paris' Left Bank and New York's Greenwich Village, Adams Morgan is one of Washington's most interesting areas. It is one of the only places in Washington were you can see such a diverse collection of people; nearly every race. creed, income group, and political inclination is represented here. Adams Morgan is one of a rare breed of neighborhoods that offers a surprise around every corner.

Adams Morgan possesses a rich history that is as varied and as interesting as the people who live there. The 1920s and 1930s marked the neighborhood's heyday, and most of its architecture dates from that era. At that time, the community included the Columbia Heights section; and it was here that much of Washington's elite made their home. After World War II, many long-time residents left Adams Morgan for the suburbs, and beautiful homes and spacious apartments were divided into smaller, low-cost units. The sections new affordability drew a whole new breed of people, and Adams Morgan began to acquire the ethnic diversity that it is known for today.

In the 1950s, integration brought Adams Morgan new life when the principals of two schools, John Quincy Adams Elementary and Black Morgan Elementary, joined forced to form the Adams Morgan Organization, a group that worked for neighborhood improvement. The community adopted the coalition's name, its present boundaries were defined, and slowly, Adams Morgan began to develop an identity. The community was further solidified in the late 1960's and early 1970's, when young idealists began moving to the area in an effort to prove that people of different races and cultures could live together.

These young idealists were successful in their experiment. Adams Morgan has become one of Washington's most integrated and ethnically diverse neighborhoods, and its varied cultural roots are evident in the French pastry shops, Cuban groceries, and Ethiopian restaurants that are often situated on the same blocks. Today, Adams Morgan is a boisterous neighborhood, whose noisy streets are filled with offbeat galleries, shops, and ethnic restaurants. Situated in a city where some of the nation's most important business is conducted, lively Adams Morgan offers visitors a pleasant change of pace.

books

BICK'S BOOKS
2309 18th Street NW
Washington D.C. 20009
Tel: (202) 328-2356
Hrs:
Monday - Thursday 10:00 a.m. - 11:00 p.m.
Friday and Saturday. 10:00 a.m. - Midnight
Sunday Noon - 8:00 p.m.
Visa, MasterCard, and American Express are accepted.

Is there a book you have been looking for and haven't been able to find? Do you yearn to dig deeply into a selection of books you never knew existed? BICK'S BOOKS is the place to discover that illusive book and it's the place to pique your curiosity with suggestions for new, stimulating and, possibly provoking, literary directions. BICK'S can open a whole new world in general interest reading. Even the most casual browser will find the widest possible choice of ideas to ponder, peruse, and study. Robby Bick insists on it's being so.

Bick's is right in the middle of Adams Morgan and leans, understandably, a little to the left. But, not to the exclusion of other persuasions. Books on Eastern and Western philosophies, poetry, sex, Santeria, best sellers, classics, the occult, women's topics and black studies give the impression that BICK'S BOOKS is orchestrating a symphony. All the instruments are in place and each provides a contribution to the overall arrangement. Completeness counts, Robby explains. For his inventory, he combines what he wants to sell with the books that are known to sell. He then adds books that he knows people will want to read.

It's an adventure to wander through the well organized stacks, especially since the layout is a bit unorthodox! Movement is linear, through a long and narrow store, which serves to make sure nothing is missed. Robby's desk is right on the floor where customers can always find him if they have questions or need a guide. In this store, any shopper is bound to come upon a delightful discovery. But, the book buff will, certainly, go wild!

health foods/gourmet

YES! NATURAL GOURMET
3425 Connecticut Avenue NW
Washington, D.C. 20008
Tel: (202) 363-1559

Hrs: Monday - Friday:	9:00 a.m. - 9:00 p.m.
Saturday:	9:00 a.m. - 7:00 p.m.
Sunday:	10:00 a.m. - 6:00 p.m.
Winter Hours	
Monday - Friday:	9:00 a.m. - 9:00 p.m.
Saturday:	9:00 a.m. - 7:00 p.m.
Sunday:	12:00 a.m. - 6:00 p.m.

Visa, MasterCard and American Express are accepted.

YES! is a positive word denoting the positive feelings that Oliver and Cris Popenoe maintain toward their food and the health of their customers. They are doing their share to help the health-conscious shopper find the kind of food that is good for body fitness and inner growth. Their emphasis is on hearty food that's good for you. Their selections are pure, natural, with no pesticides, and are often ethnic. Ollie is convinced, that to transform the world outside us, we must understand the inner self. He has been working for twenty years to help people achieve that goal.

YES! carries a full line of gourmet foods, organically grown vegetables, vitamins and body care products. And, they offer expert guidance in all departments. The staff is proud of their expertise and are ready and able to share the latest facts with their customers. Informed customers make the best clientele. High standards and personal service make the difference in a shopper's feeling confident that their selections are the safest and best quality items obtainable.

Governmental politicians, entertainers, famous rock stars and ordinary, health-motivated people have all come to rely on YES! for answers to their uncommon needs. The tradition of YES!, the length of time they have been in business, their drive for expertise and passion for quality show that they care. And, they have been doing it all successfully for so many years!

limousine rental

WELTY'S LONDON LIMOS
Suite 605
1868 Columbia Road N.W.
Washington, D.C.
Tel: (201)667-5520
Open seven days, 24 hours a day.
Major Credit Cards Accepted

Unique entertainment is the aim and the essence at WELTY'S LONDON LIMOS, and stylish transportation is the order of business! Imagine an evening at the Kennedy Center, preceded by an elegant, fully-catered meal served on Wedgewood china under the stars on Haines Point or along the bridle path in Rock Creek Park! With three hours notice, Steven Welty of WELTY'S LONDON LIMOS can make such dreams come true! WELTY'S will be delighted to provide once-in-a-lifetime details concerning your travel to and from any theater, cinema, museum, or private party in the District of Columbia or its surrounding areas.

Available 24 hours a day, the distinctive silver and blue Austins can be found at any of Washington's most distinguished social, political, or business affairs, as well as at the most intimate of gatherings. A ride in these London taxi cabs offers roomy comfort, fresh flowers, music of choice, color television and personalized service from trained drivers garbed in a choice of an authentic Bobby's uniform or tails complete with bowler hat and a Union Jack bow tie. Not to be overlooked is the practical convenience of being delivered to any place in the entire area one might wish to go.

Corporate accounts and special rates can be arranged. WELTY'S clientele consists of both regular patrons from about town as well as visitors, so do call in advance. Champagne must be properly chilled!

restaurants

I MATTI
2436 18th Street NW
Washington, D.C. 20009
Tel: (202) 462-8844

Hrs:	Monday- Thursday:	11:00 a.m.- 11:00 p.m.
	Friday - Saturday:	11:00 a.m. - 4:30 a.m.
	Sunday:	11:00 a.m. - 9:30 p.m.

Visa, MasterCard, American Express, and Diners Club are accepted.

For a little "taste" of everything, there's an answer at I MATTI in Adams Morgan! They have trolleys that bring trays of food (in the evening, it's hot) from which, for a set price, customers may make a choice of all that's on the tray. A wonderful way to sample a variety of some of the best Italian food in the area.

I MATTI was opened in 1989 by Roberto Donna, world-renowned chef/owner of Galileo, a fine Italian restaurant on P Street and was recognized by Washingtonian magazine as one of the 50 Best Restaurants in the area. The same standard of excellence prevails at both establishments, with prices a little more modest and the elegance a little more casual at I MATTI. The important similarity between the two is superb food! Traditional Northern Italian cuisine is flawlessly prepared and impeccably served at both restaurants.

At I MATTI, authentic Italian pizza is prepared in many combinations--unmatched in American pizza! For the hurried customer, any one of them can be prepared and served in five to eight minutes! Beer is available, along with 200 choices of wine. For those who enjoy grappa, an Italian after dinner drink, 20 different kinds are listed. The generous menu contains a variety of unusual dishes. Goat stew, grilled squab and fresh fish share the menu with succulently sauced linguine, chicken, fetuccine, and veal. Choices of these and other specialty dishes are offered at a Sunday Brunch Buffet. Each morsel is carefully prepared by Donna Livio Massignani who was a chef in Italy for 26 years, and a talented and dedicated apprentice, Charles Perry. Each is committed to perfection and all are concerned with delighting diners!

THAI TASTE
2606 Connecticut Avenue NW
Washington, D.C. 20008
Tel: (202) 387-8876

Hrs:	Monday - Thurday:	11:30 a.m. - 10:30 p.m.
	Friday - Saturday:	11:30 a.m. - 11:00 p.m.
	Sunday:	5:00 p.m. - 10:30 p.m.

Visa, MasterCard, and American Express are accepted.

Sooney Dejaichvitlert, with dreams of opening a Thai restaurant in the United States, searched for the best chef in Thailand! In 1984 his dream came true. He introduced Chef Siriwat and THAI TASTE to the District of Columbia. They became an immediate success! Today, they are well and thriving near the corner of Connecticut and Calvert--only steps from the Woodley Park Metro. And, the success story continues! Now, there are two more THAI TASTES--one in Georgetown and one in Rockville, Maryland. All three offer the highest quality in Thai food. Sooney, along with his brother and wife--Niphond and Jirapa and Freddy Chan, is justifiably proud of the awards they consistently earn. Most recently, THAI TASTE is one of only five Asian restaurants chosen to receive the 1989 Washingtonian People's Choice Award!

With good reason! THAI TASTE takes the finest of Chinese and Thai cooking and uniquely blends them into a best of both! The sauces are distinguished: peanut sauce for Satay (pork grilled on a stick); cucumber sauce for Tod Mum (deep fried minced shrimp); oyster, black bean, sweet and sour, asparagus, and wine sauce, all memorable, each enhancing a superior dish! Chicken soup with coconut milk is a favorite along with green or red curry. Goong Prik Gleua (shrimp sauteed with peppercorn chili) is a thrilling experience for seafood lovers.

Under pictures of Thai dancers and warriors and portraits of the king and queen, black lacquer booths line the walls while tables for four settle comfortably into the center, allowing ample seating in an elegantly cozy atmosphere. However, the food is the star of this story!

DOWNTOWN

Since its birth over two centuries ago, downtown Washington has grown and changed in numerous ways. Some of these changes, like the paving of streets and laying of sewer lines in 1874, were planned, while others were not. Whatever the changes, however, downtown Washington has managed to prosper as the hub of the city's life.

Washington has just recently finished its "third revival", and its impact on the downtown area has been tremendous. Nowhere is this more evident than on Pennsylvania Avenue. Spurred on in the 1960's by a presidentially commissioned plan to redevelop the area, Pennsylvania Avenue now appears the way Pierre L'Enfant originally planned it.

Other streets and avenues have felt the effects of the renaissance as well. For example, F Street, which was one of the city's major residential districts, has become a shopping mall; while 7th Street, where farmers once sold their wares at the Center Market, is now dotted with restaurants, nightclubs, and art galleries. Other additions to the downtown area, like the Washington Convention Center, and revitalizations of older structures, such as the one which took place at the Old Post Office Tower and Pavilion, have given the city a whole new vitality and diversity.

Few cities can offer all of the attractions that Washington does. The unique mix of monuments, historic sites, and modern structures, together with the accomplishments of its revitalization have made the downtown area one of Washington's most vital and unique neighborhoods.

accommodations

THE HAY-ADAMS HOTELS
One Lafayette Square
Washington, DC 20006
Tel: (202) 638-6600
(202) 638-2716 FAX
Hrs: Open 24 hours a day, seven days.

The John Hay Dining Room
Hrs: Monday - Friday:
Dinner 5:30 p.m. - 10: p.m.
Lunch 12:00 Noon - 3:00 p.m.

The Henry Adams Room
Hrs: Open for breakfast every morning 6:30 - 11:30 a.m.
Monday. - Friday open for breakfast and lunch
Saturday and Sunday brunch

The English Grill
Hrs: Monday - Friday: lunch and dinner

The John Hay Lounge
Hrs: Afternoon Tea daily: 3:00 p.m. - 5:00 p.m.

Everything about the HAY-ADAMS is elegant! Old World elegance, yet, up to the minute in service and style! Located across from the White House, facing Lafayette Square, near St. John's, the church of Presidents, and with a full view of the Washington Monument, this stunning hotel maintains the prestige and position enjoyed by the original homes of two very powerful, affluent and lettered men who solidly maintained a close relationship with presidents, world luminaries and, most importantly, with one another.

The original hotel, designed and built to accommodate wealthy and powerful, native and foreign visitors to the Capital city, changed hands and styles until it was recently renovated to its former elegance with many of its original furnishings and appointments.

For all of its exquisite design and luxury, the HAY-ADAMS HOTEL is a warm and comfortable place to stay. With excellent food, prepared on the premises in a kitchen that never closes, nightly turn down, full butler and concierge service, valet parking, and a solitious staff which is on call day and night, visitors thrive on the elegant history in its historical elegance.

THE JEFFERSON
Sixteenth & M Streets NW
Washington, DC 20036
Tel: (202) 347-2200 or (800) 368-5966
Hrs: Open 24 hours a day, seven days.
Restaurant hrs. 6:30 a.m. - 10:00 p.m.
Visa, MasterCard, American Express, Diners Club, and Discover are accepted.

The grand style of the 1923 Beaux-Arts building is matched only by the simple, old world, elegance befitting the name of the third president, Thomas Jefferson. Just four blocks north of the White House, one block from the business district and across the street from the historic University Club, THE JEFFERSON HOTEL is a perfect place to experience the nation's capital city. The high profile of this truly luxurious hotel has not affected the low key American Colonial atmosphere. Originally built as apartments for Washington society, it still feels more like a comfortable residence than a hotel. Each room is individually furnished with period antiques and each takes on a personality of it's own. The service is distinctive, from the white-gloved doorman to the rest of the staff. They stand ready to provide your every wish, even before you wish it! Laundry service is rapid and is returned in a wicker basket. State-of-the-art is not lost here, with an extremely modern telephone system which provides call conferencing, two line telephone and speaker phone and a FAX capability upon request. A mini bar, VCR and a CD player will be found in each of their 100 guest rooms and suites.

The restaurant at THE JEFFERSON has been completely refurbished and features its own brand of New Virginia Cuisine. Eighteenth century prints and portraits set the style. The rich, dark colored woods and leather are accented by the ornamental white plaster.

Saturday night premiere jazz entertainment, Afternoon Tea and the Sunday Jazz Brunch are highlights that make THE JEFFERSON HOTEL a unique and memorable experience!

THE WILLARD INTER-CONTINENTAL, 1401 Pennsylvania Avenue, NW, Washington, DC 20004; Tel: (202) 628-9100. This is an upscale hotel within walking distance from the White House. They have two restaurants and a lounge with live entertainment.

HOTEL WASHINGTON, 15th Street and Pennsylvania Avenue NW,Washington, DC 20004; (202) 638-5900. The rooftop restaurant and bar offer a spectacular view of the monuments and the White House. It is one of the most scenic views in Washington. Check out their Capital Family Plan.

art galleries

ZENITH GALLERY
413 7th Street NW
Washington, D.C. 20004
Tel: (202) 783-2963
Hrs:

Monday - Friday	10:00 a.m. - 6:00 p.m.
Saturday.	11:00 a.m. - 6:00 p.m.
Sunday	Noon - 4:00 p.m.

Evenings are by appointment only.

Upbeat! The art, the gallery, and the lady-in-charge! Like the proverbial phoenix, Margery Goldberg rose from the ashes of her 100-year-old hayloft studio after it burned down in 1977 and has, relentlessly, progressed to the lovely, modern, domed, atrium-flanked, two-story studio on Seventh Street near the Mall in downtown Washington, D.C.!

It was not an easy trip. There were disappointments, near disasters and true disasters, including the break-up of her Holistic Design School and Zenith Square. She said that she cried for two years about Zenith Square. It was a dream which lived for almost ten years. Artists, dancers, jewelry makers, astrologers, and writers lived and worked in community. There were 25 and there was so much happiness as they all developed their skills and knowledge and shared--everything.

And now, Margery is ensconced in her new art center. She prefers good art that's also fun! No heavy, depressing works for her! She holds a neon and humor show each year to lift everyone's spirits, including her own. She carries unique pieces of crafted jewelry and wearable art. Her sculptures are as varied and diverse as the paintings she handles. She is extraordinarily busy, but she can always find a moment to discuss art with a customer. But, mostly, her customers want to look, not talk--unless it's about an artist or a work to be ordered. It's a trip into fantasy to just BE there in her studio. The atmosphere is so light and ethereal, and provocative! One could just enjoy the respite of it. Or, buy something that you couldn't imagine before you saw it and loved it!

jewelry

TINY JEWEL BOX
1143 Connecticut Avenue NW
Washington, DC 20036
Tel: (202) 393-2747
Hrs: Monday - Friday: 9:30 a.m. - 5:00 p.m.
Saturday: Open:
Saturday: Closed: Memorial Day - Oct. 1
Sunday: Closed
Visa, MasterCard, American Express, Diners Club and Carte Blanche are accepted.

On Connecticut Avenue between L and M Streets, just one block from the Farragut North Metro station, THE TINY JEWEL BOX offers a delightful respite from the bustling activity surrounding it. The building, restored with its charming interior containing handmade walnut fixtures, looks as if it could have been plucked from a quaint city in Europe three quarters of a century ago, stocked with precious stones, coins, silver, gold, and platinum jewelry, then, carefully, placed in the heart of the city. And there it stands as a gentle reminder that beauty should be seen, enjoyed and, sometimes, possessed!

As owners of the oldest and largest location of antique jewelry in the area, Jim Rosenheim, his wife, Marcia, son, Matthew, and their friendly staff continue the family business as it was begun by his parents, with custom service and individual attention to each client, many of whom are fourth and fifth generation customers. The core of the business remains antique and estate jewelry, though Jim, who began apprenticing with his father when he was five years old, buys from 430 dealers in fifteen different countries to maintain a wide variety of choice.

Intrigued by antiques and artifacts, Jim peppers his appraisals with background information, delighting his customers with his interest and knowledge. But, it is the fading art of custom design that triumphs at THE TINY JEWEL BOX where true craftsmanship can blend dreams and reality into heirlooms of rare quality and appeal.

leather

GEORGETOWN LEATHER DESIGN, 1150 Conneticut Avenue NW, Washington DC; Tel: (202) 223-1855. For fine Leather goods. See their story under Georgetown.

maps

THE MAP STORE INC., 1636 Eye Street, NW, Washington, D.C., 20006; Tel: (202) 628-2608. They offer a very complete selection of area, state, country and world maps.

restaurants

CAFE MOZART
1331 H Street NW
Washington, D.C. 20005
Tel: (202) 347-5732

Hrs:	Monday - Friday	7:30 a.m. - 10:00 p.m.
	Saturday:	9:00 a.m. - 10:00 p.m.
	Sunday:	11:00 a.m. - 10:00 p.m.

GERMAN DELI

Tel:	(202) 347-5653	
FAX	(202) 347-4958	
Hrs:	Monday - Saturday:	9:00 a.m. - 10:00 p.m.
	Sunday:	11:00 a.m. - 10:00 p.m.

Closed: Thanksgiving, Christmas, and New Years Days.
Visa, MasterCard, American Express, Diners Club and Carte Blanche are accepted.

Everyone knows how hard it is to walk through a German Deli! But you must do it to get to CAFE MOZART, where breakfast, lunch and dinner are served continuously during everyday of the year, except

Thanksgiving, Christmas and New Years Day! Then, linger in the Deli on the way out!

After Hilde and Max Fehr bought their 1964, German Deli and moved it, in 1982, to downtown Washington, D.C., they opened along with it a new restaurant, CAFE MOZART. This authentic Viennese cafe has become a favorite for those looking for basic, home-cooked German food and tempting Viennese delicacies--a perfect place to stop for a meal, snack or just to relax at the bar. And, on Wednesday through Saturday evenings, artists entertain with both popular and classical music.

A favorite Entree is Viennese Schnitzel, but patrons like to brag about Roast Pork, Sauerbraten, Goulash and the amazing variety of sausages from Brat- to Weisswurst--and of course, tasty Red Cabbage, Sauerkraut and Potato Salad! Dobosch and Black Forest Cake and Apple-, Nut- or Poppyseed Strudel lead the list of tantalizing desserts. Can't eat another bite? Take some home to enjoy later--or perhaps, to share with family or friends!

DOMINIQUE'S FAMOUS FRENCH RESTAURANT
1900 Pennsylvania Avenue NW
Washington, D.C. 20006
Tel: (202) 452-1126

Hrs:	Lunch Monday. - Friday:	11:30 a.m. - 2:30 p.m.
	Dinner Monday. - Thursday:	5:30 p.m. - 12:30 a.m.
	Friday - Saturday:	5:30 p.m. - 1:00 a.m.
	Sunday:	5:00 p.m. - 10:00 p.m.

Reservations suggested.
Visa, MasterCard, American Express and Diners Club are accepted.

1900 Pennsylvania Avenue is about as close to the White House that most of us will ever be invited for dinner! So upon arriving there, where the greeting is wonderfully warm and friendly, it's easy to slip into a sense of importance! That's the way DOMINIQUE'S is. Fun, French and deferential!

The extravagant menu entertains as it explains the extraordinary variety and range of choices from the "Famous U.S. Senate Bean Soup"--which many experts judge to be the very best and which is packaged to take home or mail anywhere in the U.S.--to wild game, rattlesnake salad or sauteed alligator! The Chicken Nancy Reagan is so delicious and generous that a special bag is provided to take any leftovers home so every morsel can be savored! The seafood is unequaled, with trout and salmon standing out as favorites!

To enjoy the camaraderie of the crowd or to feast before or after the theater, the Prix Fixe dinner is a genuine bargain! A generous assortment of appetizers, entrees with fresh vegetables and homemade desserts are available--Lobster, Filet of Beef, Rack of Lamb, Roast Quail, or Caesar Salad for Two--but if not listed for that evening, you'll certainly find it a la carte. Do splurge on dessert--Baked Alaska, Sorbet a la Farrah (as in Fawcett!) or Liz Taylor's Les Truffles au Chocolate! Outrageously yummy! Or indulge a bit in one of the thirteen suggestions from The Cafe Bar. Or, Remy Martin??

GALILEO
1110 21st Street NW
Washington D.C. 20036
Tel: (202) 293-7191

Hrs:	Lunch	
	Monday - Friday	11:45 a.m. - 2:00 a.m.
	Dinner:	
	Monday - Thursday:	5:30 p.m. - 10:00 p.m.
	Friday - Saturday:	5:30 p.m. - 10:30 p.m.
	Sunday:	5:00 p.m. - 8:30 p.m.

Visa, MasterCard, American Express and Diners Club are accepted.

The menu changes twice a day--every day! Yet, requests for special dishes not on the menu will always be honored! That's because the owner, Roberto Donna, is one of the brightest and most innovative chefs in town. Trained in Italy before working in famous restaurants there, as well as in France, England, and Switzerland, Roberto came to the United States in 1979. In 1984 he opened the GALILEO, to immediate success, in the heart of Washington.

Deceptively housed in a typical Washington row house under a simple sign, the GALILEO is quite elegant inside with dimmed lighting, subtle colors, white linens, and attractive china and crystal. Small, it is delightfully intimate, friendly, and a bit homey--a modern Italian trattoria. Under the watchful eye of attentive and amiable waiters, dressed in proper white shirts, black ties, tuxedo pants and vests, traditional and newly created Northern Italian dishes are served to perfection. Periodically, Donna slips out of his Chef's cap and into the role of warm, gracious host to preside over the dining and ensure his customers' satisfaction.

Nationally and internationally recognized, GALILEO has been consistently chosen by Washingtonian Magazine as one of the area's 50 VERY Best Restaurants. Everything from breads, pasta, and even ice cream is prepared on the premises from the freshest ingredients! Thick fillets of fish, grilled to perfection, game and pastas are favorites. Ravioli is fantastic in a wonderfully light sauce and rivals any found in Italy. The extensive list of finest wines is personally selected by the chef, and can provide a perfect complement to any selection, on or off the menu!

THE PRIME RIB
2020 K Street NW
Washington, D.C. 20006
Tel: (202) 466-8811

Hrs:	Monday - Friday:	11:30 a.m. - 3:00 p.m.
	Monday - Friday:	5:00 p.m. - 11:00 p.m.
	Friday - Saturday:	5:00 p.m. - 11:30 p.m.

Visa, MasterCard, American Express and Diners Club are accepted.

Stick to the basics; a huge piece of prime beef, perfectly cooked and a complementary potato with all the trimmings. This is what the Prime Rib is all about! The owners Nick and Buzz BeLer believe food should be consistently good, with no surprises. It has to be fantastic the first time and every time. General Manager Garth Weldon shares that belief. Ever since the restaurant opened, when he began as a waiter, he has worked toward that goal. It's a friendly, fun place with the strains of jazz piano adding to the entertainment and enjoyment. The atmosphere is comfortable and elegant as the formally dressed staff go quietly and efficiently about their business.

The Prime Rib is, of course, the star performer with a supporting cast of Filet Mignon, New York Strip Steak, and Chicago Porterhouse. The Rack of Lamb, Pork Chops and Chicken Divan are players of equal merit. The seafood provides a royal feast of Imperial Crab that is fit for a king. The manager's personal favorite is the Norwegian Salmon. Salads demonstrate that special flair, with Hearts of Palm, Caesar and Hearts of lettuce with imported Roquefort. The deserts are delicious and the Chocolate Mousse Pie is divine. The Strawberries Romanoff and French Bread with Bourbon Sauce are begging to be tried.

THE PRIME RIB is the place for a romantic rendezvous or a dinner with friends. Whatever the occasion, The Prime Rib is the place for it!

OLD EBBIT GRILL, 675 15th Street, NW, Washington, D.C., 20005; Tel: (202) 347-5801. Washington's oldest saloon serves exceptional American food seven days a week. Founded in 1856 as a boarding house, the Ebbitt guest list read like a "Who's Who of American History." Presidents Grant, Andrew Johnson, Cleveland, Theodore Roosevelt and Harding were said to spend time at the stand-around bar refreshing themselves.

shopping

THE OLD POST OFFICE

Once the headquarters of the U.S. Postal Service, and now a thriving marketplace , the **OLD POST OFFICE TOWER AND PAVILION** (Federal Triangle Metro stop, 1100 Pennsylvania Avenue and 12th Street), is one of Washington's most exciting landmarks. Visitors to this historic spot may take a ride in a glass elevator up to the 315-foot clock tower to view Washington from its second-highest vantage point. The clock possesses ten huge bells that are replicas of those in Westminster Abbey, and tours of the bells and the workings of the clock are conducted daily. In the courtyard below, seasonal festivals , including The Cherry Blossom Festival, Oktoberfest, and the Fourth of July Celebration highlight the year. Dancers, musicians, clowns and other performers present shows each day on a stage surrounded by unique shops and foodstands, making The Old Post Office Tower and Pavilion one of Washington's most festive places. Open daily. (202) 28502598.

restaurants

PEGASUS
Old Post Office Pavilion
1100 Pennsylvania Avenue NW
Washington, D.C. 20004
Tel: (202) 371-1894
Hrs:

Summer	
Monday - Saturday	10:00 a.m. - 9:30 p.m.
Sunday	12:00 noon - 8:00 p.m.
Winter	
Monday - Saturday	10:00 a.m. - 8:00 p.m.
Sunday	Noon - 6:00 p.m.

Just to watch the Gyro meat, slowly rotating on its vertical spit, is to yearn to taste that marvelously flavored Lamb and Beef! As the huge, sharp knife flicks off the succulent slices and they are deposited onto pita to be folded, it's tough to be patient! Then the moment arrives for the first bite of the most fabulous meat in the world!

Wonderful, wonderful Gyros are to be found behind the stairs, in the Food Court of the Old Post Office Building! At a small stand called, PEGASUS, an incredible amount of tasty, fresh food is prepared and served to an enormous number of hungry visitors each day. Two partners, Joe Meredith and Nick Batsis have, for five and a half years, maintained the Greek traditions, here, at this spotless, centrally located counter, with its clear view of all the bustling activity in the newly restored building under the bell tower in the middle of the District.

Mousaka, Spinach Pie, soup and salads are all made with the freshest ingredients and are prepared from authentic Greek recipes. They are carefully cooked and arranged to perfection--as artfully as the most expensive restaurant! And, catering is available within a one mile radius. Imagine! Gyros for your next party! Or Mousaka? Perhaps, both.

THE WASHINGTON INKWELL. 1100 Pennsylvania Avenue, NW, Washington, D.C., 20004; Tel: (202) 289-4160. They offer a very complete selection of pens, cards and office supplies. A place to check out while you visit the Old Post Office Pavilion.

THE SHOPS AT NATIONAL PLACE

VIVACE
1331 Pennsylvania Avenue NW #312
Washington, DC 20004
Tel: (202) 737-0657

Hrs:	Monday - Wednesday:	10:00 a.m. - 7:00 p.m.
	Thursday - Friday:	10:00 a.m. - 8:00 p.m.
	Saturday:	10:00 a.m. - 7:00 p.m.
	Sunday:	11:00 a.m. - 5:00 p.m.

Visa, MasterCard and American Express are accepted.

For hats, hats, and more hats check out VIVACE at The National Shops. There are designer hats, Frank Olive, Adolfo, B. Michael, Canadian Hat, Don Anderson, Betmar, Kokin, Whittall & Shon and Commodore. See the Cute hats, inexpensive hats, expensive sophisticated hats, men's hats, unisex hats, and rock star hats. You can find any hat that you could imagine and some you couldn't.

Lori Goldberg left a career in radio to go into retail. She has been very successful importing beautiful women's accessories from Italy and other parts of the world. She can be particularly helpful in picking out something to add an extra accent to that new special outfit.

Vivace has beautiful handbags by Toledando, Capezio, Barganza, Unisa and M. Bianco. They have scarves, silk and wool challis by Anne Klein, Perry Ellis, Echo and Vera. Costume jewelry, sunglasses and umbrellas round out the selection. It's all beautiful and it's all fun!

MAGIC MASTERS, The Shops at National Place, 1331 Pennsylvania Avenue, NW, Washington, D.C., 20004; Tel: (202) 628-0779. They have a few tricks up their sleeve and the tricks are for sale. It's fun to watch their demonstrations of irresistible magic.

ROCKY MOUNTAIN CHOCOLATE FACTORY, The Shops at National Place, 1331 Pennsylvania Avenue, NW, Washington, D.C. 20004; Tel: (202) 638-4350. They offer a great selection of tasty chocolate treats. They boast some of the best candy apples in town.

LOOKING FOR THE DUKE

By Michael Dolan

As soon as Glenn Pearson sits down at the piano, it gets less crowded in Lucien and Martha Banister's parlor, a light-filled room in a rowhouse north of Logan Circle on 13th Street NW. Until he showed up one Saturday afternoon, the biggest thing in the Banisters' parlor was the old Gabler baby grand, its varnish gone black with oxidation. Horn rimmed and medium- complected, Glenn occupies a lot of space. He's on the outer edge of ordinary tall guyness (beyond his height of 6'5", people squint and try to remember which team you played for), and suggests an NBA guard retired into profitable announcing work.

But the long arms and big hands that would have made Glenn Pearson a threat at the top of the key gave him an edge on keys of a different sort. Instead of basketball, he took up piano, and has been playing professionally for 20 years, sometimes as a solo, sometimes leading his dance band, Floating Opera. Like many journeymen of his trade, Glenn can play anything, but when he plays what he wants it's usually something by the piano man who once lived in the house next door to the Banisters'.

The Banisters' neighborhood is among the oldest in recent Washington history, which is to say the era after the Civil War. It consists mostly of two- and three-story Victorian rowhouses, interrupted occasionally by small wooden structures or larger buildings like the derelict Whitelaw Hotel, up at 13th and T. Where left uninterfered with -- the preferred camouflage is fake stone or siding made of vinyl, aluminum, or asbestos -- the indigenous architecture is rich with insets, herringbones, corbeling, and other vocabulary words from the lost language of bricklayers. Except for modern intrusions such as the District government building at 14th and U,the skyline is low and open.

These streets can get mean -- at ten o'clock on a Saturday morning, working girls are sometimes out on the corner, and discarded hypodermics show up in the gutters like dead leaves. But the neighborhood retains an airiness and gentility, recalling a way that much of Washington once looked, and in great measure no longer does.

Glenn tentatively tries the Gabler; the tuning is off, and the sound is muffled by the piano's lid. Lucien Banister has covered it with mementoes of Duke Ellington, whose family lived in the neighborhood between 1905 and 1929, first across the street, then next door, then around the corner.

There are pieces of sheet music, souvenir programs, sepia photos. One shows a sleek young Ellington, about to leave D.C. to stalk success in Manhattan. There are 30s-vintage issues of The Flash, a local picture weekly that mixed news of black Washington with updates on life at the southern end of the Chickenbone Express. There are Ellington 78s on the Brunswick and Victor and Okeh labels, each thick as a hatbrim and probably still playable, 60 years after they were sold new for 35 cents (six bits for the top-of-the-line Brunswicks) by Reid's Music Store at "11th and You Street NW." The labels sternly forbid use of the records "for radio broadcast", carefully identifying the tunes as "foxtrots" and -- as a concession to the Latin American market -- translating their titles into Spanish, so that the sturdy-jumping "East St. Louis Toddle-Oo," for example, becomes the more languid "El Tudelo del East St. Louis." There is a sheaf of Christmas cards, posters really, that Ellington had sent over the years to his childhood friend Edith Pinn, who was Lucien Banister's business partner until she died in 1982.

Pearson tries a few chords, closing his eyes and drifting into a melancholy melody; the Gabler sounds like a dimestore harpsichord. Lucien Banister and I strain to catch the tune. "Solitude," Glenn says, shifting into "Satin Doll," more recognizable for its jauntiness but still resembling something being played by an orchestra on hallucinogens. While Pearson checks out the old Gabler baby grand, Lucien Banister told me how it came into his possession.

"I inherited the house in 1983 from Edith de Bruhl, who used to be Edith Pinn. She got the house from her parents. We had been friends for years, and I took care of her when she got sick the last time. She died in 1982. She was like family to me," he said. "We met 30 years ago, when I first came to Washington from Winchester, Virginia, to work at the Agriculture Department. I met Edith at the Recreation Center on North Kent Street in Winchester; that was a dance hall she ran with her cousin as a sideline. She taught at Garrison grade school in Washington. We got to talking and became friends, and eventually business partners. We had a little store in Middleburg. She used to hear from Duke Ellington all the time; he'd send postcards and Christmas cards. They were very close, and I've held onto these things as a memorial to her and to him." When Edith died, he bought the piano from the estate.

Sixty and seventy years ago, this was a great neighborhood for piano players. The Pinns' baby grand got tickled now and again by Ralph

Green, a cousin who gave Edward Ellington his nickname. "Duke" had no real basis; Ralph Green was just one of those fellows given to dispensing nicknames; his own was "Zeb."

Sometimes -- when he wasn't over playing baseball on the vacant lot behind the 12th Street YMCA -- little Duke would wander into the Pinns' parlor and noodle around on the Gabler. There was a piano at home as well. Both his parents played; he wrote later that one of his earliest memories was being moved to tears by his mother's rendition of "The Rosary."

As befitted their strivers' status, Ellington mere et pere favored the classics. But the neighborhood offered more secular diversions -- ragtime, the blues, jazz, and a hybrid species of dance tunes. Over at Seventh and T, alongside the Howard Theater, the old upright in Frank Holliday's poolroom was rarely still; between gigs at house hops and rent parties and saloons like the Industrial Cafe and Jack's and Mrs. Dyer's or the Poodle Dog Cafe -- a cabaret-cum-soda fountain around the corner from Griffith Stadium -- local heroes like Clarence Bowser and Lester Dishman and Oliver "Doc" Perry could be found hitting the note for the nine-ball shooters. One of their crowd-pleasing techniques came from New York courtesy of Lucky Roberts, who played the Howard, deeply impressing the D.C. crew with his trademark move of yanking a hand off the keys, as if they were too hot to handle.

Although D.C. musicians looked on New York as Mecca -- Washington didn't have a single recording studio to call its own -- the town had a reputation as a hot musical spot. The Howard was a regular stop for Lucky Roberts and the rest of the day's black stars, and their aura spilled eastward to the clubs around 14th and U -- places like the Jungle Inn, where Jelly Roll Morton, the man who claimed to have invented jazz, played his last riff. When ragtime great James P.Johnson was in town, he'd compete in "cutting contests" -- hardjamming duels of skill and stamina -- with neighborhood contenders.

According to legend, on one such sortie James P. went one-on-one with Duke Ellington, then making a name for himself with an after-school job at the Poodle Dog's piano. Johnson picked the tune: his own "Carolina Shout." First the great man himself played the number, hammering the keys and stomping the pedals and working the crowd like a ward heeler on primary day. Then young Ellington sat down. He was a sharp dresser -- every hair in place, every crease looking like it had been stropped.

the nation's capital

A student of music -- he inherited his parents' good ears and nimble hands -- Duke never had been much of a music student. As a kid, he'd grudgingly practiced under the stern ear of Mrs. Martha Clingscale (referred to variously in Ellington recollections as "Klinkscales," "Chinkscales," and so forth) and later had some private tutoring from Dunbar High music teacher Henry Grant. But Duke's main mentor was a professor of the poolroom; Doc Perry showed him a rudimentary method of reading notes. To learn "Carolina Shout," though, Duke had to run a perforated paper roll containing the song through his parents' player piano again and again, until he'd memorized the chords and pauses.

Duke laid his fingers lightly on the keys, testing the action. Once he had the feel, he began cutting loose, throwing his hands back like Lucky Roberts. He pumped up the volume, shouting "Carolina!" at the break the way James P. Johnson had; the folk in the room got behind their homeboy, and old King James got run out of the joint by the young Duke.

The trip that brought me to the Banisters' parlor and the baby grand that the baby Duke played on began with Felix Grant, the eminence grise of Washington jazz disc jockeys.

Born in Manhattan, Felix has lived in D.C. since 1945, when he mustered out of the Coast Guard with a Navy Cross and a yen to work in radio. Besides amassing an encyclopedic knowledge of jazz, Felix introduced the bossa nova to North American ears. After 30 years at WMAL-AM, he got the gate in 1984. Now he has a Saturday afternoon show on WDCU-FM. He's as easy on the ear in person as on the air. Even over the telephone, his voice sounds like midnight.

"You know, this April Duke Ellington would have been 90 years old," he said. "Remember that list I told you about, the one of the places his family lived while they were still here in Washington? I was thinking it might be a gas to go around and visit them."

"Sure," I said. "Let's go looking for the Duke."

Felix showed up casually spiffed in leather jacket and jeans, wearing a blue Chairman Mao hat he bought on a trip to China and driving a black Thunderbird he bought new in 1955. We plotted our route -- first Ward Place, then Rhode Island Avenue, then the rest -- and climbed into the T- Bird, whose small-block V-8 rumbles authoritatively, like bass notes at the deep end of a piano.

"The first time I met Duke Ellington was 25 or 30 years ago, when I was working at WMAL," Felix said, aiming the Thunderbird downtown. "We used to run into one another when he was in town. One time he came to Capitol Hill; he was the most elegant guy who ever hit the place. We were walking down one of those old marble hallways with Edward Brooke and George Murphy, the song- and-dance man who'd gotten into Congress.

"Duke was striding along with this belted polo coat over his shoulders. He spotted four women standing off to one side. You must remember, he was a tremendous ladies' man, not in the sense of hitting on everyone, but just. . . appreciative. He sees these gals and he rolls his eyes at us and says, 'Hey, why don't we all stand over here awhile?' And we did."

We were rolling down the Whitehurst headed for Washington Circle; despite their age, the T- Bird's springs were giving as good as they got.

"The last time I saw him was in 1974. There was a presentation on his behalf at the Sumner School at 17th and M," Felix said between potholes. "He was on his last legs; they had to carry him in. I'd brought my copy of Music is My Mistress, his autobiography, in a manila envelope; I asked if he'd sign it. He wrote, 'To my friend, Felix Grant.' He died a few months later."

We rounded the circle and took New Hampshire to 23rd, heading north past the few remaining houses in that part of the West End. "The way this list came about was, one night on the air back in '72, I mentioned that Duke had told me he was born near Georgetown, but I didn't know exactly where. Right after that I got a letter from Mathilde Williams listing every place the Ellingtons lived in Washington."

Mathilde Williams wasn't just a Grant fan; she was a curator with the D.C. Public Library at Wisconsin Avenue and R Street NW. Hearing of Felix's curiosity, she dusted off her Boyd's Directory and went to work. The Boyd's Directory testifies to a long-vanished sense of permanence in American life. No longer published, it was a yearly inventory of each city's residents by address and occupation; some editions show who owned and who rented. Mathilde Williams began with the Boyd's books of the 1890s. Before Duke Ellington developed velocity sufficient to break the pull of hometown gravity, she found, he and his family traveled a tight little orbit around black Northwest. Between 1898 and 1922, the directory lists Duke's father, James E. Ellington (and later his family), living at 1462 Rhode Island Avenue NW, 2129 Ward Place NW, 420 Elm

Street NW, 1805 13th Street NW, 1816 13th Street NW, and 1212 T Street NW. Later entries show "Edward K. Ellington, student" at the family address; the 1922 Boyd's lists "Edward K. Ellington, musician" at 2728 Sherman Avenue NW.

Felix drove past Blackie's House of Beef and turned onto Ward Place, a short curve of concrete between 23rd Street and New Hampshire Avenue NW. Ward Place was thick with construction workers putting the finishing touches on an enormous hole in the ground where Blackie's used to stack the oak for its fireplaces.

"I thought it would be nice to put a marker on the Ward Place house -- 'Duke Ellington was born here,' that sort of thing," Felix said. "I called the Ellington Society, where someone suggested that I get confirmation on the address. I went to the D.C. Bureau of Records, where, if you have $5 and the names of the mother and father, you can get a copy of the birth certificate of anyone born in Washington. I don't think the guy who handled my request even knew who Duke Ellington was.

"These days they spit something out of the computer, but back then -- in '72 or '73 someone physically copied the original certificate on a Xerox machine. It said Duke was born at 2129 Ward Place NW on April 29, 1899, and that his birth was attended by a midwife who lived on 19th Street. All that remained was to find the actual spot. When I came by here I saw that the house was gone and that the real estate boundaries essentially had been erased," Felix said while we waited for a truck to run the gauntlet of double- parked vehicles on Ward Place. "At first it looked as if the house had stood on what's now the site of an apartment house owned by the World Bank. We asked the Bank, and they said it was cool to put up the plaque. But someone at the Bank checked the plats and squares and found that their building wasn't the right place, either. Blackie Auger had bought 2129 Ward Place years ago; the house had been torn down, maybe even before he bought it. When we couldn't find a place to put it, the plaque went into a display case at the Ellington School."

A hole appeared in the traffic jam. We cruised past the postal facility across from Giorgio's Restaurant, located at 2128 Ward Place. Felix found a parking space, and we hoofed it back in the chill morning shadows, dodging delivery trucks and messengers on mountain bikes.

Felix pointed out the red herring World Bank apartment house; an alley led behind it. We followed the alley, which, it turns out, is Ward Court. For decades, the alley was just that -- sixty yards of no-name narrowness.

Then Warren Publishing, which puts out newsletters covering the communications industry, built offices there.

In a business that depends on the arrival of subscription payments, good postal service is paramount. Unfortunately, the Post Office won't deliver mail without an official address, and "you know, back there, on the alley behind Ward Place" wasn't official enough an address to get the messengers to make their appointed rounds. So Warren Publishing petitioned the city to create Ward Court, most of which is either parking spaces or Warren Publishing; across from its offices, the company leases an old two-story stable that once was a watering hole popular with the denizens of the CBS News Bureau on nearby M Street. Most of the stable's exterior is clad in white vinyl siding, but one wall isn't; it features half a dozen bricked-up openings, each about the size and height of a horse's head. We rounded the corner and knocked on the door. Warehouseman Bob Gobbett let us in. There wasn't much to say, or see. Where horses once whinnied and reporters once howled stand silent stacks of newsletters, promotional materials, and stored documents.

Back on Ward Place, amid the bustle outside the Post Office, we tried to gauge where 2129 might have stood. If 2128 was there, then 2129 should be here, but there wasn't much hope of pinning things down without access to official records, so we prepared to march. Our next stop was easy -- 14th and Rhode Island; the one after wasn't. I buttonholed a courier for directions to 420 Elm Street NW. "LeDroit Park," he said. "Up above Florida Avenue."

We settled into the T-Bird again, this time for the short hop to 1462 Rhode Island. "You know, one of Duke's big influences was Willie 'The Lion' Smith, the great stride player who worked the bars and clubs on the Lower West Side of Manhattan in the Twenties," Felix said. "One Willie's things was to call everybody 'Jumbo,' as an affectionate salutation. "I was born on the Upper West Side in 1918. My father was a salesman for a whiskey wholesaler who made the rounds of the taverns, and of course he knew The Lion. Shortly before she died, my mother told me that when I was quite small, my dad started calling me 'Jumbo' -- which I guess he picked up from Willie the Lion."

The visit to 1462 Rhode Island was as brief as our ride. The house, which had abutted the alley east of 14th Street on the south side of Rhode Island, had been erased. In its place: the General Scott Inn, a hotel distinguished by its utter lack of distinguishing marks.

the nation's capital

Although gone, 1462 Rhode Island Avenue was an important stop on the Ellington journey. It had been home to Middleton Cuthbert, MD, who hired James Ellington and his brother George in the 1890s, soon after their father encouraged his sons to emigrate to Washington from the family homestead in Lincolntown, N.C. to escape a plague of lynchings triggered by a regional recession. Eventually the whole family came to the capital.

Four Ellington men had been renting rooms in a boarding house at 1735 H Street NW and working as day laborers. James and George joined Cuthbert's household, probably occupying quarters over the carriagehouse. At first they were butlers -- sometimes moonlighting at the White House and at embassy parties -- and later drivers, handling Dr. Cuthbert's carriage and eventually his electric automobile, one of the first in the city.

Cuthbert encouraged the brothers to use his extensive library; James Ellington was an enthusiastic autodidact. Surrounded by the object lessons of Cuthbert's life and holdings, he began to develop the keen sense of style and class that he passed along to his children. He learned about wines and food, and how to recognize good silverware, good china, and good manners. In Music Is My Mistress, Duke wrote, "J.E. always acted as though he had money, whether he had it or not. He spent and lived like a man who had money, and he raised his family as if he were a millionaire."

James Ellington worked 20 years for Dr. Cuthbert, first living under Cuthbert's roof, then commuting from his various residences. In 1898, when he married Daisy Kennedy, they moved in with her folks -- her father was a police captain -- on 20th Street NW, then into his father's house at 2129 Ward Place, where Duke was born. Except for a brief period when the family lived again at Cuthbert's, the Ellingtons stayed at 2129 until 1906, when they moved to 420 Elm Street, in LeDroit Park, at the edge of Howard University.

Felix aimed the car north on 14th and east on T, through the theater zone and the car repair district, past blocks where the battle between ruin and revival hasn't been settled. At Seventh Street, T suddenly went one way -- east -- past the Howard Theater. Felix chuckled. "This stretch of T Street is one way because of Duke Ellington," he said as we passed the shuttered theater and then Andrea's Barbecue, doing serious noontime business. "It was to accommodate his fans. Shep Allen, who managed the Howard, started bringing in the big bands. He noticed that when the Ellington unit was playing, the traffic on T Street was unbearable. So he got the street one-wayed. By the way, Andrea's used to be called Cecilia's, and it was the backstage hangout for the musicians." We crossed Florida Avenue into LeDroit Park. The sense of desolation so powerful a few blocks back diminished. It took a while to get oriented. Although the enclave is part of the city's alphanumerical grid, its streets' signs also show their former names, which are mostly those of trees -- Maple, Linden, Elm. Elm? Turn here!

At 420 Elm Street NW, a compact brick house painted tan, we encountered our first real property, and first real person. A knock at the door drew Tina Penny, who studies marketing at Howard University. During the school year, she lives with her aunt, Sylvia Lawson, who bought the house in the early '70s from her father. Ms. Penny said she hadn't known the Ellingtons preceded her by 85 years or so as tenants, but volunteered to introduce us to her grandfather, who lives around the corner on U Street in a big house that was his father's.

Milton Piper, a big man in a gray cardigan sweater and hair to match, came out onto his front porch to talk with us. "I've lived in this house on and off since '22. Walter Washington lives around the corner," he said. "I bought 420 Elm in '48, when I got married. I'd heard Duke Ellington had lived there.

"I was in the show business myself in my younger days. When I was 15 and 16, I was a champion tapdancer. In about 1927, I won the dance contest at the Lincoln Theater. My partner Francis Brown and I went on the road as a duo, Brown and Piper. We played Baltimore and Philadelphia and were going to go on up to New York City, but at the Hippodrome in Philadelphia the child labor people snatched us up and sent us home and I had to go back to the Mott School." We thanked Mr. Piper and headed west, bound for the trio of houses the Ellingtons occupied between 1910 and 1929, when Duke could afford to move everyone up to Manhattan.

The trail went temporarily cold at 1805 13th Street, a two-story, seemingly uninhabited red rowhouse. But across the street we hit a main vein. Not only were the current owners, Matt and Gloria Andrea, home; they are enthusiastic conservators of the Ellington memory. Their house is one of three identical structures; at some point after the Ellingtons moved out, it became a rooming house. But in 1978, when Matt and Gloria Andrea bought it, 1816 13th Street NW was essentially what it had been during World War I - - a gracious, well-appointed city house, with its ornate Eastlake fireplace mantles and pocket doors still intact and chestnut trim still unpainted. What preserved the house was decay -- in the pocketbook of the developer who sold it to the Andreas, having run out of money before she could do any extensive work.

"When we moved in, the first thing we heard from Edith, the lady next door, was 'You know, Duke Ellington lived in your house.' She used to say he got into music from playing her piano, and I'd think, 'Sure, right,'" Gloria said. "But she had all these mementoes from him, and in 1981 or 1982 this guy was outside taking pictures of our house. I asked him why and he said, 'Because Duke Ellington lived in your house when he was a boy.'"

It was while living at 1816 13th Street that Duke Ellington got serious about music. After his encounters with Mrs. Clingscale, he seemed to prefer the baseball diamond to sharps and flats. Who knows what turned him around? It might have been listening to his parents play, or to Zeb Green tinkering on the Pinns' piano next door. He was moved by out-of-town players like Harvey Brooks, whom he heard on one of the extended summer vacation trips he took with his mother to Philadelphia and Asbury Park, N.J. But probably it had to do with Edna Thompson, whose family had lived on Ward Place and then moved to 13th Street around the same time as the Ellingtons. Edna was sweet, smart, and far more diligent in her piano studies. She went to Dunbar High -- academically superior to Armstrong, where Duke enrolled after attending Patterson Elementary and Garrison Junior High -- and helped Duke learn to read music.

When a cold confined him to the house for a couple of weeks in 1913, Duke fooled around on the keys and came up with "Soda Fountain Rag," and "What You Gonna Do When the Bed Breaks Down?" The next time he went out of the house he played them, and discovered the philosopher's stone. Word got out that Duke Ellington could play something danceable, and he became a social commodity worth speculating in.

"I was invited to many parties where I learned that when you were playing the piano there was always a pretty girl standing down at the bass clef end," he wrote. Then came the hanging out at Holliday's, the tips from Doc Perry, the cutting contest with Johnson, the gigs at Mrs.Dyers' and the Poodle Dog, and the jam sessions at True Reformer's Hall, where in Room 10 Duke began in earnest to invent himself as a musician, putting together a band with his pal and neighbor Otto (pronounced "Oh-toe," and later replaced by "Toby") Hardwick, who started out on bass but switched to saxophone. Duke began practicing started out on bass but switched to saxophone. Duke began practicing two or three hours a night. The noise through the walls at 1814 13th Street got on the neighbors' nerves.

"He'd plunk and plunk and plunk it out," Mr. Pinn told Ellington biographer Barry Ulanov. "He wasn't a very good pianist then, and two or three hours of plunking out the same chord or a few notes running away from it got to be pretty wearisome." One day, out front, Mr. Pinn told Duke as much. But Duke persisted, and later asked if Mr. Pinn knew anyone who might need a little orchestra. Mr. Pinn did, and sent Duke Ellington on his way as a bandleader.

The only vintage items Matt and Gloria found in their house were some pages from a 1934 or 1935 Washington Post. Otherwise, they must content themselves with considering that the dining room where daughter Marie Claire watches herself on "Sesame Street" (she was one of 10 D.C. kids chosen to perform in the show's opening sequence) once housed the upright piano on which young Edward Ellington struggled to satisfy Mrs. Clingscale and later, to learn by heart the rolling-thunder rhythms of James P. Johnson.

"You really should talk to Lucien Banister," Gloria said. "He still has the piano that was here in those days." She called next door. Mr. Banister was busy, but said he'd be happy to see us another time, so we strolled around the corner to 1212 T Street, the Ellingtons' last house as a family. No one answered my ring, so we hit the road again, this time for 2728 Sherman Avenue, Duke Ellington's first and last address on his own in Washington.

The house is still standing, occupied by a children's clothing boutique run by Annette Reid, who couldn't say much more about the Ellington connection than that she knew it existed. We tried the corner market across the street, where we began to slip out of the realm of fact and into the kingdom of belief.

"Sure, Duke Ellington lived around here. He lived all up and down here," said a man in line at the grocery, gesturing vaguely up Sherman Avenue. "I'm too young to have known him personally, but I heard he lived in that big old house up there a couple of blocks."

We had run out the list. Felix dropped me off and promised to send a postcard from Rio de Janeiro, where he was headed on his annual pilgrimage to carnival. I decided to check back with Lucien Banister, who invited me to visit, and to see what else I could see. I rounded up a few books about the Duke, and made a note to try again at 1212 T.

According to Ellington's biographers, Duke moved into 2728 Sherman Avenue in 1918. He and Edna had married and were expecting a child (son Mercer was born in 1919), and Duke was trying to support his young family with both of his talents -- art and music.

He didn't have much choice. He'd quit Armstrong High one course short of his diploma. What could a baccalaureateless young father and husband who was good with his hands do but run a sign-painting shop by day and play piano by night? The break came when Louis Thomas, a fellow piano player, sent him Duke a job -- a little party, background music, nothing more. The fee was $100, of which Duke kept $10. Dumbfounded at the possibilities, he looked in the phone book and saw advertisements for band bookers like Meyer Davis. He promptly took out one on his own behalf. Since no one knew who Duke Ellington was, he could -- and did -- field five or six bands, each known as the Duke Ellington Orchestra, every night.

Within a year he gave up sign-painting -- he was bringing home $150 or $200 a week from booking his bands into the Industrial Cafe and Dreamland and even his old stomping ground, the Poodle Dog. By 1921, Duke was thinking seriously about New York. In 1922 his drummer, Sonny Greer, got the call from bandleader Wilbur Sweatman to move on up, but Greer wouldn't go without his main men Duke Ellington and Otto Hardwick. Duke and Sonny and Otto made a few trips in Otto's Pullman, a cantankerous car they dubbed the "Dupadilly," playing at a swank Harlemboite called Barron's. Finally, in 1923, Duke moved to Manhattan, never to return. He installed Edna and Mercer back at 1212 T, which had room for an extended family, until 1929, when his star became a comet.

Later, Ruth Ellington told me a little about the house at 1212 T, the first one her family owned. The Ellingtons were prospering. James had left Dr. Cuthbert's employ to become a blueprinter at the Navy Yard. Daisy had worked briefly as a printer's devil at the Bureau of Engraving, until she became pregnant with Ruth, who was born in 1915. Among all his part-time jobs as a delivery boy, messenger, soda jerk, scene painter at the Howard Theater, and sometime musician -- the going rate for sitting in to replace a more established player was 75 cents a gig -- 17 year-old Duke was pulling down some money. It was time to buy a house, which the Ellingtons did.

"That's the first house I remember," Ruth Ellington said. "We had two pianos -- one in the living room and one in the dining room. My mother's brother, James Kennedy, lived with us. He brought his piano, and my parents had a piano. My brother used to practice on both of them. He was always playing the piano. It was marvelous to watch him play. He played rags, with a fast left hand. He was influenced by James P. Johnson and Willie the Lion Smith. He taught me one of the rags, but I started classical piano lessons at age five, and I cannot play jazz to this day."

"The house had a very large kitchen that led to a porch and a garden. There was a garage. The dining room had french doors; there was a suite of mahogany furniture. My father kept the house as he had at Cuthbert's -- cut glass and silver, with lace curtains in the living room. Every spring someone would come and pick up the carpets and replace them with rattan summer rugs, and take down the drapes and curtains and replace them with cloth shades.

"We had our bedrooms on the second floor. Before he moved out, my brother lived in two rooms on the third. My earliest memory of him is of being in the living room and having him walk in and pick me up and hug me so tightly that I became a little frightened and ran underneath the dining room table to get a better look and figure out who this was."

After Glenn and I visited with the Banisters, I stopped by 1212 T again, and this time met Mrs. Viola Clipper, a retired nurse whose brother, Charles Whitby, bought the house in 1949. She lived there with him until she married and raised a family out on Sargent Road, moving back when her brother died and left the house to her. The house still has a big kitchen and a pleasant garden. The back windows look out onto the vacant lot behind the old 12th Street YMCA, where little Edward Ellington played baseball instead of practicing piano. The third-floor rooms where the maturing musician lived are Mrs. Clifford's attic; when her brother was alive, he rented them out to roomers.

"I was a little bit of an Ellington fan," she told me as we sat in the living room, with blue, gold, and green light streaming in through stained-glass transoms in the bay that faces onto T Street. "My brother knew about the Ellingtons. He wrote to the government to ask about getting an historic designation."

"The neighborhood is coming back. It was rough for a while. The house next door was a rooming house, and I tell you, they made some racket! But it's coming up. There's a mixture of black and white; some of the black families are in their third and fourth generation of ownership. In the Thirties, of course, it was all black. The Whitelaw Hotel was nice -- the ladies' barber there, Mr. Coffee, did all the neighbors' haircuts."

In many ways the house has the same feel as the one in Ruth Ellington's memories -- the pine floor gleams (Mrs. Clifford had it sanded before she moved back), the bull's eye moldings are still intact. The furnishings are an elegant mixture of antiquities.

We went upstairs to the third floor. A brilliant band of sunlight was pouring in through the rear window, which opens onto a low, pleasing skyline little different from when Edward K. Ellington, student, lived here.

"On the Fourth of July, you can stand at this window and see every bit of the fireworks downtown," Mrs. Clipper said, opening the door to the first room, a small space full of Charles Whitby's things -- interesting oddments such as a brass spittoon and three or four oil-fired railroad lanterns. "After my brother retired, he liked to go to the fleamarket in Englishtown, New Jersey, near where he lived. He brought back all these things," Mrs. Clipper said. Besides a battered two-bulb ceiling fixture, the room's only vestiges of the Ellington era are a couple of closed-off gas jets that once provided light and heat. There are two big windows looking out on the YMCA lot, a small closet, and an alcove leading to a door that opens into the front room.

Low-ceilinged and warmed by the radiators on the floors below, the room where Duke Ellington began to see why he could dream of being famous is dark, even on a bright day. It has one large and two small windows, all facing north, toward New York.

Michael Dolan is a Washington writer whose work appears in City Paper, The New Yorker, the Washington Post Magazine, Travel & Leisure, Washingtonian, and other publications. This article appeared in slightly different form in Washingtonian Magazine.

DUPONT CIRCLE

Originally planned as a device to slow invading armies, Dupont Circle has become one of Washington's loveliest areas. Located at the eastern edge of Embassy Row, Dupont Circle has long been known for its style and charm. Beautiful homes, galleries and museums, and tree-lined streets have made Dupont Circle a favorite among Washingtonians and visitors alike.

Following the Civil War, Washington began a program of expansion which led to the development of Dupont Circle. Prior to the 1870's, it had only been a defensive device, but an improvement program that included landscaping and street paving soon made it one of the city's most popular residential areas. By the 1920's, Dupont Circle was known for its grand embassies, spectacular mansions, and gracious townhouses.

Today, a walk through Dupont Circle reveals many architectural styles, including Victorian, Georgian Revival, and Spanish Mission. Many of these grand old buildings have been restored, and are now home to businesses, museums, and research institutes, as well as families. Walk through some of the streets surrounding the Circle, and you are bound to come across quaint shops, bookstores, art galleries, and outdoor cafes.

One of the most pleasant features of Dupont Circle is its park-like setting. The terminus of Massachusetts, New Hampshire, and Connecticut Avenues, three of Washington's grand boulevards, Dupont circle is sprinkled with trees and benches, making it a perfect place for people-watching. A tranquil haven in the midst of one of the country's most bustling cities, the charming streets and beautiful buildings of Dupont Circle have earned it a place on any visitor's itinerary.

books

SECOND STORY BOOKS
2000 P Street NW
Washington, DC 20036
Tel: (202) 659-8884
Hrs:
Open seven days 10:00 a.m. - 10:00 p.m.

4836 Bethesda Avenue Row
Bethesda, MD 20814
Tel: (301) 656-0170
Hrs:
Open seven days 10:00 a.m. - 10:00 p.m.

12276 Wilkens Avenue
Rockville, MD 20852
Tel: (301) 770-0477
Hrs:
Warehouse 10:00 a.m. - 6:00 p.m.
Seven days a week, by appointment.
Visa, MasterCard and American Express are accepted..

Enter a world of deja vu! Find amazing books from the past and present. Most have been previously experienced, but all have a great deal of enjoyment remaining. Allan and Kim Stypeck have assembled a selection guaranteed to delight the most ardent booklover. Allan began his business by collecting several interesting books for himself. He sold a few to buy some more. Since then, he has spent the last 17 years delving into the book business and enjoying the opportunity to travel and handle the rare and antique books he has a passion for.

Wonderful books--new, used, rare, antiquarian, out of print, remainders, and review copies, all are for the finding at Second Story Books. Such a large selection is hard enough to find, but quality books at such affordable prices are usually out of the question. Decorative art, graphic art and posters are, also, available. At the Rockville store, Asian and African antiques and a large supply of wicker furniture are for sale. And, wicker pieces can be left for expert repairs.

On Saturday and Sunday, the warehouse book and record sale offers new and used hardbacks at half off and paperbacks for three-fourths off the list price. Try the Rockville weekend Dollaramma. Everything goes for just one dollar!

restaurants

FOOD FOR THOUGHT
1738 Connecticut Avenue NW
Washington, D.C. 20009
Tel: (202) 797-1095

Hrs:	Monday:	11:30 a.m. - 3:00 p.m.
		5:00 p.m. - 12:00 midnight
	Tuesday - Thursday	11:30 a.m. - 1:00 a.m.
	Saturday:	12:00 noon - 1:00 a.m.
	Sunday:	5:00 p.m. - 12:00 midnight

Visa, MasterCard, American Express, Diners Club and Carte Blanche are accepted.

One of the most eclectic areas in the District of Columbia happens to be Dupont Circle! The mix and match are distinct and unique. The blend is beautiful! Presiding over food fortunes and foibles, during seventeen years of change on the circle, is the popular, community-minded, good-and-good-for-you food emporium, FOOD FOR THOUGHT, complete with a newsy, neighborhood bulletin board.

In 1973, Bobby Ferrando left his family business of catering fancy foods for fancy affairs and launched into his own vision of alternative living. His aim was to have a no-frills, unpretentious place to serve good, healthy food for an honest price. An absolute devotee of pure, organic foods, he grills meat to perfection, serves fresh vegetables and meatless entrees (Lasagne is a favorite), and offers grain fed trout, vegetarian burgers, homemade soups, open-face Melts and pita pockets stuffed with assorted, wholesome goodies. Desserts are honey-sweetened and fresh--superbly delicious! American and imported beer, wine and a pleasing choice of mixed drinks are available. But, it's the camaraderie that really counts!

In the evenings, entertainment is provided by soon-to-be knowns and unknowns who enthusiastically share time and talent for a mere passing of the hat. Some now well-knowns, like Mary Chapin Carpenter, have appeared in the past. Rhythm and Blues, Classical, Jazz and Folk spell one another's styles, ensuring variety that is as wholesome and diverse as the food is healthy and tasty and the clientele, fun.

RUTH'S CHRIS STEAK HOUSE
1801 Connecticut Avenue
Washington, D.C. 20009
Tel: (202) 797-0033
Hrs: Seven days a week; 5:00p.m. - 11:00 p.m..
Visa, MasterCard, American Express, Carte Blanche and Diners Club are accepted.

The quality of the steak must be in the top 2% of beef sold in the U.S., (just for starters!). It must be corn-fed U.S. Prime, richly marbled, and never frozen. The magnificent piece of beef must be custom aged, hand-cut daily at the restaurant, broiled to perfection and then, and only then, it must be rushed to your table still sizzling. In this manner, RUTH'S CHRIS STEAK HOUSE has been satisfying the most finicky steak fanciers for eight years, and that says a lot. It's not just the steak, it's the whole process that makes that one bite of tender beef melt in your mouth like butter.

Their menu offers Filet, Ribeye, New York Strip, Porterhouse and mouth watering seafood. The swordfish, which is juicy and tender, comes highly recommended. There is a wonderful selection of vegetables, potatoes and salads. Try the Lyonnaise potatoes and the Caesar Salad for something special. The deserts like the Bananas Foster are guaranteed to tempt.

The Dungeon Cocktail Lounge offers a happy hour from 5:00 p.m. - 7:00 p.m. Mon. -Fri.. It's a great place to meet and have a drink before dinner. Valet parking is complementary so parking is never a problem. Repeat customers make up the majority of their clientele. Business just keeps getting better and better at Ruth's Chris. Reservations Suggested.

restaurants/bookstores

KRAMERBOOKS & AFTERWORDS CAFE
1517 Connecticut Avenue NW
Washington, D.C. 20036
Tel: (202) 387-1462
Hrs:
Monday - Thursday 7:30 a.m. - 1:00 a.m.
Friday 7:30 a.m. -1:00 a.m.
Open 24 hours on weekends.
Visa, MasterCard and American Express.

Alone or with a friend, KRAMERBOOKS & AFTERWORDS CAFE is a friendly place to go for a good time. Dupont Circle has long been a bit Bohemian in style. KRAMERBOOKS continues the tradition of the beat generation. It was the first bookstore cafe when it opened in 1976. The store carries an eclectic selection of books and has reported more sales per square foot than any other store in the country.

When first opened, the cafe was an Espresso bar that served food. Now it has become a full service restaurant with a small, but interesting menu and an impressive choice of wines and beer. Wine is available by the glass so people can choose what they prefer or sample different kinds. The Menu offers such intriguing items as Fettuccine New Orleans, a popular favorite, and Baked Seafood Antipasto, the manager's choice. They prepare everything in house, even smoke meats and bake breads. Salads and specialty beverages are remarkable, Duck Salad & Ginger Dressing and Iced Cappuccino. Desserts are sweet and luscious, like Kahlua Walnut Pie, Cafe Snowball and Turtle Tarts. Yummy!

Manager, Michael Winters, says there is a very high incidence of people getting engaged at Kramerbooks. He ran into such a couple recently in Costa Rica. Old customers remain loyal and in touch. Kramerbooks has been flattered by many restaurants, both in the U.S. and Europe, who have asked for their formula for success!

Late night and early morning crowds blend together. It's not at all unusual to find the place crowded at four in the morning! On weekends, it's open all night with live music at ten. Anytime is a good time to slip in for some company, a Chocolate Truffle and a glass of Chardonnay!

FOGGY BOTTOM

Washington's original residents would never recognize Foggy Bottom today. One of Washington's oldest neighborhoods, it began life as little more than swampland, and was continuously plagued by thick fogs and mosquitoes. In the course of its lifetime, Foggy Bottom experienced many changes, both good and bad, before becoming the vibrant place it is today.

Nothing much happened in Foggy Bottom until the industrial boom of the 19th century; the factories, breweries, and coal works sprang up along the riverfront, filling the air with something more serious than swamp fog. By the 1900's, the industrial boom was over, and the factories were closing. Still, Foggy Bottom had earned such a horrible reputation that no one wanted anything to do with it, until its southern end was suggested for the site of the Lincoln Memorial. Despite protestations from those who warned that the swamp air would prove harmful to it, the monument was placed here. Slowly, Foggy Bottom's luck began to change.

By the 1950's, Washington's city officials were seeing new possibilities in Foggy Bottom. When they chose it as the site for the John F. Kennedy Center for th Performing Arts, Foggy Bottom was suddenly considered upscale. Today, the dreary breweries have given way to radiant office complexes, and working-class rowhouses have been replaced by elegant condos, making Foggy Bottom one of the most coveted addresses in Washington.

GEORGETOWN

It is a surprising fact to many people that Georgetown was named after King George II, not George Washington. Georgetown was chartered as George, Maryland in 1751, long before George Washington had earned the kind of acclaim that would make him the nation's first President. Then, it was nothing more than a station used for the inspection and shipping of tobacco. Since that time, Georgetown, which has seen both good and bad times, has become one of Washington's most well-known areas.

As a Maryland Tidewater town, Georgetown was home to many of the South's tobacco barons. Rich and upwardly mobile, these men built grand mansions in Georgetown, turning it into one of Maryland's most prosperous towns. When Georgetown was incorporated into Washington in 1791, it looked as though the town would continue to thrive. The population exploded, as government officials and workers moved in to await the completion of the capital city; and Georgetown University, founded in 1789 by the Jesuits, attracted distinguished visitors such as George Washington and General Lafayette to the neighborhood.

Unfortunately, once Washington was completed, Georgetown declined. Shipping, so vital to the neighborhood's prosperity, all but ended when bridge construction in Washington made the harbor impassable, and to make matters worse, the tobacco crop began to fail. Fortunately, the completion in 1828 of the Chesapeake and Ohio Canal, which connected Georgetown to Cumberland, made the town an important commercial center once again.

By the 1870's, Georgetown was once again one of the most prosperous areas of Washington. Up until that time, it had been an independent entity as well, electing its own mayor and town council. Then, in 1871, Congress decreed that all of Washington would be administered by one territorial government.

Despite the Congressional decree, Georgetown remained, and still is, a separate spiritual entity. Today, it is home to unique shops, restaurants, and galleries, as well as some of Washington's leading citizens. The entire area has been declared a historic landmark, making it possible for many of its old buildings to be restored, and enabling it to retain some of its small-town character.

antiques

JUSTINE S. MEHLMAN, 2918 M Street, NW, Washington, D.C., 20007; Tel: (202) 337-0613. They offer a beautiful selection of art, antiques and period jewelry. See fine, detailed and intricate jewelry created by expert craftsman long ago.

M. SINDLER & DAUGHTERS ANTIQUES, 1206 Thirteenth Street, NW, Washington DC, 20007; Tel: (202) 625-1767. This is the place to find fine American and English furniture and accessories from the 18th and 19th centuries.

boat & bike rental

BIG WHEEL BIKES, 1034 33rd Street, NW, Washington DC, 20007; Tel: (202) 337-0254. They provide bike rentals for short trips on the C & O Canal, as well as high tech mountain bikes for the long haul.

FLETCHER'S BOAT HOUSE, Georgetown, under the Whitehurst Freeway, NW, Washington D.C., 20007; Tel: (202) 244-0461. Boats are available for boating on the Potomac River or the C & O Canal. They also provide bike rentals.

bookstores

MODERN LANGUAGE BOOKSTORE, 3160 O Street, NW, Washington D.C., 20007; Tel: (202) 338-8963. This is a bookstore that has really a diverse selection of new and used books. They specialize in books from other countries and in different languages.

jazz and supper clubs

D.C. BLUES: A MOVEABLE FEAST

by Michael Dolan

Huddie Ledbetter thought Washington was a bourgeois town; at least, that's what Leadbelly called the capital in his "Bourgeois Blues", written to commemorate an unhappy interlude that the legendary bluesman had in D.C.

"Listen here people,
Listen to me.
Don't try to find no home
Down in Washington, D.C.
'Cause it's a bourgeois town,

the nation's capital

It's a bourgeois town.
I got the bourgeois blues,
Gonna spread the news around.
Some white folks in Washington,
Ain't no telling how,
Toss the black man a nickel
Just to see him scrape and bow.
This is the home of the brave
And the land of the free,
Don't wanna be mistreated by no bourgeoisie
In that bourgeois town.
I got the bourgeois blues
Gonna spread the news around.*

Bourgeois or not, Washington offers a moveable feast of blues music: the acoustic
piedmont blues played by John Cephas and Phil Wiggins, the gutbucket downtown blues that Nap Turner sings, the electric howl of The Nighthawks, and all the shades in between. Whether at the Smithsonian or the Kennedy Center, or sandwiched in among the rockers at the Bayou, the blues is a key part of Washington's music scene.

Once strictly an inner-city phenomenon, Washington's blues scene nearly disappeared after the riots of April 1968, which put the torch to the entertainment districts of 7th and 14th Streets NW. But instead of withering, the scene diversified and spread, eventually extending into even the outermost suburbs, as the blues underwent another rebirth.

Singer Nap Turner, who grew up in D.C.'s Shaw neighborhood, remembers hearing the blues everywhere, including Simpson's Drug Store at 7th Street and Rhode Island Avenue NW, where the chief cook and bottle washer was the late Bill Harris. Harris, then beginning a long innovative career as a jazz and blues guitarist, ran the lunch counter at Simpson's during the day. Evenings, he played guitar around the club circuit frequented by the younger Turner.

"When I was coming up, it wasn't unusual in the Black community to find two to five joints in the same block with live music," says Turner. "D.C. was a pretty wide-open town in the '40s."

"It was the age of the blues -- doo-wop on the corner, R&B in the clubs," Turner said backstage at a benefit for Harris held in late 1988, just before the guitarist died. "You had the Howard Theater, and along 7th Street from M north to Florida there were one or two clubs in every block. At 7th and T, Clore's restaurant had live music upstairs. That was one of the first first places Thelonius Monk heard Charlie Rouse. Two doors down was Little Harlem, with the Off Beat next door, and across the street was an after-hours club, the Old Rose Social Club, which was a speakeasy-type arrangement where you could buy liquor and listen to the jam sessions."

Then, as now, blues and blues-rooted jazz and R&B drew listeners both black and white. "The blues have the ability to transcend the superfluous," says Turner. "They're very basic. They express feelings common to all people. Everybody laughs, cries, hurts, feels pleasure. There's nothing new about young whites getting into black music; whites have always supported jazz and the blues. Even now, 40 years later, I see young white musicians coming to black joints and sitting in."

Turner started out his musical career as a be-bop bassist, but soon learned that bop was a hard financial row to hoe. He payed the rent in R&B bands but fell prey to the occupational hazards -- bad companions and worse habits. Turner made his way back onto the stage in the early 70s as a singer. Now he works as a drug-abuse counselor for the city and sings weekends. In 1988, he was among nearly two dozen DC blues figures to travel to Italy to play at the San Remo Blues Festival.

"D.C. has a sound as distinct as in Chicago or Kansas or Texas," says Turner. "It's an amalgam of musicians from all over, colored by the experience of being in Washington."

Jerry "Bama" Washington disagrees. 'Bama says he hears a melting-pot mix of Texas, the Mississippi Delta, Chicago, and the Piedmont, but no distinct D.C. blues sound.

"People come up from North Carolina, South Carolina, Louisiana, but after they've moved here revert back to the things they heard at home," says Washington, who adds a unique vitality to the local blues scene by hosting "The 'Bama Hour," a WPFW-FM radio show named for Washington's gruff, grits-ain't-groceries persona. "My daughter calls D.C. home, but I go back to her grandfather's roots in Georgia, which she's seen only fleetingly. She hears her Daddy play Sonny Rollins, but I also play Blind Boy Fuller and Tampa Red.

"It's a familiar sound -- it goes back to the church, when the church was the social center for blacks -- rich and poor, they had the same church, the common ground of fellowship. Church music is familiar to everybody, and the blues is the flip side of church music."

the nation's capital

In the late Fifties, Mark Wenner was growing up in Arlington and Bethesda, listening to Wheaton station WDON.

"That was a real neat time," says Wenner, a founding member of The Nighthawks, one of the city's best-known blues bands. "From sign-on time until school started, WDON played rock 'n' roll. During school hours they played country. From after school until sign-off, rock 'n' roll again, with the blues mixed in. Side by side you heard Joe Turner, Mississippi blues, Jimmy Reed, John Lee Hooker, rockabilly, doo-wop, R&B -- with a dash of country and pop novelty songs, all in there together, not boxed up and separated."

Eventually Wenner found WOL, WUST, and WOOK -- black-oriented stations that played James Brown and Wilson Pickett before, during and after school hours, however, they played B.B. King and Elmore James. "If you stayed home from school you could listen to non-discriminatory radio," says Wenner, who gradually homed in on Muddy Waters and Elmore James as his favorite musicians. "By the time I graduated from Bethesda-Chevy Chase High School in 1966, I was deep into the hard Chicago blues that were enjoying a revival. I was the smartass who kept pointing out that the Rolling Stones' songs were just remakes of Bo Diddly and Chuck Berry numbers."

Like many a suburban blues fan of the mid- 60s, Wenner went off to college with harmonica in hand. Majoring in English at Columbia University, he made his performing debut as the leader of B- Town Slim & His Rhythm Review. "B-Town" was Bethesda; the music was twelve-bar blues with a funky beat, straight out of the songbooks of Slim Harpo and Junior Wells. During Wenner's extended tour of duty at Columbia, the group went through a zillion incarnations and got nowhere. Finally Wenner looked homeward and saw Bobby Radcliff, another B-CC bluesman, doing what Wenner wanted to do -- play the blues in Washington clubs five nights a week.

Radcliff was a fixture on the Washington club circuit in the early 70s, playing Chicago- style riffs at places like the Far Inn (now Club Soda) on Connecticut Avenue. After helping to crystallize Washington's blues scene, Radcliff lit out for New York, where he's still playing. Wenner came back as Radcliff was packing up, sitting in here and there and eventually teaming up with guitarist Jimmy Thackery to form The Nighthawks.

The "Hawks" began reaching audiences around the country with their blend of energetic live shows, well-regarded albums such as Jacks & Kings, and grueling tours. Their Blue Monday showcases at the Bayou (where the band's New Year's Eve appearance has become a tradition) brought in aces they'd met on tour -- acts such as J.B. Hutto, Hound Dog Taylor, Otis Rush, Big Walter Horton, James Cotton, the Chicago Allstars, George Thorogood, the Fabulous Thunderbirds, Stevie Ray Vaughn, and others. Washington became known as a place to hear blues as hot and greasy as those served up anywhere.

Why? Wenner cites radio station WHFS-FM, an oasis of blues programming in the desert of commercial radio.

"WHFS had a loyal audience of sophisticated, funky people. Washington has always been a good music town, and until recently, it was a Southern town," he says. "In the South, white people listen to Black music. Any white boy in Mississippi can play slide guitar. He might not want to eat in a restaurant with somebody black, but Black music is all he's got at home. White people in D.C. walk differently than white people in other places -- because there's a black influence. White people in D.C. dance better than white people in Boston, for example -- you should see the way they hop around up there."

Unlike The Fabulous Thunderbirds, Robert Cray and the late Stevie Ray Vaughn, The Nighthawks never were able to translate roots music into large dollars, and ultimately broke up. But the Hawks are flying again, this time with guitarist Jimmy Nalls and vocalist Jimmy Hall, with music that Wenner calls "less Chicago blues and more of a soul thing."

Ever the purist, Wenner himself has brought out a fine a solo LP on the local Powerhouse label. Singing and playing harmonica, backed only by electric guitar and stand-up bass, he attains the feel of classic recordings by Muddy Water, Lightning Slim, and Little Walter.

The lure of acoustic blues is evident in Washington's blues sound: the finger-picked Piedmont style played by John Cephus. With his partner, harmonica player Phil Wiggins, Cephus won the 1987 W.C. Handy Entertainers of the Year Award, which honors pre-eminent practitioners of the blues. Other names in the circle are Eleanor Ellis, Rick Franklin, Neil Harpe, and Ben Andrews.

Former WRC-TV anchorman and sometimes singer Dave Marash calls Washington a haven for acoustic music. Marash occasionally sits in with Ben Andrews at Glover Park's venerable Grog & Tankard.

the nation's capital

"In Washington you have an older generation -- John Cephus, John Jackson, Archie Edwards, the late Flora Moulton -- whom you could almost call first-generation players," says Marash. "They encompass a variety of styles, with Piedmont the dominant style. Ben Andrews is one of the third- generation players, most of whom seem drawn to acoustic folk blues styles."

Richmond native Marash has been a blues fan for 36 of his 46 years. When he was 10 his father gave him a set of Leadbelly records, to which the boy listened compulsively, learning to imitate the bluesman's high, lonesome sound even though it was a full octave above his natural range. As an undergraduate at Williams College, Marash sang at clubs and coffeehouses in western Massachusetts. In 1964, while he was in graduate school at Rutgers, he and his first wife, Megan, made the Greenwich Village scene, singing together at The Nightowl on Bleecker Street. Then Dave went to work at radio station WINS-AM, where, he says, "I got a bug for the news and forgot about the blues" -- that is, until he arrived at WRC in 1985.

"Washington may be the best city in the U.S. for acoustic music," Marash says. "D.C. is a small conservative music town, where people are interested in conserving music. All national capitals are full of archives and museums, and the courts and legislature are tradition- oriented. That's expressed a lot in this city's aesthetic life -- Washington is weak at the avant garde end of the scale, but strong on conserving, which is a boon in terms of preserving indigenous acoustic American music. We have a cadre of great blues performers here -- the late Bill Harris, Archie Edwards, John Jackson. Forget about Chicago! There ain't a city in the country that has that wealth of talent."

Once or twice a month -- "when I can get my aged bones down there" -- Marash sits in at the Grog & Tankard. No matter where they come from or how they get here, blues musicians seem to direct their careers the way Phil Wiggins did.

"I didn't leave myself any way out," says Wiggins, an Army brat who grew up in Europe and Northwest D.C., graduated from Fort Hunt High School in suburban Virginia in 1973 and put in some time in college, but dropped out to play music. He'd begun listening to the blues at home, and took up the harmonica after a brief stint on the saxophone. He hit the streets, playing the corners for quarters.

Wiggins terms his time playing with Flora Moulton his first "serious" work, and Washington a fine place to learn country blues. Members of his circle of musical acquaintance revolving around Fairfax County blues paterfamilias John Jackson, Wiggins and Cephus hit it lucky in 1981, when scouts from a German record company came to town looking for talent to put on vinyl and on tour in Europe. Since then Cephus and Wiggins have been off the streets and in the record bins, as well as participating in international tours sponsored by the State Department, the Smithsonian Institution, and the Kennedy Center for the Performing Arts.

"We play in a lot of different countries -- we've been to Africa, to Central and South America, the Caribbean, Russia, China," says Wiggins, a soft spoken man with a holsterful of harmonicas. "The blues is a very emotional music, straight from the heart, from everyday life. It tells stories so basic that no matter who you are, you can relate to it."

WHERE TO FIND THE BLUES IN D.C.

Like the music it features, Washington's blues circuit varies night by night and endlessly reconstitutes itself. Be sure to check in advance for who's playing what and where. And remember that the blues can strike anywhere, anytime; Blues Alley once booked Albert Collins for Sunday brunch -- hardly a standard setting for the fiery Texan, who nonetheless cranked up his Telecaster and tore the house down, leaving nothing intact but lukewarm mimosas and plates full of eggs Benedict. Besides this list, more information is available from the D.C. Blues Society (Box 11817, Washington DC 20008; 202/369- 6781)

This material originally appeared in the February 1989 issue of Washingtonian Magazine.

BLUES ALLEY JAZZ SUPPER CLUB
1073 Wisconsin Avenue
Washington, D.C. 20007
Tel: (202) 337-4141
Hrs: Open seven days a week.
Dinner 6:00 p.m. -
Shows Weekdays 8:00 p.m. & 10:00 p.m.
Fri.day and Saturday Midnight Show
Reservations and proper dress are required.
Visa, MasterCard, American Express, Diners Club and JCB are accepted.

Stand in line? In an alley? With reservations, already?? Well, that's just the BEGINNING of the fun of it! An evening at BLUES ALLEY JAZZ SUPPER CLUB always starts in the alley. That's why Georgetown named the alley for the club. People have been gathering there, happily, for twenty-five years! So, go early, on purpose! This small piece of Jazz Heaven is nestled in the heart of Georgetown, but, it can't stay hidden! Performers and patrons, alike, are drawn to the music, the food and the fun. The music is all it promises to be--big names and absolutely top entertainment Jazz; the food has been fantastically Cajun since BEFORE Cajun became the national rage; and the fun is, simply, in BEING THERE.

Big names and budding artists can be on stage performing or sitting at the next table, or both. You'll know them before you leave! In a room that can accommodate 125 people, there isn't a bad seat in the house. Some prefer watching from the vantage point of the bar, while others like seats where they can watch hands or hear certain notes. Whatever is your pleasure, you can find it in this small, casual but classy Georgetown night spot. It has been called, "a living monument to the American Art of Jazz" performed by the best musicians in the field, accompanied by the best of New Orleans cuisine, within windowless walls that enclose the best example of 18th century early elegance and shared with the best and liveliest audience anywhere to be found. We just call it the BEST!!

leather

GEORGETOWN LEATHER DESIGN
Washington, D.C.
1150 Connecticut Avenue NW
Tel: (202) 223-1855

3265 M Street, Georgetown
Tel: (202) 333-9333

Mazza Gallerie
Tel: (202) 363-9710

Virginia
Tysons Corner Center
Tel: (703) 893-1620

Springfield Mall
Tel: (703) 418-6702

Maryland
White Fling
Tel: (301) 881-4677

Landover Mall
Tel: (301) 322-7773

Out of a plethora of leather craft shops in the late sixties, a very select but modest one named "Sandal Shop," rose to become GEORGETOWN LEATHER DESIGN and is today, the area's foremost quality leather specialty store. With many convenient locations in the Metropolitan area and a Catalogue Center in Beltsville, Maryland, they have also expanded to Pennsylvania, New Jersey, Massachusetts and Connecticut. However, the policies on which they were founded are carefully maintained. Today's customer can still expect the highest quality, the latest in fashion, the most attentive service and the lowest prices possible.

Top value wearing apparel for men, women and children, handbags, business cases and a wide variety of accessories have been carefully produced with attention given to the very latest in technology, styling and quality. Each skin is individually selected, treated and crafted with an eye toward a finished article of superior distinction. And, with no middle market to satisfy, savings are passed on to the consumer.

Extensive training enables store personnel to be helpful, friendly and extraordinarily knowledgeable. The entire staff welcomes browsers and delights in answering questions. They do not need to sell their customers, rather they inform and educate. GEORGETOWN LEATHER DESIGN sells itself by offering the ultimate in leather--innovative and classic designs in superior and enduring quality which make any purchase an investment for a most rewarding return!

restaurants

DONATELLO
2514 L Street NW
Washington, DC 20037
Tel: (202) 333-1485

Hrs:	Monday - Thursday	11:30 a.m. - 3:00 p.m.
		5:00 p.m. - 11:30 p.m.
	Friday.	11:30 a.m. - 3 p.m.
		5:00 p.m. - 12:30 a.m.
	Saturday	5:00 p.m. - 12:30 a.m.
	Sunday	5:00 p.m. - 11:30 p.m.

Visa, MasterCard, American Express, and Diners Club are accepted.

DONATELLO is snuggled into the edge of Georgetown, near the corner of 25th and Pennsylvania Avenue NW. It's ideal for lunch, dinner and before or after the theater! One can select from a full, fixed-price menu for theater dining from 5:00 p.m. until 7:00 p.m. and, later, from 10:00 p.m. until closing. Or, if you have time for a more leisurely dinner the list of fine Italian, California, and French wines is the place to start enjoying this cozy restaurant that specializes in Northern Italian cooking.

Do begin with one or more of the delectable appetizers! Perhaps Funghi Ripieni mushrooms, crisply capped with baked crabmeat or Antipasto Caldo a very tasty mixture of baked clams, baked shrimp, and snails served on mushroom caps. Whether you succumb to the delicately fried puffs of Mozzarella in garlic butter and anchovies, or the Mussels, succulent in white wine, or choose among the Antipasti Freddi, room must be saved for tastes from the rest of the menu. You will obtain supreme enjoyment from home made pasta in the Combinazzione Di Pasta, when Cannelloni, Agnolotti, and Tortellini, each in its own delicate sauce and stuffed to tender puffiness with veal, spinach, and cheeses, are served together in gourmand glory! Chicken, beef and veal are offered in the finest Italian tradition and the freshest of seafood is often a daily special.

The owner and his staff are thoroughly committed to their customer's comfort and pleasure. Old world attentiveness pampers the diner from the moment the coat is taken to be hung until it is returned at the end of a delicious and delightful experience.

FILOMENA ITALIAN BRASSERIE
"On The Canal in Georgetown"
1063 Wisconsin Avenue NW
Washington, D.C. 20007
Tel: (202) 33-PASTA - 338-8800
Hrs:
Monday and Tuesday 5:00 p.m. - 11:00 p.m.
Wednesday. - Sunday 11:30 a.m.- 11:00 p.m.
Closed Dec. 24 & 25; Jan. 1; and July 4.
Visa, MasterCard, American Express and Choice are accepted.

It is rumored that customers will wait as long as two hours to get into Filomena's! Maybe. But then, that's not so bad when you think how entertaining it is to watch through the front window to see the Pasta Mamas stroking strings of pasta and coaxing them into neat, little, curious and colorful, nest-like shapes! But then, one doesn't go to FILOMENA'S for quick eating anyway. That would be sacrilegious! One goes to FILOMENA'S for a wonderful dining experience, for becoming a star for the evening as JoAnna Filomena's valued guest where the meal is a feast, especially prepared from beginning to end with no one else in mind, but YOU!

Given the fact that the food is absolutely superb, the service perfectly punctilious, the setting elegant and romantic, overlooking the C&O Canal, there is another element not to be found anywhere else in town! It's the warm, gentle and gracious ambiance emanating from the great lady, herself--owner, JoAnna Filomena! Customers are charmingly welcomed as her personal guests. Whether partaking of the fixed price buffet on the upper level or going to the more formal downstairs, which is beautifully decorated with exquisite antiques, statuary, delicate china and sparkling crystal, guests feel pampered.

A long list of celebrity friends are regular customers, who enjoy Rigatoni Filomena; delightfully flavored shrimp in Gamberi Alla Diavola; lobster in sweet and tasty tomato sauce, Aragosta Alla Diavola and uniquely wonderful bread bowls, made from a recipe straight from her mother and the old country. The name and logo for her restaurant also come from her mother, whose picture is displayed in honor!

NATHANS
3150 M Street NW
Washington, D.C. 20007
Tel: (202) 338-2000
FAX: (202) 333-2509

Hrs: Lunch:	Monday - Friday:	11:00 a.m. - 3:00 p.m.
Brunch:	Saturday - Sunday:	9:00 a.m. - 3:00 p.m.
Dinner:	Sunday - Wednesday:	6:00 p.m. - 11:00 p.m.
	Thursday - Saturday:	6:00 p.m. - 12:00 p.m.

BACK ROOM DISCO
Friday - Saturday until 3:00 a.m.
Reservations are encouraged.
Visa, MasterCard, American Express, Diners Club, and Carte Blanche are accepted.

Wisconsin and M, the corner where beats the pulse of Georgetown! On this corner, since 1969, NATHANS has drawn the discerning and the sophisticated out of the crowds and gathered them in to enjoy fine wines, delicious food, and dancing. Most of the regulars are residents, but business visitors swell their ranks during the week, while on weekends, suburbia comes to town and queues in long lines on the doorstep!

Casual, cosmopolitan and classic, NATHANS boasts a long, cozy bar which serves good drinks, 400 imported and domestic wines, and an unusually large variety of fine champagnes. The Italian kitchen specializes in fresh, homemade pastas and one of the finest chefs in the area creates and supervises daily specials that include Basil Pappardelle with Lobster, Grilled Norwegian Salmon, Brace of Quail, Soft Shell Crabs, and luscious deserts!

Howard Joynt, the owner, takes an active hand in managing NATHANS. He gives thoughtful attention to every detail, even going as far as creating the descriptions that help to clarify choices on wine, lunch and dinner menus. The old wood floors, the wooden bar and stools, the red and white tablecloths adorned with a single flower, and the dark walls covered with wonderful pictures of horses and more horses, all add up as the place to stop for food, drinks, and night life, in comfortable ambiance, on THE corner that IS Georgetown.

TANDOOR RESTAURANT
3316 M Street NW
Washington, DC 20007
Tel: (202) 333-3376
Hrs: Open seven days a week.
Lunch: 11:30 a.m. - 2:30 p.m.
Dinner: 5:30 p.m. - 11:00 p.m.
Visa, MasterCard and American Express are accepted.

Open the door and stand there a moment! SAVOR the aroma!! Indian spices! Permeate your senses? Tickle your appetite? Now, enter TANDOOR on M Street in Georgetown, the first Indian restaurant to introduce Tandoori cooking to the Washington area. Owner, Jack Katyal, and his wife, Mona, have since expanded to include a restaurant in Boston, one in Baltimore, and four in the District: Tandoor and Katmandu, both on Connecticut Avenue, Tandoor and Madurai on M Street, as well as, Tandoor of Alexandria at 719 King Street in Old Town.

Small, cozy and intimate, yet bright and colorful with chairs and decorations imported from India, the Georgetown Tandoor is dominated by a large glass window through which the chef can be seen as he prepares and grills skewers of chicken, meats and seafood, hanging them over charcoal in a clay oven. It's hard to resist wanting a taste of it ALL! Number six under Appetizers, Kofta Kabab, is a perfect beginning, as is a platter of Samosas or lightly fried Shrimp Pakoras. The Murgh Tandoori Chicken, marinated overnight in yogurt, herbs and spices is a popular specialty, as are the Fillet of Lamb and the Number nine, Platter Tandoori, a selection of Shrimp Masala, Chicken Vandalu and Butter Chicken are recommended, mildly flavored, family favorites and bread cooked in the tandoor oven is a must!

This delightful restaurant is frequented by Embassy and State Department people--perhaps because of the comfortable, private room upstairs that is perfect for luncheon and dinner parties. Or perhaps it is the attentive service afforded by Massi and Terry, manager and assistant manager. It could be the ambiance, or exotic desserts, or, how about deliciously authentic food?

TONY AND JOE'S SEAFOOD PLACE
Georgetown
3000 K Street NW
Washington, D.C. 20007
Tel: (202) 944-4545
Hrs: Sunday - Thursday: 11:00 a.m.- 1:00 p.m.
Friday - Saturday: 11:00 a.m. - 2:30 a.m.
Visa, MasterCard, American Express, and Diners Club are accepted.

On cool summer evenings, dining outside affords a magnificent view of the Potomac River and the splendid Kennedy Center. When the weather chills enough to move inside, a beautiful picture of the Virginia shoreline, wrapping itself around the curve of the Potomac, is every bit as impressive! Extraordinary windows afford a clear view for diners at TONY AND JOE'S SEAFOOD PLACE in Washington Harbour of Georgetown.

This elegant setting encases one of the largest selections of the freshest, fresh seafood in the Washington area. No pretenses here; they call it, "straight forward, simple, fresh seafood." But, there's nothing simple about oysters from Long Island, Swordfish from the Gulf of Mexico, Crab Legs from Alaska, Alligator from Louisiana, and Scallops, Lobster and Flounder from New England! Its more than simple, when ten to fifteen different species can be represented on a menu, and offered to be prepared to your choice. It's not simple when the chef can grill, steam, broil, or saute to your pleasure and then serve your fish accompanied by a tasty seasoned butter calculated to compliment the dish. The butters range from a sweet Basil to garlic, to a spicy Cajun, each perfect for the kind of fish with which it is served!

Steak and Chicken are deliciously prepared on the grill. The Filet Mignon, particularly, is tasty and tender. TONY AND JOE'S specialize in group parties, banquets, business meetings, and River Tours coordinated with dinners! But, know what is SIMPLY the best? Maryland Crab cakes! Tops!

1789 GEORGETOWN COMPLEX:
1226 36th Street, NW, Washington, DC, 20007.

1789 RESTAURANT, Tel: (202) 965-1789. On March 4, 1789 the Constitution of the United States was adopted, beginning the first year of the Federal Government. On April 30, 1789, George Washington was inaugurated in New York, on July 1789 The Department of State was organized and on December 25, 1789, the village of Georgetown was incorporated. The 1789 Restaurant was established to serve these three communities.

F. SCOTTS, Tel: (202) 342-0009. This is a romantic jazz-age nightclub, with an Art Deco interior, small dance floor and two intimate dining rooms. It features thirties and forties music, classic cocktails and a sophisticated atmosphere.

THE TOMBS, Tel: (202) 342-0009. The first establishment of its kind in the country addressing itself strictly to a university population. The walls are decorated with fine graphics, and with premium Hamburgers on the menu, it isa congenial meeting place for Georgetown faculty and students.

CLYDES, 3236 M Street, NW, Washington, D.C., 20007; Tel: (202) 333-9180. One of Washington's most celebrated saloons located in the heart of historic Georgetown. Checkered tablecloths, Tiffany shades and turn-of-the-century decor create a warm, cheerful and friendly atmosphere.

restaurants and nightclubs

THE RIVER CLUB
3223 K Street NW
Washington, D.C. 20007
Tel: (202) 333-8118
Hrs: Monday - Thursday: 6:00 p.m. - 11:30 p.m.
Friday and Saturday: 6:00 p.m. - Midnight
Dancing until 3:00 a.m
Sunday: Private parties only.
Reservations are recommended.
Valet parking is offered.
Visa, MasterCard, AMEX, Diners Club, and Carte Blanche are accepted.

In Georgetown, on a quiet street above the banks of the Potomac River, the epitome of gourmet fare is served in a manner guaranteed to suit one's fancy--amidst a glitzy blend of frosted etched glass, a cascading waterfall, striking wall murals, and a seventy foot sweep of bar that is topped with marble and sparkled with neon. Delightful ambience for cocktails, dinner and dancing is found at THE RIVER CLUB!

The kitchen is inspired under the direction of a young chef from Texas, Jeff Tunks, who has an unusual talent for brilliantly mingling taste and texture to both startle and please the palate. He calls it American Cuisine with an Asian influence. Each dish is a work of art and can be ordered as an entree or as an appetizer. This affords a unique opportunity to sample a wide variety of menu choices. Fresh salmon, whose delicate sauce is infused with Thai basil and papaya, or Chinese Style Smoked Lobster with crisp fried spinach are among the menu choices that can be as special as the mood of the evening warrants.

Big band/swing music from the 30's and 40's sets the mood and is enhanced by ample floor space to accomodate dancing by both dinner guests and the bar crowd. Two sound systems allow private parties to be intimate and cozy in the Empire Room or celebrated in the entire club. Upbeat glamour, glitz and glitter offer the ultimate experience in dining, entertainment and celebrity gazing!

UPTOWN

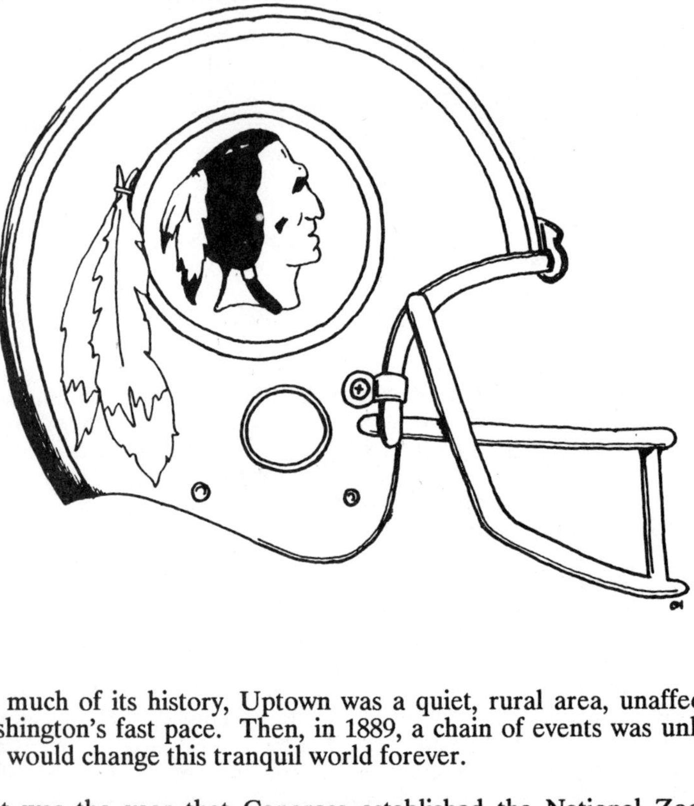

For much of its history, Uptown was a quiet, rural area, unaffected by Washington's fast pace. Then, in 1889, a chain of events was unleashed that would change this tranquil world forever.

That was the year that Congress established the National Zoological Park, and soon, people were crowding into Uptown to visit the park. Eventually, these visitors discovered that Uptown, with its lack of crowds, and somewhat cooler climate, was a pleasant place to live, and it became a fashionable summer enclave for Washington's wealthier residents. In 1890, trolley service was brought to Uptown, making it accessible to nearly every part of Washington, and it was finally enfolded by the Capital city. Three years later, Congress decided to have the Washington National Cathedral built here, and Uptown finally came of age.

A century later, Uptown is celebrating the birth of these historic landmarks. In that time, it has gone from being a suburb to an integral part of Washington. In addition to its most famous landmarks, Uptown is home to Embassy Row, the Hillwood Museum, and many other attractions

apparel

AFRICAN EYE
2134 Wisconsin Avenue
Washington, D.C. 20007
Tel: (202) 625-2552
Hrs: Tuesday - Saturday: 10:00 a.m. - 8:00 p.m.
Sunday: 11:00a.m. - 4:00 p.m.
Visa, Mastercard, American Express and Carte Blanche are accepted.

Three sisters, Mozella Perry Ademiluyi, Katherine Perry and Shirley Perry, grew up in Africa and developed an eye for fashion with an emphasis on comfort and flare. Collectively they see the world and uniquely use fashion to bring it's elements together, offering a unique blend of African, Asian and European designs.

They work with six African designers to fabricate hand-woven, on-of-a-kind garments. Every effort is made in both countries to provide a style and quality that is distinctly African, but at the same time a contemporary innovation. Wearing the elegant colorful evening wear will demand notice of all those you meet, and the comfort of each creative design must be experienced to be believed.

Their line of home accessories is as distinct and different as their clothing. Their jewelry and scarves will add the perfect accent to their own designs, or will spice up any outfit you already own. The warm and friendly atmosphere of the AFRICAN EYE make shopping there a pleasure. They make you feel like a welcome guest in their home. All three sisters are proud to represent their African designers and offer their customers a comfortable ambiance.

gourmet foods

SUTTON PLACE GOURMET
3201 New Mexico Avenue NW
Washington, D.C. 20016
Tel:
Washington, D.C. (202) 363-5800
Alexandria, Va. (703) 549-6611
Bethesda, Md. (301) 564-3100
Hrs:
Monday - Saturday 9:00 a.m. - 9:00 p.m.
Sunday 9:00 a.m. - 8:00 p.m.
Visa, MasterCard, and American Express are accepted.

SUTTON PLACE CAFE
Franklin & South Washington streets
Old Town Alexandria, Va.
Tel: (703) 739-0404

"One of the most respected specialty food stores in the United States," is a statement recently attributed to SUTTON PLACE GOURMET. Developed in the European style, each Sutton Place location has 17 different specialty food shops, including a traiteur restaurant, quality prepared foods perfect for picnics and parties, an extensive bakery with daily selections ranging from the heartiest breads to an exquisite chocolate Grand Marnier Cake, an award-winning delicatessen with sumptuous sandwiches made to order, and a gift department specializing in personalized, elegant baskets for every occasion. In addition, there are full-service departments in seafood, meat, produce, wine, cheese, candy, coffee, housewares, and flowers.

For ten years, SUTTON PLACE GOURMET has been introducing its customers to the highest quality products combined with a knowledgeable and courteous staff. There are at least two experienced chefs at each store, a customer service department that can handle all special orders and home delivery, and an experienced management team ready to assist you.

kitchen supplies

KITCHEN BAZAAR

The Galleria at Tysons II
Tel: (703) 883-1313

Seven Corners Center
Tel: (703) 534-0220

Fair Oaks Mall
Tel: (703) 385-0990

Pentagon City
Tel: (703) 415-5545

Montgomery Mall
(301) 365-5555

Lakeforest Mall
(301) 869-0600

Annapolis Mall
(301) 224-4414

Baltimore
(301) 547-COOK

4401 Connecticut Ave. N.W.
Washington, D.C.
Tel: (202) 244-1550

Bright, shiny, coppery and colorful, THE KITCHEN BAZAAR flaunts its organized clutter into a warm, fascinating, and irresistible welcome! Every inch of space is utilized without ever crowding the customer! High style, top tech, and prominent names are displayed on walls, shelves and in neat, charming piles on the floor! For books, baskets, necessities or whimseys, it's pure pleasure to browse, and it's intriguing to search for the latest gadget or the miracle-tool-of-all-time. If it's been invented, it most likely is available at the KITCHEN BAZAAR!

In 1964, the first store opened on Connecticut Avenue, with twelve more following in the biggest and best malls about town. Dedicated to creative cookery and catering to the flair of gourmand within us all, the staff is committed to the customer and is fully trained to answer questions, demonstrate products, and help select, wrap and mail gifts.

Simply sign for a free subscription to the "Kitchen Bazaar Times." You'll keep abreast of all sales, book signings, press parties, instructional seminars, and appearances of big name celebrities in the field of the culinary arts!

GEORGETOWN LEATHER DESIGN, Mazza Gallerie; Tel : (202)363-9710. For fine leather goods. See their story underGeorgetown.

NEIMAN MARCUS, Mazza Gallerie, 5300 Wisconsin, NW; Tel: (202) 966-9700. See their story under The Galleria at Tysons II.

NORTH EAST/SOUTH EAST

CAPITOL HILL, HOUSE SIDE

The House side of Capitol Hill shares much of the same history as that of the Senate Side. Like the other neighborhood, it also took the House side some time to become a community in its own right. Unlike the Senate side, however, the House side possesses fewer national monuments, making the neighborhood more typical of residential Washington.

What Capitol Hill's Senate side lacks in monuments, however, it makes up in other attractions. Among other things, the house side boasts the Sewall-Belmont House, one of the oldest homes in Washington. Home of the the National Women's Party, it is filled with memorobilia from the women's suffrage movement. Another attraction is the Capital Children's Museum, one of the country's first "hands-on" museums. Finally, you will not want to miss the crowning glory of this neighborhood, the newly refurbished Union Station, which is home to more than 100 retail shops, restaurants, and a nine-screen move theater.

The House of Capitol Hill is easily forgotten by many tourists, but it has a character of its own that makes it very different from the Senate side. A visit to this unique area will surely enhance your visit to Washington.

restaurants

ANTON'S LOYAL OPPOSITION
400 First Street SE
Washington, D.C. 20003
Tel: (202) 546-4545
Hrs: Monday - Friday:

Breakfast	7:00 a.m. - 10:30 a.m.
Lunch/Dinner	11:30 a.m. - 11:45 p.m.
Saturday - Sunday:	
Brunch	10:00 a.m. - 5:00 p.m.
Piano:	
Tuesday - Saturday:	6:30 p.m. - 12:00 midnight

Bar closes at 2:00 a.m.
Reservations recommended, especially for lunch.
Visa, MasterCard, American Express, Discover, Carte Blanche, Diners Club and Choice are accepted.

When Congress is in session, Democrats and Republicans alike gather at ANTON'S LOYAL OPPOSITION. Just a short walk from the Capitol, they relax and enjoy a cup of coffee, a meal, or conversation and count on not missing the role call for assembly. Whenever two bells sound the fifteen minute warning, there is a dash out the door while waiters gather up orders and return them to the kitchen to put on hold. After results of the vote are announced on the intercom, Congressional customers straggle back to finish whatever they had begun! And wide-eyed tourists watch and revel in the mystic of Washington, D.C.!

ANTON'S LOYAL OPPOSITION is a spacious, classy, art deco restaurant and piano bar. It glasses in the corner of First and D, Southeast, and its upbeat interior memorializes power, past and present, with autographed pictures of famous statesmen, movie stars, and astronauts. At tables sprinkled around the room, there are always many news-familiar faces. It's the in-place on Capitol Hill.

It also serves memorable food! Bill Anton, its affable, ebullient owner, innovated Grazing--choosing three out of two dozen appetizers for one low price! Rumor is that Steak Tartare, Oysters in Champagne and Buffalo Mozzarella are the favorites! Seafood is plentiful and fresh. In the fettuccini, it is magnificent! Variety in beef, lamb and capon plus an extensive wine list offer the diner an unusual opportunity for adventurous eating. And, Bananas Foster, served tableside? By all means, go for it!

Breakfast is available after 11:00 p.m. With twelve kinds of beer on tap, more in bottles, terrific burgers and sandwiches, and Capitol Hill Bean Soup available every day, it's not a surprise that twenty three years of success continues to succeed!

HAWK 'N' DOVE
329 Pennsylvania Avenue
Washington, D.C. 20009
Tel: (202) 543-3300
Hrs: Open seven days, except Christmas!
Sunday - Thursday: 10:00 a.m. - 2:00 a.m.
Friday and Saturday:. 10:00 a.m. - 3:00 a.m.
All major credit cards are accepted.

After 20 years, draft beer is still a buck! Luncheon Martinis are up to $1.25, however! Waiters still wear jeans, the menu is the same and no one is about to put tablecloths on the tables. We're talking "no frills" here! The HAWK 'n' DOVE is determined to remain what it was intended to be--a neighborhood pub with "America's favorite truck stop food." Well, why quarrel with success!

In 1967, when Stuart Long and Michael Lange merged the city's first gas station with the tobacco shop and taffy factory next door to it, the one hundred year old buildings adapted to their new mission with ease and grace. The dark, rustic interior remains mysterious and inviting. The juke box keeps on playing. Fish 'n' Chips, Crab Reubens, and King Club Sandwiches are still favorites. And members of Congress continue to forget their differences and blend happily with Supreme Court Justices, visiting dignitaries and tourist constituency!

Situated only two blocks southeast of the Capitol on Pennsylvania Avenue, there is always a good size night-time crowd there. Brunch is popular on weekends and Midnight Breakfast is available after 11:00 p.m. With twelve kinds of beer on tap, more in bottles, terrific burgers and sandwiches, and Capitol Hill Bean Soup available every day, it's not a surprise that twenty three years of success continues to succeed!

CAPITOL HILL, SENATE SIDE

"A pedestal waiting for a monument" was how Pierre L'Enfant, Washington's first city planner, described what is now called Capitol Hill. Home of the Capitol Building and the Supreme Court Building, Capitol Hill is perhaps one of the most important sites in this country. What many Americans don't realize is that Capital Hill is home to more than major government buildings, for Capitol Hill also boasts unique shops and restaurants, as well as one of Washington's more interesting residential neighborhoods.

Like the neighborhoods of Foggy Bottom and Dupont Circle, Capitol Hill was not immediate a popular place to live. While construction on the Capitol Building began in 1793, it was not until the turn of the century that Capitol Hill emerged as a residential neighborhood with an identity of its own. Up until that time, Capitol Hill consisted of the Capitol Building, which housed both houses of Congress, the Supreme Court, and the Library of Congress, eight boarding houses, a washer woman, a shoemaker, a general store, an oyster house, and several tobacco farms. A massive building program, spurred by the completion in 1897 of The Library of Congress, brought new life to the area. By 1935, a new Supreme Court Building, the grand Union Station, and several thousand red brick rowhouses had sprung up in the area.

Today, Capitol Hill offers visitors much more to do than just tour landmarks. On the Senate side of the Capitol Building, you will find "the other Capitol Hill", a lovely neighborhood of older homes, gardens, parks, churches, shops and museums. A walk through this area reveals several attractions that are easily missed. Along 7th Street and Pennsylvania Avenue, around Eastern Market, you will find a number of specialty shops, as well as some reasonably priced restaurants. Another overlooked attraction is Lincoln Park, which possess a statue of Black educator Mary McLeod Bethune. Standing with the figures of two children, it has been called the happiest statue in Washington.

When you are visiting the Capitol Building, do not overlook the neighborhood surrounding the Senate side of the building, This often-ignored neighborhood offers visitors some of Washington's loveliest and most unique attractions.

LA COLLINE
400 North Capitol Street
Washington, D.C. 20001
Tel: (202) 737-0400
Hrs:

Breakfast	Monday - Friday	7:00 a.m. - 10:00 a.m.
Lunch	Monday - Friday	11:30 a.m. - 3:00 p.m.
Dinner	Monday - Saturday	6:00 p.m. - 10:00 p.m.

Closed on Sundays.
Visa, MasterCard, AMEX, Diners Club and Carte Blanche are accepted.

Warmth, friendliness, elegance and charm underscore classic French cuisine at LA COLLINE! Situated directly across from both Union Station and the Capitol Building, it attracts the nation's famous visitors, politicians, and lobbyists! And, while dining "on the Hill" IS exciting, it's the preparation, quality, and service of the food under the watchful eyes of the owners--Paul Zucconi, Chef Vatche Benguian, and Executive Chef Robert Greault--that merit rave reviews for this popular restaurant!

Selected each year by Washingtonian Magazine as one of the "Top 50" Restaurants, LA COLLINE continues to offer its customers an extensive selection of fresh, seasonal seafood with home-smoked Salmon a key specialty on a daily changing menu. Regular diners favor the "Special Complete Dinner" --a variety of choices at a fixed price. Excellent Bouillabaisse and Dover Sole are favorites, as well as the light and tasty Salade Maraichere, with its special Walnut Dressing. Home made Pastries are NOT to be resisted, except in favor of one of the other tempting choices of luscious desserts on the menu. A variety of French and American wines are offered by the glass.

LA COLLINE boasts a private party room for meetings, receptions or fund-raisers, and the casual cocktail hour is the preferred choice of many for a bit of relaxing, and perhaps, some people/politician gazing!

NORTHEAST

restaurants

COLONEL BROOKS' TAVERN
901 Monroe Street NE
Washington, D.C . 20017
Tel: (202) 529-4002
Hrs:

Monday - Thursday	11:00 a.m. - 3:00 a.m.
Friday	11:00 - 3:00 a.m.
Saturday	11:30 - 3:00 a.m.
Sunday	11:00 a.m. - 2:00 a.m.

Visa and MasterCard are accepted.

Colonel Brooks wouldn't believe what he would see today on what was once his land! However, he certainly would be delighted with the tavern that is named for him and sits near the site of his former mansion. After his death, the huge expanse of property was subdivided and sold. The building that is now COLONEL BROOKS' TAVERN was built in 1917 by an Italian tailor. It was classic style of that period, with living quarters above for the family. Many business have been at this location including a cigar store, a pool hall, church, and Chinese laundry.With the help of friends. Jim Steigman has developed it into an attractive, innovative, neighborhood gathering place with excellent food and Washington D.C.'s largest selection of draft beer! The building was purchased and renovated more than a decade ago.

The menu changes seasonally in order to take advantage of the freshest ingredients. Lighter selections are featured in the summer, with heavier soups, stews and roasts being reserved for the cold winter months. Dinner is served until eleven o'clock in the evening and there is a Late Night Menu that continues to be available until 1:00 a.m. with an amazing mix of customers from the neighborhooh and beyond.

The food is delicious and attractively served. Virtually everything is prepared on the premises, the hand made bread, deserts--they even smoke their own meat and grind their sausage. Cajun Mixed Grill and Stuffed Coho Salmon are unsurpassed and the quiche is great! Jim's favorite is a Grilled Swordfish Sandwich, served on Pita bread! Actually, its hard to have a favorite! It's all so good!

SOUTH WEST

accommodations

LOEWS L'ENFANT PLAZA
480 L'enfant Plaza SW
Washington, DC 20024
Tel: (202) 484-1000
Hrs: Open 24 hours a day, seven days.
Visa, MasterCard, American Express and Diners Club are accepted.

LOEWS L'ENFANT PLAZA defines the term "ultra deluxe." Elegant furnishings include entertainment armoires with remote control, color T.V./video cassette players, miniature bar and fully stocked refrigerator. The nightly turndown is accented with Godiva Chocolates.

The hotel is located in the heart of Washington's business and governmental centers and is within walking distance of the Smithsonian Institution and the Washington Monument. Occupying the bottom two and top four floors of the 15-story office building, the hotel offers sweeping vistas of the Potomac River, Waterfront, Capitol Hill, National Monuments and Loews L'enfant Plaza. A shopping promenade is located directly underneath the hotel featuring 50 specialty shops and eateries. One of the largest metro stops is also located directly beneath the hotel. They cater to the business traveler and have all the amenities needed to conduct business when away from home.

The Fitness and swim center has a trained staff on hand to help establish or maintain a guests' workout program and to lead exercise and aerobic classes. Massages are available upon request, and the rooftop pool dons a seasonal cover to allow year-round swimming. Seniors, do check on the Capitol Memories or Cabinet Class accommodations. A discounted rate is offered, free parking and Continental Breakfast, all based on availability.

restaurants

THE MARKET INN
200 E Street SW
Washington, D.C. 20024
Tel: (202) 554-210
Hrs: Sunday - Thursday: 11:00 a.m. - midnight
Visa, Mastercard, American Express and Carte Blanche are accepted.

The specialty of the house is Lobster, but they also prepare Chateaubriand for two, Swordfish, Salmon Steaks, Shrimp Scampi in garlic butter, Soft Shell Crab and many other entrees, with the same care and expertise they have demonstrated with Lobster for the past 31 years. THE MARKET INN is owned by the Mandis family who have been restaurateurs for three generations and they are particularly proud of their seafood, soups and sauces. They offer Imperial Crab baked with fresh lump meat crab, Fresh Blackened Redfish Seared Cajun Style and Brook Trout. The vegetables are cooked to perfection and the deserts tempting and delightful. The service is prompt and friendly and the manager, Michael Kipp began his career at the market Inn as a waiter when it first opened.

The sound of a Jazz piano permeates each of the distinctly different dinning rooms. They have an antique bar in one room that was built in Civil War days. In the colorful Hanger room, there are red and burgundy table cloths and plates accented by the eclectic wall decoration. Pictures of military aircraft are shown together with antique guns and trophy fish. It's a striking effect.

Just off Capitol hill The Market Inn is convenient for lunch or dinner while visiting the Smithsonian or a lovely dinner before or after attending the theater. Be sure and try their "New Orleans Jazz Brunch," served Saturday and Sunday 10:30 a.m. till 2:30 p.m..

THE WATERFRONT

The picturesque waterfront are all the best that the greater Washington, D.C. area has to offer into one lovely package. Located just blocks from the museums and attractions of the Mall area, the waterfront offers fabulous entertainment, superb, fresh seafood, fine military museums, and picturesque views of the Potomac River.

Established in the 17th century, the waterfront thrived as travelers took advantage of the river to travel south, and as fishermen brought their catches into the wharf to sell. Pierre L'Enfant chose this section of the city to be for military development because of it strategic location near the river, so a fort, arsenal, and prison were erected. The area saw its heyday during the Civil War, when the wharfs here acted as the debarkment site for federal soldiers.

In the 1950s, shopping, office buildings and other new facilities were built at the waterfront, modernizing the area.

attractions

More than 5,000 Navy artifacts are housed at the **Navy Museum** (9th and M streets SE). Opened in 1963 at the Washington the Navy Yard, major draws to the museum include the fighting top from the *Constitution*, gunmounts from World War II fighting ships, the bathyscaphe *Trieste*, and submarine periscopes.

For submarine fans, **The Navy Museum Annex** features four World War II Midget subs, a submarine-launched Poseidon missile, and underwater weapons systems.

Learn the history of the U.S. Marine Corps at the **Marine Corps Historical Center** (9th and M streets SE). Artifacts trace the Marines' beginnings in the Revolutionary War to the present.

events

One of the most spectacular summer sights in Washington is the colorful **Evening Parade**, held every Friday from mid-May through August, at the Marine Barracks (Eighth and I streets, SE). The parade is presented by the Marine Drum and Bugle Corps and the Silent Drill Platoon, who thrill audiences with their precision twirling of bayonets. Reservations to view the parade are required three weeks in advance.

The Washington Waterfront Association holds its **"Restaurant Olympics"** in the early fall of each year. All of the events take place bewtween Ninth St. and M St. The "olympic" events include a chowder cook-off, a keg roll, a waiter's race, a vegetable carving, a tray press and a waiter's marathon. All of these events are designed to demonstrate the skills of area employees and to provide fun activities in the area.

The Washington Waterfront Association holds its annual **Festival of Lights** in mid-December of each year. This event begins with a ceremony in the park between the Hogates and Phillips Flagship restaurants. Santa arrives at this time and conducts the judging of displays presented by ships docked in the Washington Yacht Club area. At the same time that evening each, of the adjacent restaurants light their Christmas decorations and caroling is conducted by local school and church choirs.

restaurants

THE GANGPLANK RESTAURANT
600 Water Street S.W.
Washington, DC 20024
Tel: (202) 554-5000

Hrs:	Lunch		11:30 a.m. - 3:00 p.m.
	Dinner	Sun. - Thu.	5:30 p.m. - 10:00 p.m.
	Dinner	Fri., Sat.	5:30 p.m. - 11:00 p.m.
Tower Lounge		Sun. - Thu.	5:30 p.m. - midnight
		Fri. - Sat.	5:30 p.m. - 1:00 a.m.

Visa, Mastercard, Americaqn Express and Diners Club are accepted.

Seafood just seems to taste better the closer you get to the water. You can not get any closer to waterfront dining than the GANGPLANK'S floating restaurant. Here, it's waterfront dining the way it was meant to be, quiet, intimate and with one of the best views in the city. During the day there is much to see with the comings and goings of the hundreds of power cruisers and sailing yachts that live at the Gangplank Marina. At night the Washington Channel lights reflect from the river and create a beautiful effect when shining together in the reflection of the moon. It doesn't get any better than this when you want to do something special with an intimate friend or to commemorate an anniversary with a spouse.

Only the finest freshest, ingredients are used to create the succulent delights of fancy. At lunch, appetizers like Fried Calamari with Lemon butter or Timbale of Smoked Salmon filled with Fresh Crabmeat are sure to spark an appetite or the Grilled Chicken and Artichoke salad might just be enough for the light luncher. Try the Smoked Salmon Fettucine for a real pasta treat. The Gangplank Shellfish Combination, Grilled Sea Scallops and Grilled Catfish are sure to please. For dinner the Smoked Combination of Salmon, Trout and Shrimp comes highly recommended as an appetizer and the Caesar Salad is wonderful. Veal and Crabmeat and the Seafood Mixed Grill are two favorite entrees and the desert menu changes daily to provide an untold scrumptious finale.

HOGATE'S
800 Water Street SW
Washington, DC 20004
Tel: (202) 484-6300
Hrs: Mon. - Fri. 11:00 a.m. - 11:00 p.m.
Sat. 12:00 noon - 12:00 midnight
Sun. 10:30 a.m. - 10:00 p.m.
Visa, MasterCard, American Express, Diners Club and Carte Blanche are accepted.
Reservations are suggested.

Famous landmarks take priority when planning a trip to Washington, DC! Statues, monuments and museums--and, for over fifty years, HOGATE'S FAMOUS SEAFOOD RESTAURANT! HOGATE'S is known, both nationally and internationally, as the place-of-choice for absolutely fresh, perfectly prepared seafood, for the most fantastic view of the Potomac River and for its delicious Rum Buns! It is a favorite stop for group tours from all around the world! Each day, buses pull into the wide, circular drive on the waterfront and unload hungry patrons, who happily compare glowing recommendations as they filter into one of the oldest and largest of the city's most noted restaurants.

Upon entering, the temptation is to stop and shop at the glassed-in, colorful expanse of tucked-in-ice seafood that is always just-delivered from the prestigious firm of Steve Connolly in Boston, Massachusetts. Or, to purchase a handful of soft, warm Rum Buns! Do it--on the way out!

It is wise to make a reservation but the waiting area is comfortable and cozy. All rooms are pleasantly appointed with old seafaring artifacts decorating the walls. Some patrons wait for a window table, but, the incomparable vista is framed by large windows which open the view toall as they enjoy HOGATE'S famous specialties--such as the enduring, original Mariner Platter and the New England Clambake. The Norfolk Sampler and the Captain's Platter are also familiar favorites. Each is a generous serving, artfully arranged, flawlessly prepared--worth the trip!

PHILLIPS FLAGSHIP
900 Water Street SW
Washington, D.C. 20024
Tel: (202) 488-8515

Hrs:	Sunday - Thursday:	11:00 a.m. - 11:00 p.m.
	Friday - Saturday:	11:00 a.m. - Midnight
Winter		
	Sunday - Thursday:	11:00 a.m. - 10:00 p.m.
	Friday - Saturday:	11:00 a.m. - 11:00 p.m.

Visa, MasterCard, American Express, Diners Club, and Discover are accepted.

The most delicate part of a crab cake is the tender crab meat lump. It must remain unbroken and free of bits of shell and other foreign objects. It's the finesse and care given to this very important ingredient that permeates the entire philosophy at PHILLIPS FLAGSHIP RESTAURANT. The customer is king; only the best is good enough and the price must be reasonable.

Seated in a beautiful, Chesapeake style, seafood house, the view of the waterfront and glimpse of Haynes Point across the Washington Channel help to develop a heightened craving for seafood. Phillips specializes in your pleasure. They have the traditionally remarkable Crab Cakes and Crab Imperial, the house specialty, to feast on. The Broiled Seafood Platter is the most popular, and it comes highly recommended. The Surf and Turf with Lobster or the Filet Mignon with Stuffed Shrimp satisfies the hearty eater who is unable to make up his mind. Everything on the menu is prepared and served with the utmost care.

Shirley and Brice Phillips, with their son Steve and his wife Olivia, have created an eating place charged with high energy that is capable of delighting everyone, from a celebrated star to a powerful politician, to a family of tourists. No trip to the Waterfront would be complete without sampling the food and hospitality of Phillips Flagship.

SECTION TWO: MARYLAND

BALTIMORE

accommodations

ADMIRAL FELL INN, Fell's Point, 888 S. Broadway Street, Baltimore, MD, Tel: (301) 522-7377 or (800) 292 Inns. Open 24 hours a day, seven days. Visa, MasterCard and American Express are accepted. A historic inn located at Fell's Point. Rooms are individually furnished with antiques and antique reproductions.

KNOXVILLE

rafting

RIVER & TRAIL OUTFITTERS
604 Valley Road
Knoxville, MD 21759
Tel: (301) 695-5177
Hrs:
April 1 - October 31
Open seven days: 9:00 a.m. - 5:00 p.m..
Winter
Monday - Friday: 9:00 a.m. - 5:00 p.m.
Also open for ski trip weekends.
Visa and MasterCard are accepted.

Experience the beautiful and historic waters of the Shenandoah, Patomac, and Antietam for the perch of a raft, canoe, or inner tube. fe. Glowing recommendations say these river tours are fun and great for families.

Their entry level raft trip near Harpers Ferry is a half day of majestic mountain and river scenery. The outfitters provide a guide in each raft, U.S. Coast Guard approved safety equipment, a picnic, and transportation to and from the river.

For a more personal experience in a boat on the river, you can explore the many waterways that are open to a canoe. The outfitters canoe rental program maps out the Shenandoah, Potomac and their tributaries for a day, weekend, or weeklong paddle.

Named by Washingtonian Magazine as one of the areas best summer activities is River & Trials guided tubing trips down Antietam Creek. This spring-fed stream will refresh you even when the air temperature is breaking through the 90s.

River & Trail Outfitters is a year-roud operation providing cross-country ski tours to New Germany, Maryland and Blackwater Falls, West Virginia during the winter.

notes notes notes notes notes notes

the nation's capital

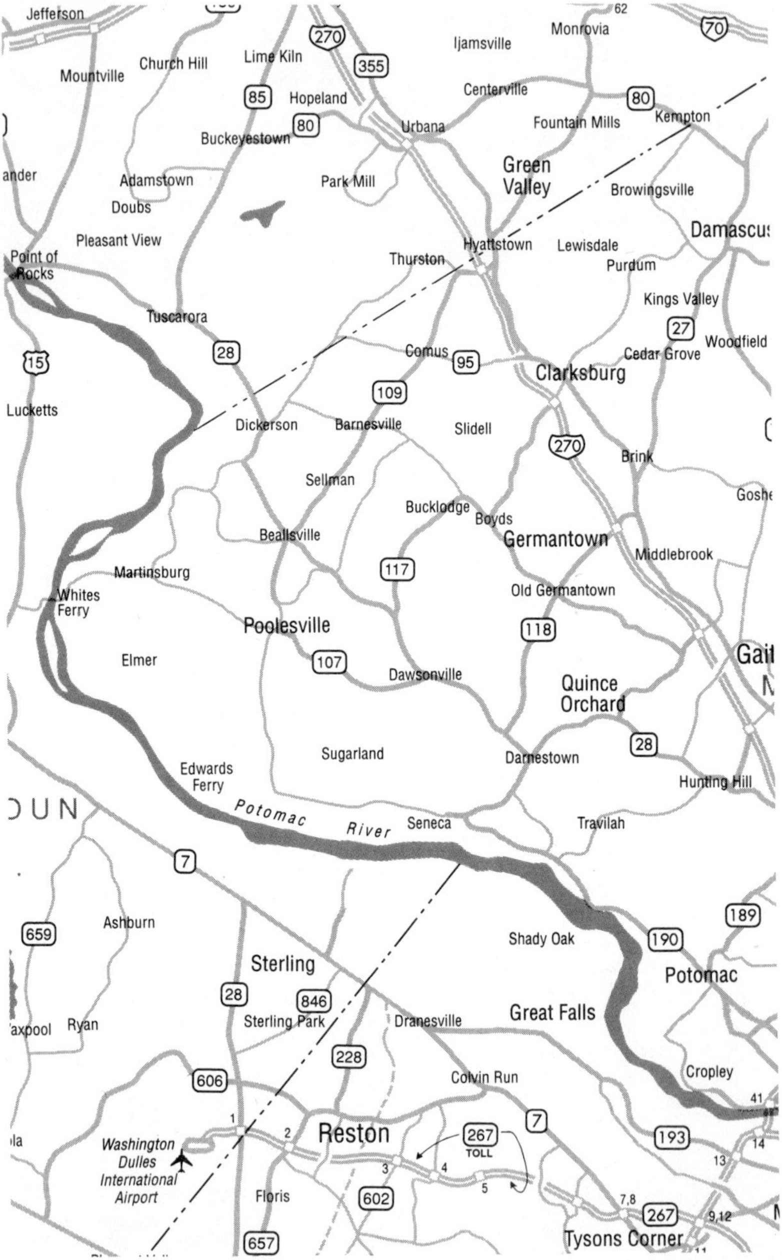

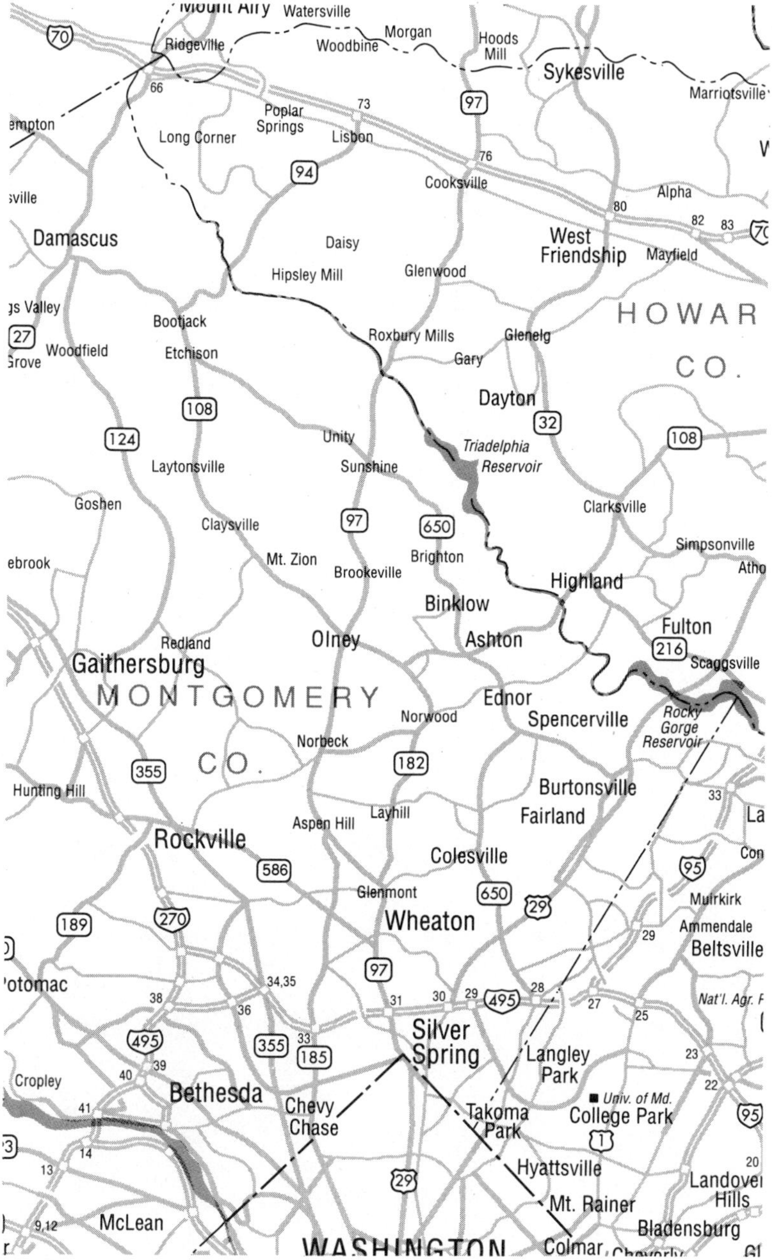
Mount Airy
Watersville
Morgan
Woodbine
Hoods Mill
Sykesville
Marriotsville
Ridgeville
Poplar Springs
Long Corner
Lisbon
Cooksville
Alpha
West Friendship
Mayfield
Damascus
Daisy
Hipsley Mill
Glenwood
HOWARD CO.
Bootjack
Etchison
Woodfield
Roxbury Mills
Glenelg
Gary
Dayton
Triadelphia Reservoir
Unity
Sunshine
Laytonsville
Goshen
Clarksville
Simpsonville
Claysville
Mt. Zion
Brookeville
Brighton
Highland
Binklow
Fulton
Scaggsville
Redland
Olney
Ashton
Gaithersburg
MONTGOMERY CO.
Ednor
Spencerville
Norwood
Rocky Gorge Reservoir
Norbeck
Hunting Hill
Burtonsville
Fairland
Layhill
Aspen Hill
Rockville
Colesville
Muirkirk
Glenmont
Ammendale
Wheaton
Beltsville
Potomac
Nat'l. Agr.
Silver Spring
Langley Park
Cropley
Bethesda
Chevy Chase
Univ. of Md.
College Park
Takoma Park
Hyattsville
Landover Hills
McLean
Mt. Rainer
Bladensburg
WASHINGTON
Colmar

MONTGOMERY COUNTY

Montgomery County had rebellious beginnings, and has continued to be a trail blazer ever since. Chartered in 1776, the county took its name from Revolutionary War Hero Richard Montgomery instead of from English nobility, which was usual for that time.

From that time forward, Montgomery County was a haven for wealthy city dwellers, but now it has evolved into a high-tech region and retail Mecca.

Montgomery County is the home of the National Institutes of Health, one of the world's foremost research centers, the National Naval Medical Center, Johns Hopkins University Montgomery County, and the National Institute of Standards and Technology. Smaller research and technology firms also fill the county, making for one of the richest research facilities in the country.

attractions

President James Madison's hideout after escaping the British in 1812, the Caleb Bentley Home, est. 1808, is part of **Brookeville** (Georgia Ave and Brookeville Road), one of the country's earliest settlements.

Step into yesteryear with a visit to **Garrett Park** (north of Grosvenor Metrostation between Rockville Pike and Connecticut Ave.). Established in 1898, this is an entire town that is registered as a "Historic District" in the National Register of Historic Places.

For a rich, historic experience, visit **Poolesville** (Md. Route 107 and Md. Route 109), a lovely town brimming with homes built in the 18th and 19th centuries. Features are the John Poole House, Poolesville's first house and the home of the town founder; Town Hall; St. Peter's Episcopal Church; Seneca Schoolhouse; and White's Ferry, the last working ferry on the Potomac River, accommodating vehicles up to 40,000 pounds.

Established in 1817, the **Sandy Spring Meeting House** (Md. Route 108 and Meeting House Road) is an important piece of Quaker history. Visitors are intrigued by the Colonial-style church with its original benches and unusual, wavy-paned windows.

An amusement park until the 1950's, **Glen Echo Park** (MacArthur Blvd. and Goldsboro Road) has evolved into a one-of-a-kind arts and cultural center with an original Dentzel Carousel still in operation. Showcased are artisans demonstrating their crafts in 19th century-style studios; summer entertainment; puppeteers, dancers, painters, and the oldest year-round theater for children.

The home of the founder of the American Red Cross, the **Clara Barton National Historic Site**, is open to the public from 10:00 a.m. to 5:00 p.m. daily.

It is still possible to take a old-fashioned barge trip at **Chesapeake And Ohio (C&O) Canal Park** (11710 MacArthur Blvd, Potomac). Operated by the National Park Service, the park offers barge rides and a 180-mile tow path. Within the park, **Great Falls Tavern Museum** features exhibits of the canal's history.

Open daily from 6:00 a.m. to one hour after sunset, **Black Hill Regional Park** (13440 W. Old Baltimore Road, Boyds), is 2,000 picturesque acres of parkland, complete with picnic areas, hiking and biking trails, and horseback riding paths. Located within the park is **Little Seneca Lake**, a wildlife and waterfowl observatory offering boating and fishing.

The historic **Beall-Dawson House** (103 W. Montgomery Ave.)is the home of the Montgomery County Historical Society. This restored Federal-style building is now a museum.

One of the highest quality and most challenging golf courses in the Metropolitan Washington area, **Redgate Golf Course** (14500 Avery Road) is open to the public.The 18-hole, 72 par course offers 6,486 yards of greens.

events

The Civil War comes back to life at Rockville's **Civil War Re-Enactment** (on the grounds of the Beall-Dawson House). This two-day summer event includes a camp, complete with soldiers, officers, and physicians, and gives guests the chance to see how a Civil War wedding might have taken place.

BETHESDA

The area now known as Bethesda was once part of St. Mary's, the name given to the whole state by Lord Cecilius Calvert, who inherited it from his father. Lord Calvert sent his brother Leonard to establish a colony in 1634, and to call it Terra Maria (Maryland) in honor of Queen Henrietta Maria.

Near 1820, a group of Presbyterians built a church, which they named the Bethesda Presbyterian Church, after the pool of Bethesda in Jerusalem. The surrounding area also adopted the name.

Once a rural retreat for those seeking religious freedom, Bethesda is now a thriving cultural, educational, and commercial community

attractions

The world-famous Federal health research complex, the **National Institutes of Health** (Cedar Lane, Bethesda), has a visitors information center, featuring model lab, slide show, exhibits, and a theater which hosts cultural programs throughout the year.

Located within the National Institutes of Health is the **National Library of Medicine**. Free tours are conducted Monday through Friday at 1:00 p.m. The reading room is open Monday through Thursday, 8:30 a.m. - 9:00 p.m.; Friday and Saturday 8:30 a.m. - 1:00 p.m.

A local tradition, the **Montgomery Farm Women's Cooperative Market** (7155 Wisconsin Ave., Bethesda), offers fresh produce and handmade craft sales. Hours are Wednesday and Saturday, 8:00 a.m. - 3:00 p.m.

Concerts and art exhibitions are presented all year long at **Strathmore Hall Arts Center** (10701 Rockville Pike, Bethesda), a beautiful turn-of-the-century mansion that serves as Montgomery County's performing and literary arts center.

Open April through September, **Cabin John Regional Park** (7777 Democracy Blvd., Bethesda) offers entertainment for the young at heart. Focal points of the park are **Noah's Ark Petting Zoo**, train rides on their miniature train; and the **Locust Grove Nature Center**, which offers nature-related classes, hikes, lectures, and films.

A garden consisting of 750 varieties of azalea, 300 varieties of holly, rhododendron and other exotic plants awaits visitors at **McCrillis Gardens and Gallery** (6910 Greentree Road, Bethesda). The gallery features contemporary drawings, prints, and watercolors. Garden hours are 10:00 a.m. - sunset, seven days; Gallery hours are Tuesday - Sunday Noon - 4:00 p.m.

bookstores

ROGUES' GALLERY MYSTERY BOOKSTORE
4934 Elm Street
Bethesda MD 20814
Tel: 301) 986-5511
Hrs: Tuesday - Saturday: 11:00 a.m. - 7:00 p.m.
Sunday: 1:00 a.m. - 5:00 p.m.
Visa and MasterCard are accepted.

It was a damp, dark night and the fog was thick and heavy. I was in a mysterious room with blood red walls and carpeting. A chalk outline of a body was on the floor and yellow police tape barred the bathroom door ... Whodunit and where and why? Am I dreaming? Am I in some ghastly horrible place or am I shopping for a good murder mystery? It would be hard to say, because at ROGUES' GALLERY they have all that and more. Fred and Shelley Wegner have created a bookstore devoted to the art of Mystery. The atmosphere, with all those thousands of solved and unsolved mysteries, can be exhilarating and intense. It's a perfect environment for the mystery addict in search of a fix that will turn the night into an thrilling and enjoyable reading experience.

Fred Wegner says the most rewarding facet of his business are the customers. He is a devoted mysteryphile himself, and enjoys the relationships with readers who share his passion. He is eager to help anyone find the mystery novel that interests her or him the most. And he has a large selection of thousands from which to choose. He has classics and contemporary mysteries for adults and children, true crime, espionage, reference books, and games for the really hooked.

Come on in and browse, increase your heart rate, and get into a really good mystery book tonight.

TRAVEL BOOKS UNLIMITED AND LANGUAGE CENTER
4931 Cordell Avenue
Bethesda, MD 20814
Tel: (301) 951-8533
FAX: (301) 951-8546

Hrs:	Tuesday - Sunday:	10:00 a.m. - 9:00 p.m.
	Sunday:	noon - 5:00 p.m.

Visa, MasterCard and American Express are accepted.

Never before has so much information been so carefully and selectively garnered, gathered and grouped as is available to be explored in Bethesda, Maryland, next door to our Federal Government and the foreign embassies assigned to this country! Rochelle Jaffe's sixteen-hundred square feet of fascinating space is appropriately called TRAVEL BOOKS UNLIMITED AND LANGUAGE CENTER! Unlimited! That's precisely the point!

Nearly every book in print, on anything related to travel, can be found either on her shelves, in her catalogue, or at her fingertips! Neophytes as well as experienced travelers pour through the books, tapes and maps hoping to enhance their travel or their reverie. Rochelle appreciates the armchair traveler since she is so busy with her popular store that much of her own exploration is accomplished in the same manner! With a sharp eye, she culls the best and is totally intolerant of misinformation or inaccurate facts.

With a table to spread out maps, and deft hands to refold them, the visitor is able to reminisce, chart a course, or dream ahead! With a courteous, unusually knowledgeable and experienced staff (they get to travel more than she does!), the time spent becomes extraordinarily fruitful. Material in foreign languages encourages customers from other countries as well as those planning trips abroad. This is, indeed, the something-for-everyone place! And, too, there are nearly one hundred of the finest ethnic restaurants located nearby--and a book on the shelf to help you choose one to your liking!

SECOND STORY BOOKS, 4836 Bethesda Avenue, Bethesda, MD, 20814; Tel: (301) 656-0170. See their story under Dupont Circle.

delicatessens

LE GOURMET MARKET
4550 Montgomery Avenue
Bethesda, MD 20814
Tel: (301) 656-6167
Hrs: Monday - Friday 10:30 a.m. - 8:30 p.m.
Saturday 1:00 p.m. - 6:00 p.m.
Visa and MasterCard are accepted.

LE GOURMET MARKET is a corner carry-out in the Air Rights Center Building in Bethesda, Maryland. The story of this small and bustling business begins three years ago with their opening and continues with their ever-abiding devotion to food preparation and service, and providing the best Deli food in the whole area.

Melody Willson, at LE GOURMET MARKET is the woman who oversees the plans, purchases and preparation to provide the best and most unusual Deli food to be found in the Metropolitan area! They make magnificent sandwiches of imported meats, sausage, cheeses and jumbo shrimp, served on a choice of eight different breads. Everyday brings forth a unique and delectable "special," always with soup, which stands as the star of that day! Regular customers come early for it. their personally concocted Chicken Salad and Chinese Sesame Noodles are eagerly sought after and are often ordered ahead for luncheons. Upon order, they are delighted to cater!

They insist that everything must be absolutely fresh. And they start from "scratch," carefully building and blending each step herself, as if each dish, each sandwich, was the only one offered. They want it to be attractive and delicious and they strive to make it healthy, too. No mayonnaise on the special-for-dieters Gourmet Chef Salad and no monosodium glutamate is used. Chinese heritage, French expertise and a big heart are blended to perfection at this Deli, a veritable show case of culinary art!

restaurants

BETHESDA CRAB HOUSE
4958 Bethesda Avenue
Bethesda, MD 20814
Tel: (301) 652-3382
Hrs: Open seven days 9:00 a.m. - 12:00 midnight

Authentic Maryland crabs! BIG ones, too! And all the old-fashioned ambiance of picnic tables covered with newspaper, wooden mallets, beer on tap, by the pitcherful and deliciously spiced shrimp in shells. Maryland is famous for its seafood and the BETHESDA CRAB HOUSE is famous for the way they spice, steam and serve Maryland crabs in season and Louisiana crabs 12 months out of the year.

When Henry Vechery opened his place in 1961, there were just a few restaurant/carry outs in Bethesda. Now, there are over 100 restaurants! And, Henry's place remains the favorite for steamed crabs and shrimp. He knows his loyal customers by name and he is so helpful and friendly that new customers immediately become loyal ones. His five children have all worked there over the years, zipping around the tables, like their father, replacing crab and shrimp trays and drinks as many times as happy customers give the signal.

Reservations are a must if you'd prefer eating to waiting. Whether eating in or carrying out, it's best to reserve the crabs, not just a table! Henry is glad to pack for trips so a visitor can take a real treat to the peopleback home. They take big parties on the premises and cater to a lot of individual office parties, workint out package deals for them. But, to savor an evening of Old Maryland tradition, whether you're a visitor from near or far, it's shirt sleeves and slacks for the time of your life and crabs you'll never forget!

SHANDIZ RESTAURANT, 4550 Montgomery Avenue, Bethesda, MD 20814; Tel: (301) 961-8989. Excellent ethnic cuisine.

specialty shops

BIG PLANET COMICS, 4865 Cordell Avenue 2nd Floor, Bethesda, MD 20814, Tel: (301) 654-6856, Hrs: Monday - Saturday 11:00 a.m. - 6:00 p.m.., Friday 11:00 a.m. - 8:00 p.m.,Visa and MasterCard are accepted. New comics come in every Friday and you better be there if you want to get the hot new issues. Joel Pollack started into business for himself to do something he really enjoyed. Together with Steve Hauk the manager they will help you discover what the comics are all about. They cater mostly to adults and boast that they have the most intelligent clientele in D.C.

THE LIBRARY STORE, 7720 Wisconsin Avenue, Bethesda, MD, 20814; Tel: (301) 652-8811. Mail-order number: (800) 233-8959. This amazing store features everything one could possibly imagine being connected with a library or a book collector, except the books.

toy stores

LOWEN'S IMAGINATIVE PLAYTHINGS
7201 Wisconsin Avenue
Bethesda, MD 20814
Tel: (301) 652-1289
Hrs:
Monday, Wednesday,Friday and Saturday: 9:30 a.m. -6:00 p.m.
Thursday 9:30 a.m. - 9:00 p.m.
Sunday Noon - 5:00 p.m.
Thanksgiving to Christmas:
Monday - Friday 9:30 a.m. - 9:00 p.m.
Visa, MasterCard, American Express and Discover are accepted.

A store uniquely centered around children of all ages and their amusement! Sound like a fantasy? It is! LOWEN'S offers a playground for toy testing in an environment designed to stimulate thought and wonder! No violence promoting toys here, just good, clean fun with toys that give pleasure and evoke curiosity and an atmosphere that intrigues and fascinates. For example, a 300-gallon Aquarium of colorful, tropical fish captivates a child's eye and allows parents to keep watch on the other side.

To read, children often choose to sit in an 1920s, roller coaster car and, then, play or rest in the 1920s bumper car. There are opportunities to interest and enthrall the child in all of us! For a future builder, there is a massive Lego model, complete with moving parts. A full size Steif tiger, named Lowenstripe, welcomes everyone to the third floor. A nostalgic soda fountain provides a treat of frozen custard, in an area reserved for birthday parties. The emphasis is on providing a truly enjoyable setting for the child of any age to shop and play. With the large variety of toys they have, they are committed to safety and quality. Convenience plays an important part, as well, with "Old Fashioned Delivery Service" available for personal service from 10 feet to 10 miles!

The Community-minded owner, Scott Goode, presents a weekly Parents' Night with local and national child experts advising on the problems of raising children--from playing games to helping with homework. This extraordinary toy store offers an experience no one would want to miss!

CHEVY CHASE

In 1751, Col. Joseph Belt acquired a patent for his new estate, which he named "Chevie Chace." Named after the hunting song, "The Ballad of Chevie Chace," his property spanned 560 acres and is believed to have once been a hunting club. That acreage is now the location of the Chevy Chase Golf Club, at the intersection of Bradley Blvd., and Connecticut and Wisconsin avenues.

By the late 19th centuries, the Chevy Chase Land Company started acquiring property between Dupont Circle and Jones Bridge Road. The village of Chevy Chase was incorporated in 1914, and has been growing ever since. Though the old amusement park and Chevy Chase Lake are memories, Chevy Chase continues to be a rich community in which to live and work.

attractions

Nature lovers will delight in the **Audubon Naturalist Society** (8940 Jones Mill Road, Chevy Chase). An impressive Georgian mansion called Woodend Mansion, was built by John Russell Pope, architect of the Jefferson Memorial. This 40-acre estate is now a wildlife sanctuary and nature education center. Hours are Monday - Friday, 9:00 a.m. - 5:00 p.m.

One of the most prestigious shopping centers in the greater Washington area is **Downtown Chevy Chase**. Dozens of designer boutiques and department stores, such as Saks Fifth Avenue, Gucci, Saint Laurent, Rive Gauche, and Saks-Jandel, are concentrated in a three-block area.

restaurants

HOULIHAN'S OLD PLACE, 4444 Willard Avenue, Chevy Chase, MD; Tel: (301) 654-9020. A great place to dine. they have live music on Thursday, Friday and Saturday nights.

GAITHERSBURG

Gaithersburg, the center of Montgomery County, has tripled its populations since 1970, but has still managed to maintain its rural ambiance.

Benjamin Gaither built the first house here in 1802, thus establishing the settlement. Referred to by some as "Bio Tech" Valley, Gaithersburg is renowned for being the heart of the scientific community in the East.

attractions

The Federal science and engineering laboratory, the **National Institute of Standards and Technology** (I-270 and Quince Orchard Road) features studies on productivity and quality control.

The **National Geographic Society Membership Center** (Darnestown Road, Gaithersburg), offers a book and map store, along with exhibits, in a park-like setting.

For lovers of all things equestrian, **The Maryland Horse Center** (Quince Orchard Rd.) is the perfect place to spend the day. The horse center has shows nearly every weekend.

events

The East Coast's largest county fair, the **Montgomery County Fair** (16 Chestnut St.), is held the third week in August.

There's sure to be something to please everyone at the **Autumn Crafts Festival** (Montgomery County Fairgrounds, 16 Chestnut St., Gaithersburg. The craft boasts 250 professional artists and craftspeople displaying and selling their original creations, demonstrations, music, and a petting zoo.

KENSINGTON

Kensington is most well known for its antique shops. There are an amazing 40 shops within a five-block stretch along Howard Avenue, known as "Antique Row.". Many of these shops, which are located in lovingly restored Victorian structures, also feature artisans and art galleries.

attractions

Three revolving stages with life-sized figurines are the focal point of the visitors center of the Washington Temple of the **Church of Jesus Christ of Latter Day Saints**. Exhibits and formal gardens are available for public viewing. Hours for the visitors center are 10:00 a.m. to 9:30 p.m., seven days; the garden is open Tuesday - Friday, 6:30 a.m. to 9:30 p.m.; and Saturday, 6:00 a.m. to 3:00 p.m. Private tours for the garden may be scheduled on Sundays and Mondays.

antiques

GONAZLES ANTIQUES, INC.
4119 Howard Avenue
Kensington, MD 20895
Tel: (202) 234-3336
Hrs: Monday - Saturday: 9:30 a.m. - 5:30 p.m.
Visa, MasterCard, and American Express are accepted.

After forty years in Washington, this fascinating shop loaded up its exceptional artifacts of by-gone eras and moved to Kensington, Maryland. The new floor space is covered with unusual examples of fine, old furniture that is mostly European. On the walls, among clocks and candelabra, are pictures and portraits, delicately framed or displayed in ornate gold leaf, and mirrors of all sizes and shapes that are perfect for hanging just anywhere! Rare pieces of porcelain, brass and silver clutter delightfully on desks and table tops.

And, above it all, are chandeliers and more chandeliers of all descriptions and affordability! Here, beats the heart of GONZALES ANTIQUES, and herein, lies the magic of Franco Ercolano, the owner. This is the ideal place to find the chandelier you've always dreamed of, and it's the shop for mending dreams as well! A fixture can be brought to Franco, in any condition, and he will restore it to its original beauty! After years of studying and collecting crystal, he has come to prefer those from France in cut glass, and has become an expert in salvaging damaged fixtures of any style or age. He enjoys everything about chandeliers--

rewiring, redesigning, repairing, rebuilding and refurbishing old frames to sell.

To begin with a bare metal frame and develop it into a lovely crystal chandelier takes practiced skill and an artistic eye, as well as patience and devotion to integrity! A visit to this delightful shop furnishes an opportunity to view all of these talents in action. Often, there are chandeliers hanging about in various stages of progress. With walls and floors filled with eclectic treasures as well, this shop can be a difficult place to leave!

OLNEY

Olney is one of the few communities in the greater Washington area where people can "get away from it all." Though there has been a big jump in population in the last 20 years, the town is surrounded by pastureland, quaint, historic villages, and relatively undeveloped ground.

attractions

The ancestral home of poet William Cowper, **Little Olney Manor House** (Georgia Ave. and Md. Route 108) is now a delightful crafts center.

theatres

OLNEY THEATRE
2001 Olney-Sandy Spring Road (Rt. 108)
Tel: (301) 924-3400
Hrs. May - October
Tuesday - Saturday 8:00 p.m.
Sunday 2:30 p.m. & 7:30 p.m.
Visa, MasterCard, American Express, and Discover are accepted.

For over 44 years, hundreds of known and unknown actors, actresses, and technicians have slept in this homey, sprawling, 19th century farmhouse, fondly called "Camp Olney!" The picturesque, verandahed, white frame building, next door to the OLNEY THEATRE and a short drive from the heart of downtown Washington, D.C., houses the season's performers, making it possible to maintain the demanding schedule of having a show in rehearsal while one is in performance. As an independent, non-profit, Equity organization, the Olney Theatre Corporation presents five different plays, for four weeks each, from may to October.

OLNEY THEATRE, long recognized and appreciated for its level of excellence, has been granted status as a Major Arts Organization and is designated the State Summer Theater of Maryland. It has become a show case for many venerable stars and a learning opportunity for bright new talent in every phase of theater. It is home to the National Players, "Americas longest running classical touring company.

The OLNEY THEATRE, built in 1942 on 11 beautiful acres of peaceful Maryland countryside, closed during World War II, then triumphantly reopened, with Helen Hayes as star, in 1946. Shows have continued to be highly professional and the charming theater remains popular with performers, visitors and its diligently supportive local community. There's plenty of parking space and the drive out Georgia Avenue is pleasant. Tables and chairs on the patio by the theater allow for relaxing and savoring of the country air before a play and during intermission, with flavored coffee, sodas and homemade goodies. It's all delightful!

ROCKVILLE

The City of Rockville, the county seat of Montgomery County, occupies nearly 12 square miles in Montgomery County. Rockville may have become a city in 1860, but its roots go back to pre-Revolutionary War days.

The land was settled in the early 1700s and was called Exchange and New Exchange Enlarged, with tobacco as its main crop. Since a main road ran through the settlement from Frederick to Georgetown, there were many taverns and inns in and near Rockville to accommodate travelers, and one of the establishments was the site of a history-making event.

In 1774, it was at Owen's Ordinary that a group of citizens met and drafted the Hungerford Resolves, calling for boycotts against British goods. The group also elected delegates to attend Maryland's general committee of correspondence in Annapolis, which eventually led to the First Continental Congress. The tavern was later renamed Hungerford's in honor of the event.

Such auspicious beginnings been a solid foundation for Rockville. The community incorporated and became a city in 1860, daily round-trip stagecoach trips began going to Washington and back, and later, the B&O railroad came to the city and made it easily accessible.

Despite its accessibility, Rockville remained a relatively quiet town until the 1950s, when it began annexing land and expanding. Today, Rockville is the second largest city in Maryland and is known for being a lovely area in which to live and visit, as well as a vital commercial area.

History still remains on the forefront in Rockville, and the town boasts four renovated historical sections, which transport visitors to a simpler time and place, and remind natives of their roots.

attractions

Over 100 Victorian structures, recognized for their historic and architectural value, can be seen at the **West Montgomery Avenue Historic District.**

A 100-acre park with antebellum mansion, the **Rockville Civic Center Complex** (Edmonston Dr. and Baltimore Road),features a museum, the F. Scott Fitzgerald Theatre, and formal, outdoor gardens. Tours of the mansion are held Monday - Friday, from 9:00 a.m. -4:30 p.m.; and the gallery is open Monday - Friday from 9:00 a.m. to 4:30 p.m., Thursday, from 7 to 9:30 p.m.; and Saturday, from 9:00 a.m. to 11:00 a.m.

Visitors can view the gravesites of F. Scott Fitzgerald and his wife, Zelda, at **St. Mary's Catholic Cemetery** (Viers Mill Rd. and Rockville Pike). Their remains were moved from their original graves in Rockville Cemetery in 1975

A 3,600-square-foot mural, by artist Gerardo Gomez Morena is on display on the southern exterior wall at 232 N. Washington St., Rockville. The piece is an impressive Cubist depiction of Rockville's buildings.

The best that nature has to offer awaits guests at **Rock Creek Regional Park.** Picnic and recreational areas, and hiking and biking trails. Lake Needwood in the park has boat rental and a golf course, while Meadowside Nature Center, has a recreational area.

events

Rockville pays tribute to its residents the first Sunday in May on **Rockville Day** (Civic Center Park). All those who attend are welcome to enjoy games, contests, and free entertainment.

A two-day long traditional **Oktoberfest** is celebrated each autumn, featuring ethnic food, music, and entertainment.

One of the most popular events of the year is the city's annual **Antique and Classic Car Show** (Civic Center Park).

bookstores

SECOND STORY BOOKS, 12276 Wilkens Avenue, Rockville, MD, 20852; Tel: (301) 770-0477. See their story under Dupont Circle.

SILVER SPRING

Silver Spring takes its name from a spring which sparkles with the tiny bits of mica on its bottom. Formed in 1918, it is now known as the fastest growing central business district in Montgomery County.

transportation

REGENCY LIMOUSINE SERVICE, INC.
12055 Tech Road
Silver Spring, Md. 20904
Tel: (301) 622-0200 (800) 262-5466
Hrs: Open seven days.
All major credit cards are accepted.

When ordering a limousine, are you apt to assume that it will arrive where and when you want it? Often, this is not the case! And for this reason, Paul Rodberg, when he began his company, with one vehicle in 1983, made a commitment to provide consistently excellent service to his customers. Since then, his integrity, dependability and service have propelled him into owning one of the largest fleets in this area!

Each limousine belonging to REGENCY LIMOUSINE SERVICE, INC. has a telephone, TV, VCR, stereo, sunroof, bar console, and a knowledgeable driver who, for no extra charge, will delight you with a guided tour! Paul is proud to offer a variety of vehicles--including sedans, stretch and ultra-stretch limousines, vans, mini-buses and coaches--to handle most any transportation requirement.

A visit to REGENCY'S bright, cheerful office and garage in Silver Spring is fascinating! There's a friendly, well organized, efficient atmosphere with personnel interacting cooperatively as they answer phones, make assignments, clean cars, and move routine business at a brisk pace. The employees are as happy working for Paul as customers are in dealing with him. He's a man of his word! There is no haggling over price! REGENCY'S rates remain as quoted and service is delivered as promised! So,if you need a shiny, spotless limousine, complete with professional chauffeur, to be delivered to the right location, at a specific time - then, call REGENCY and relax!

TAKOMA PARK

Takoma Park, which borders the District of Columbia, is a bustling, populous suburb that has managed to maintain its old-fashioned charm. Once strictly a resort community, its tree-lined streets and wonderful examples of Victorian architecture have earned it a designation as historically significant by the National Register of Historic Places.

attractions

A visitors center, tours, and presentations are highlights of the **Seventh Day Adventist World Headquarters** (6930 Carroll Ave.). This major educational complex is the site of Columbia Union College.

events

Takoma Park comes alive with color in the spring, during the **Takoma Park Flower Show** held yearly in late April, and the **Takoma Park House and Garden Tour,** held annually in early May.

catering services

B & B WASHINGTON'S CATERER
7041 Blair Road NW
Washington, DC 20012
Tel: (202) 829-8640
Hrs: Open 24 hours a day, seven days.
Visa, MasterCard and American Express are accepted.

Fashion, flavor, flair and festivity is what you see and what you get from B&B WASHINGTON'S CATERER! Whether you prefer sedate and serious, light and lovely or propriety and protocol, you dream your dream. THEY will create the reality! They'll blend your ideas, hopes and desires with their years of experience in dealing with food, fun and foibles of the Washington social scene. They have the answer to every question, the solution to any problem!

The B&B team has carefully developed a gifted, skilled approach to entertaining that is solidly based on the notion that with every moment there comes the opportunity for the extraordinary! B&B doesn't concern itself ONLY with food and service. They mastered that long ago. Their people are all highly trained professionals, all highly competent in their fields and proud of what they do. And they do it flawlessly! They serve an endless variety of clients, from Supreme Court Justices and Heads of State to average citizens from anywhere! They're at their best in all situations. And the numbers game? It's unimportant to them! They are delighted to provide for two or for four-thousand. And, for instant entertaining, they will prepare a morning order, for two to twelve, and deliver it in the evening with complete instructions. You can warm and serve it yourself and be the star for an evening!

The main thrust with B&B is to help make your occasion memorable for you and your guests. In a city where entertaining has elevated and destroyed many a host and hostess, it is wise to turn to professional help that can advise as well as provide. After getting to know you and your reason for having your party, B&B will offer suggestions for creating the perfect scene in which all who attend will enjoy every moment. Dreams do come true!

WHEATON

Named for a Civil War general, Wheaton is an area without borders that has experienced major growth in the last 25 years. It offers an abundance of shopping opportunities, and is well-liked by residents for its more affordable housing.

attractions

Family fun abounds at **Wheaton Regional Park** (1500 Glenallen Ave.) Some of the great family-oriented activities available at the park include Old MacDonald's Farm Petting Zoo, a carousel, train rides, camping, and horseback riding.

Wheaton Regional Park is the site of **Brookside Gardens** (1500 Glenallen Ave.). These 50 enchanting acres include a conservatory and greenhouse with stream, specialty gardens, and an impeccably-kept outdoor formal garden. The conservatory is open daily from 9:00 a.m. to 5:00 p.m.; the grounds are open to the public from 9:00 a.m. to sunset.
Visitors can take a ride into yesterday - literally - at the **National Capital Trolley Museum** (Bonifant Road.). Tourists delight at the demonstrations of the electric railway and the trolley rides that are available for a fee. An informative visitor's center makes the facility complete. The museum is open Saturday and Sunday from Noon to 5:00 p.m., and Wednesdays in July and August from Noon to 4:00 p.m.

events

Scores of nationalities are represented at the annual **Ethnic Heritage Festival**, held each September in Wheaton Regional Park.

A celebration of electric transit is held each April and September at the **National Capital Trolley Museum**.

Brookside Gardens is the site of two fabulous annual flower shows -- the colorful **Easter Show** in April and the **Fall Chrysanthemum Show**, held in mid-October.

WHITE FLINT

leather

GEORGETOWN LEATHER DESIGN, White Flint; Tel: (301) 881-4677. For fine Leather goods. See their story under Georgetown.

WHITE'S FERRY

White's Ferry may be a bit off the beaten path, but it is certainly worth the trip.

After the Civil War, a Confederate officer named Elijah Viers White purchased a ferry service that connected Montgomery County with Loudon County, Va. The ferry remained in service through various owners until 1942, when a flood destroyed the barge that served as ferry boat.

In 1946, William Altizer, Edwin Brown, and Lucas Phillips bought the service, using a wooden boat that could carry no more than three cars. In 1953, the first steel ferry was put in use.

The ferry service is now located on a five-acre site that offers, in addition to a unique river crossing, picnic and recreation facilities available on the Maryland side. The ferry runs from 6:00 a.m. to 11:00 p.m. daily during the summer. During the winter months, the schedule is 6:00 a.m. to 8:00 p.m.

PRINCE GEORGE'S COUNTY

A 341-acre national park located on the graceful banks of the beautiful Potomac River, **Fort Washington Park** (off Route 210) offers nature trails, picnic grounds, and military structures. There are military programs on weekends with guides in 19th century clothing leading visitors through the park. Fort Washington was completed in 1824 to guard and stem attacks on the Capitol. The fort is surrounded by a dry moat and is entered by using a drawbridge.

During the Revolution, William Smallwood commanded the Maryland Line of the Continental Army. He was later elected governor. Now, visitors can tour his homestead at **Smallwood State Park** (off Highway 224, south of Marbury). Visitors can see his brick, pitched roof, and view his grave.

An 80-year-old hand-carved, hand-painted carousel is the centerpiece of **Watkins Regional Park** (Route 566, Kettering). Park hours are Tuesday - Thursday, 11:00 a.m. - 3:30 p.m., and 6:00 - 9:00 p.m.; Saturday, 11:00 a.m. - 9:30 p.m.; and Sunday, Noon - 6:30 p.m.

The Clearwater Nature Center is a major attraction in Prince George's County, and is located within the **Louise F. Cosca Regional Park** (near Clinton). The park also has a lake with boating and fishing, indoor tennis courts, ballfields, campground, and picnic area.

The U.S. Department of Agriculture's largest research center, the **USDA Agricultural Research Center** (Powder Mill Road, Beltsville), is open to visitors Monday through Friday, from 8:00 a.m. to 4:00 p.m.

For a controversial piece of history, visit **The Surrat House and Tavern** (Routes 381 and 223, Clinton). In the mid-1800s, the Surrat House served as the local post office, polling place, tavern, public dining room, and a safe house for Confederate couriers, in addition to being the home of the Surrat family. John Wilkes Booth stopped at the tavern after shooting President Abraham Lincoln. After being accused of conspiring with Booth in the assassination, Mary Surrat was convicted and was the first woman hanged in the United States.

Visitors can view artists at work at the **Montpelier Cultural Arts Center** (12826 Laurel-Bowie Road, Laurel). This facility offers a full curriculum of visual arts classes, and is home to over 30 artists. Three galleries, which span many different types of art forms, are open to the public.

A trip into a more gracious era is easily accomplished by touring the **Montpelier Mansion** (Muirkirk Road and Route 197, Laurel). This recently restored Georgian structure, once belonging to Major Thomas Snowden, one of Prince George's County's early settlers, is an impressive sight and worth a trip to Laurel. The mansion is open Sundays from Noon until 4:00 p.m. The gift shop is open Saturdays and Sundays from Noon to 4:00 p.m.

Farming is done the way it was in the old days at **Oxon Hill Farm** (Route 210, Oxon Hill). Visitors can see farm animals, watch demonstrations of daily farm chores, and take part in enjoyable activities. The farm is open 8:00 a.m. to 5:00 p.m. daily.

The history of space flight is carefully catalogued at the **NASA/Goddard Visitors Center and Museum** (Greenbelt Road, Greenbelt). This center features space craft, flight articles, and displays dealing with the U.S. space program. Model rocket launches take place the first and third Sunday of each month at 1:00 p.m.

The agricultural methods of a mid-18th century farm are still in use at the **National Colonial Farm Museum** (Bryan Point Road, Accokeek). Farm exhibits are also on display.

For sports and concert lovers, **The Capital Centre** (Landover Road, Largo), is the perfect choice. This entertainment center seats over 18,000 and offers concerts and sporting events, including ice hockey, basketball, and professional wrestling.

Fun for the family awaits visitors of **Wild World** (Exit 15A, off I-95, Largo). This 300-acre amusement park offers water slides, a wave pool, six live performances per day, and video arcade.The park also inlcudes three separate children's areas, offering play facilities, small rides, and kiddie pool.

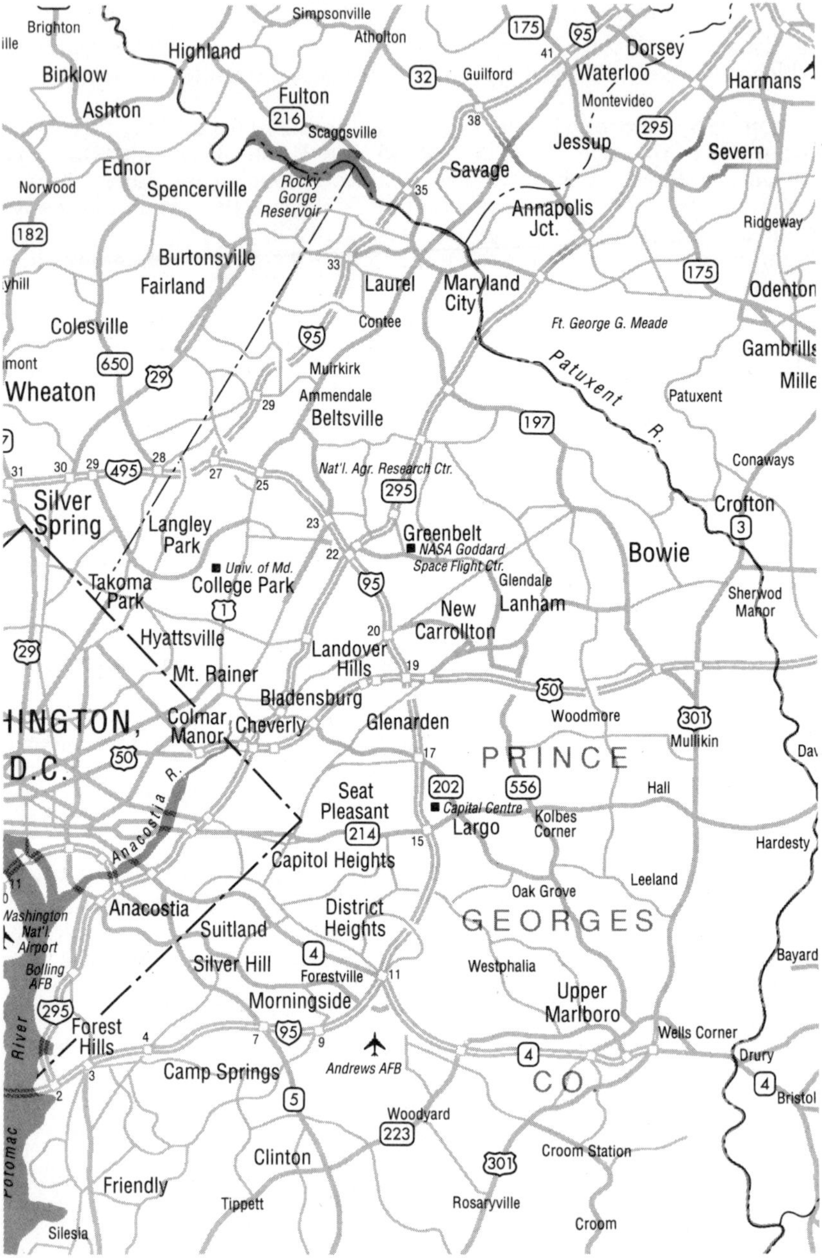
Simpsonville
Brighton
Atholton
Highland
Binklow
Guilford
Dorsey
Waterloo
Harmans
Fulton
Montevideo
Ashton
Scaggsville
Jessup
Severn
Ednor
Savage
Norwood
Spencerville
Rocky Gorge Reservoir
Annapolis Jct.
Ridgeway
Burtonsville
Fairland
Laurel
Maryland City
Odenton
Colesville
Contee
Ft. George G. Meade
Gambrills
Muirkirk
Patuxent R.
Wheaton
Ammendale
Patuxent
Beltsville
Conaways
Nat'l. Agr. Research Ctr.
Silver Spring
Crofton
Langley Park
Greenbelt
NASA Goddard Space Flight Ctr.
Bowie
Univ. of Md.
College Park
Takoma Park
Glendale
Sherwood Manor
New Carrollton
Lanham
Hyattsville
Landover Hills
Mt. Rainer
Bladensburg
Woodmore
Colmar Manor
Cheverly
Glenarden
Mullikin
WASHINGTON, D.C.
PRINCE GEORGES CO.
Seat Pleasant
Hall
Capital Centre
Kolbes Corner
Largo
Hardesty
Anacostia R.
Capitol Heights
Leeland
Oak Grove
Anacostia
District Heights
Washington Nat'l. Airport
Suitland
Westphalia
Bayard
Silver Hill
Forestville
Bolling AFB
Upper Marlboro
Morningside
Wells Corner
Forest Hills
Drury
Andrews AFB
Camp Springs
Bristol
Woodyard
Croom Station
Clinton
Potomac River
Friendly
Tippett
Rosaryville
Croom
Silesia

COLLEGE PARK

attractions

The history of flight blends beautifully with the functions of a modern airport at **College Park Airport and Museum** (6709 Cpl. Frank Scott Dr.). Touted as being the "World's Oldest Operating Airport," the Wright brothers taught here and the first Army Aviation school was located here in 1911. The museum depicts the history of flight, beginning in 1909.

LANDOVER

leather

GEORGETOWN LEATHER DESIGN, Landover Mall; Tel: (301) 322-7773. For fine Leather goods. See their story under Georgetown.

LARGO

amusements/waterparks

WILD WORLD
13710 Central Avenue (I-95, Exit 15A Central Avenue)
Largo, Md. 20772
Tel: (301)249-1500
Hrs:
Memorial Day Weekend - Labor Day Weekend
Open seven days 10:00 a.m. - 9:00 p.m.
Visa, MasterCard, American Express, and Discover accepted.

Yes, WILD! The second largest wave pool in the world and a roller coaster, rated sixth, are located just 20 minutes from downtown Washington and can be reached by both metrorail and the bus system. Situated on 68 of 460 acres of beautiful countryside in Prince George's County, Maryland, the ONLY amusement/water park in our Nation's Capital offers space, thrills and pleasure as well as both in and out of water activity--and all for one price! Season tickets are popular.

WILD WORLD has evolved into an extensive amusement center containing one of the largest water parks on the East Coast. The WILD WAVE, which generates waves up to four feet, is the highlight! Its pool and deck area can comfortably accommodate over 4,000 people. PARADISE ISLAND features a 30,000-square-foot pool area with two 360-degree spiral flumes and two high-angle slingshot flumes. Shoot the rapids on RAFTERS RUN or gently relax on an inner tube and cruise down the LAZY RIVER. Small kids can splash in the TADPOOL over and over, under the watchful eye of lifeguards who preside over every attraction. Since bathing suits are required on all water rides, bath houses and lockers are easily accessible.

There is live entertainment with daily shows, ranging from song and dance and magic to kiddie shows as well as weekend special events. The park has thrill rides, including the WILD ONE roller coaster, a spine-tingler boasting a 98-foot drop and a 380 degree helix finish! It easily dominates other rides which range from a train to a topsy-turvy SKYSCRAPER. There is also a special KIDDIE CITY with rides especially for the youngsters. Food, games and gifts are available throughout the park to complete your day of fun!

SILVER HILL

attractions

Visitors can see where the restoration work of historic airplanes takes place at the **Paul E. Garber Facility** (Silver Hill Road, Silver Hill). This is the suburban facility of the Smithsonian Air and Space Museum and is where all the preservation work for the museum's displays occurs. Tours are offered.

UPPER MARLBORO

attractions

Nature is at its finest at the **Merkle Wildlife Sanctuary** (11704 Fenno Road, Upper Marlboro). Interpretive and nature-related programs are available. A visitor's center is on-site.

Tobacco is a mainstay of this region, and the annual **Tobacco Auctions** (Old Marlboro Pike, Upper Marlboro) take place Mondays through Thursdays from mid-March through May.

SECTION THREE: VIRGINIA

ALEXANDRIA

Once the center for Virginia's commerce and culture, modern-day Alexandria is a lovely combination of past and present. Take a stroll through the beautiful tree-lined walks of this charming town, and you are sure to be struck by the way sophisticated shops and boutiques, art and craft galleries, and restaurants mingle harmoniously with the cobblestone streets and restored Colonial buildings of Old Town Alexandria. This blending of the old and the new has made Alexandria one of Northern Virginia's most popular residential areas.

Alexandria was founded in 1749 by Scottish merchants, and you are bound to find evidence of this heritage all over the city. For example, Alexandria has its own tartan (Cameron), and bagpipes and drum corps are present at almost every town festival. During the Revolutionary and Civil Wars, Alexandria was a strategically important port. It was here that General George Washington plotted with other patriots to overthrow the British, and during the Civil War, Alexandria was vital in defending the capitol city from Confederate invaders.

The townspeople of Alexandria have gone to a great deal of trouble to preserve their colonial heritage. Old Town Alexandria, a section of the city that has been designated a historic landmark, has been charmingly restored. More than one thousand 18the and 19the century buildings have been preserved here, with the oldest dating back to 1724. It was in Old Town that George Washington maintained a townhouse, became a Mason, and attended church services.

Today, Alexandria is a thriving city, rich in history, yet firmly rooted in modern times. Scores of artists have made their home here, and the city is teeming with galleries. Unique shops, boutiques, and restaurants are found on every corner, and it seems that antiquing has become everyone's favorite pastime.

A leisurely stroll through Alexandria, both old and new, is sure to open your eyes to the charms of this lovely Southern town. The people of Alexandria are very friendly, and their hospitality is sure to enhance your stay in this pleasant city.

the nation's capital

antiques

STUDIO ANTIQUES AND FINE ART, 628 N. Washington Street, Alexandria, VA 22341, Tel: (703) 548-5188, Hrs: Monday - Saturday 10:00 a.m. - 5:00 p.m., Sunday. Noon - 5:00 p.m. Visa and MasterCard are accepted. Studio Antiques has rapidly established itself as an important and reputable source for fine antiques, including English, American and French furniture, 18th and 19th century oil paintings, lamps and other antique decorative accessories.

dinner theaters

WEST END DINNER THEATER 4615 Duke Street, Alexandria, VA 22341. Tel: (703) 370-2500. Hrs: Tuesday - Sunday evenings: dinner: 6:00 p.m.; curtain, 8:00 p.m. Wednesday and Sunday matinees: dinner, 12 noon; curtain, 2:00 p.m. Visa, MasterCard, and American Express are accepted. Enjoy expertly prepared gourmet meals served at your table and professional productions of Broadway favorites. Minutes from Washington D.C. Free parking, reasonable prices. Discounts for seniors, children, students and groups.

OLD TOWN ALEXANDRIA

Nestled within the confines of modern Alexandria, and graced by tree-lined, cobblestone streets, is Old Town Alexandria. Designated a historic landmark, Old Town is known for its restored 18th and 19th century buildings, as well as numerous historic landmarks. A visit to Old Town takes visitors back to the time when Alexandria was one of Virginia's most important seaports, as well as its center for commerce and culture.

In addition to historic landmarks, Old Town is well known for its wide variety of shops and boutiques. Make a point to venture down side streets, as over 200 import and specialty shops are hidden away in the nooks and crannies of Old Town. Many artists have studios and galleries here, and the great number of antique and craft shops have made shopping a popular Old Town pastime.

attractions

A wave pool, water slides, and batting cages are found at **CAMERON REGIONAL** Park.

Housed in a restored 18the century building in the heart of Old Town Alexandria, **THE RAMSAY HOUSE VISITORS CENTER** (221 King Street) is indispensable to visitors. The Center's knowledgeable staff can provide you with maps, brochures, block tickets for historic museums, and special free-parking permits.

Known for its central hall staircase and Adamesque woodwork, **THE BOYHOOD HOME OF ROBERT E. LEE** (607 Oronoco Street.) gives visitors a glimpse of the famous general's childhood. Throughout the year, important dates in the history of the house are marked with festivals that include tours and entertainment.

The 18the Century home of wealthy merchant and landowner John Carlyle, **CARLYLE HOUSE** (121 N. Fairfax Street) is patterned after a Scottish Manor. It was in this house in 1755 that General Edward Braddock made his headquarters and planned some of the first campaigns of the French and Indian War.

Built in 1773, both George Washington and Robert E. Lee once belonged to **CHRIST CHURCH** (118 N. Washington Street). Known for a cut-glass chandelier that is representative of the best type of lighting fixtures available in the 18the century, Christ Church remains practically unchanged from the time it was built.

Located in what was once an integral part of the defensive ring around Washington D.C during the Civil War, the **FORT WARD MUSEUM AND HISTORIC SITE** (403 W. Braddock Road) takes visitors back to those tense days when the future of the United States was at stake.

Once the center of Alexandria's social and political life, **GADSBY'S TAVERN MUSEUM** 134 N. Royal Street) is full of history. The tavern is the site of the annual Birthnight Ball, which celebrates George

Washington's Birthday, and it was here that the first President made his last appearance in a military capacity.

Inspired by the ancient lighthouse in Alexandria, Egypt, the **GEORGE WASHINGTON MASONIC NATIONAL MEMORIAL** (101 Callahan Drive) is dedicated to George Washington, the Mason. Visitors to this site can see some of the original furnishings of Alexandria-Washington Lodge No. 22, over which Washington was Worshipful Master.

About 35 members of the Lee family lived at the **LEE FENDALL HOUSE** (614 Oronoco Street) from 1785 until 1903. Now, the house serves as a museum and is filled with period antiques, many of which belonged to the Confederate general.

A repository of Alexandria's history, the **LYCEUM** (201 S. Washington Street) sponsors changing exhibits, lectures, concerts and other educational programs throughout the year.

A reconstruction of an 18the century mill built by George Washington, **THE GEORGE WASHINGTON GRIST MILL** (Mount Vernon Memorial Highway) was originally built on this site in 1770. The three story stone mill contains informative exhibits about milling techniques.

A wedding gift from George Washington to his foster-daughter, Eleanor Parke Custis, and his nephew, Major Lawrence Lewis, **WOODLAWN** (U.S. Highway 1) was originally part of Mount Vernon. The house, restored 19the-century rooms, and magnificent formal gardens are open for viewing. Also on the grounds is the **POPE-LEIGHEY HOUSE**, designed by Frank Lloyed Wright.

Attended, and possibly even designed by George Washington, **POHICK CHURCH** (9301 Richmond Highway) has been restored to its original grandeur. The interior, which had been destroyed by Union troops during the Civil War, still bears the carved initials of the soldiers.

Housing the grave of the Unknown Revolutionary War Soldier, **THE OLD PRESBYTERIAN MEETING HOUSE** (321 S. Fairfax Street) is still in use today. Built in 1744, this church was the site of George Washington's funeral.

Discover how medicine was practiced in Colonial times at the **STABLER-LEADBEATER APOTHECARY SHOP** (105 S. Fairfax Street). Everything is arranged as it had been in 1792 when George

Washington, Henry Clay, Daniel Webster, and others had prescriptions filled here.

Built at the close of World War I to manufacture torpedoes, **THE TORPEDO FACTORY ART CENTER** (N. Union, between King and Cameron Streets) is now divided into 38 studios and 5 art galleries. The works of 200 artists are on display and available for purchase.

Designed by Benjamin Henry Latrobe, the interior of Gothic-style **SAINT PAUL'S EPISCOPAL CHURCH** (228 S. Pitt Street) was patterned after Christopher Wren's St. James Church in London. At the start of the Civil War, Union forces occupied the cathedral, and supposedly carried off the rector when he refused to pray for Lincoln.

events

Old Town celebrates **ROBERT E. LEE'S BIRTHDAY** on January 20, with candlelight tours of his Boyhood Home and the Lee-Fendall house.

A 10K run, 18the-century banquet and ball, and a Revolutionary War Encampment highlight **GEORGE WASHINGTON'S BIRTHDAY WEEKEND.**

Alexandria's **SAINT PATRICK'S DAY PARADE** is held on March 16.

Private residences are opened to the public for the **OLD TOWN ALEXANDRIA TOUR OF HOMES AND GARDENS** in mid-Aprilas part of Virginia's Historic Garden Week.

Visiting ships, ethnic food, local entertainment, and health and safety displays are all part of the **ALEXANDRIA RED CROSS WATERFRONT FESTIVAL**, held in early June.

Alexandria commemorates its Scottish roots with the **VIRGINIA SCOTTISH GAMES** on the Episcopal High School grounds (3901 West Braddock Road) in late July.

Auctions, mock court sessions, and people in period costumes are among the attractions at **GADSBY'S TAVERN MUSEUM 18TH CENTURY FAIR**, held Labor Day Weekend.

Held in mid-November, **THE HISTORIC ALEXANDRIA ANTIQUES SHOW** benefits the preservation and restoration programs of Alexandria.

Celebrate Christmas in the Scottish tradition with a **SCOTTISH CHRISTMAS WALK** through Old Town in early December.'

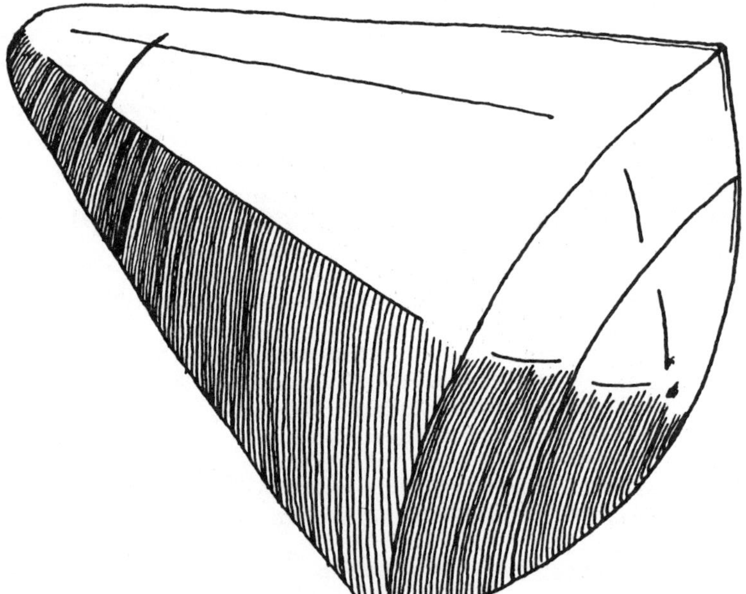

bookstores

SECOND STORY BOOKS, 602 King Street, Alexandria, VA, 22314. Tel: (703) 548-2742. See their story under Dupont Circle.

craft shops

AMERICAN ARTISAN
118 King Street
Alexandria, Va. 22314
Tel: (703) 548-3431
Hrs: Monday - Saturday at 10:00 a.m.
Sunday at 11:00 a.m.
Open late every night.

Visa, MasterCard, American Express, Diners Club,Carte Blanche, and Discover are accepted.

There are times when only "American" will do! That's when we go to the corner of King and North Lee Streets in the heart of Old Town Alexandria, George Washington's home town, where we find AMERICAN ARTISAN, a store sparkling with hundreds of stained glass suncatchers of every shape and color and filled with music from a wide array of windchimes, including the popular Woodstock chime. Here, we find affordable, high quality, handcrafted gifts and household items--all produced in the United States.

AMERICAN ARTISAN features pottery for every need and taste, from whimsical to sophisticated and from traditional to contemporary--pitchers, bowls and serving pieces, beautiful and practical, made to be used. AMERICAN ARTISAN has the area's largest selection of handcrafted stoneware lamps in styles and colors to suit every decor. Stoneware name mugs are an inexpensive gift that's always appreciated. You will also find an exquisite collection of handcrafted jewelry in porcelain, fabric and metal. There are, in a variety of woods, fun and practical items including music boxes, bookracks, desk accessories and cutting boards in every size. Always intriguing are the Wood that Works Kinetic wall sculptures, kept in motion by delightfully complicated assemblies of gears, weights, springs and pulleys.

This warm, friendly store reflects the patriotism and dedication of its owner, Joel Blanchette, and manager, Dan O'Day. Along with their accommodating staff, they welcome browsers and shoppers and are pleased to help you choose the perfect gift. There is gift wrap available and your purchase can be shipped UPS. Do visit AMERICAN ARTISAN!

gift baskets

BASKETS OF JOY
125 South Fairfax Street
Alexandria, Va. 22314
Tel: (703) 684-2120
Hrs: Tuesday - Saturday 10:00 a.m. - 5:00 p.m.
Sunday Noon - 5:00 p.m.
Closed on Mondays.
Summer & holiday hours extended.
Visa and MasterCard are accepted.

One-half block south of King Street, three blocks from the river--near the Visitor's Center--is a typical old townhouse shared by two specialty gift shops. BASKETS OF JOY offers a most unique concept in gift-giving. Its byline says it all: "Custom Gift Baskets for Every Taste, for Every Occasion." Wishes in White for brides, The Welcoming Basket for new friends, clients, or employees, or The Particular Palate for gourmets are among the more than 75 baskets displayed in the shop. Although a visit allows you to enjoy the wide variety of choices available, telephone orders may be more convenient for busy shoppers. Delivery and shipping services are provided.

Beneath clusters of hanging baskets is an incredible selection of items which may be arranged in baskets for a creative gift. Proprietor Susan Lozinyak freely offers her talent and time in creating lovely, color-coordinated or clever theme baskets. Customers can choose from a list of basket ideas tailored to meet any price range or have fun creating their own, as they prefer. Exploring the nooks and crannies of this shop is an adventure! It is literally brimming with treasures which may be purchased separately as well as for basket-ing. While you are busy looking, children will love the adjoining room, called DEFINITELY DINOSAURS, a shop owned by Susan's sister.

A personalized gift is the ultimate in gift-giving! BASKETS OF JOY offers a rare opportunity for creating a gift as distinctly special as the person receiving it.

gift shops

THE IRISH WALK
415 King Street
Alexandria, VA 22314
Tel: (703) 548-0118
Hrs: Monday - Saturday 10:00 a.m. - 6:00 p.m.
Sunday 12:00 noon - 5:00 p.m.
Closed on major holidays.
Visa, MasterCard and American Express are accepted.

There's a bit o' blarney on the Tavern Square in Old Town, Alexandria! Probably, wee folk, too--but, it's tough to see a Leprechaun! Slip into THE IRISH WALK and ask Bernadette Troy. She and her husband, Pat, literally have the corner on the Irish. They own IRELAND'S OWN--the top o' the line in Irish eating, drinking, and merriment, and THE IRISH WALK, a few steps across the courtyard. And, they're proud of PAT TROY'S RADIO SHOW on Sundays at 2:00 PM on station WNTR, 1050-AM, where the latest and best of news and music keep Irish Americans informed and happy!

When Bernadette Troy discovered fifteen years ago that there were no shops for her to find the beautiful Irish woolens, crystal, linens and china she had left in Ireland, she decided to open one herself! She sent for the best -- gorgeous Waterford crystal; Belleek and Royal Tara china and porcelain, classic Aran sweaters in styles and stitches developed by fishermen's wives and handed down over generations; soft mohair and Aran 100% wool scarves, gloves, mittens and hats; Heraldic, Family Coat-of-Arms in mugs, key rings, plaques; lovely linens; Irish tee-shirts and sweatshirts for all ages; Claddagh rings; and a complete line of baby sweaters, shirts and kilts, even bottles decorated with shamrocks!

A bit of Ireland it is! Step onto the Kelly green carpet and wander under the hanging Irish pendants that represent thirty-two counties in Ireland. You'll catch sight of Leprechauns surrounded with history, humor and story books. And watch! You might notice a wink!

THREE WISHES GIFTS AND TOYS
8401-G Richmond Highway, Potomac Square
Alexandria, Va. 22309
Tel: (703) 360-2332
Hrs: Monday - Saturday: 10:00 a.m. - 5:30 p.m.
Hours are extended in November and December.
Open Sundays in November and December.
Closed all major holidays.
Visa, MasterCard, American Express, Discover, and personal checks are accepted.

From whimsy to the sublime and in-between! A bit of .all or any of it can be discovered on a visit to this fascinating gift shop. It is eclectic in flavor, yet cozy, casual and comfortable. Managers Rebecca and Pamela Chase, or the clerks, will help with your selections

Being surrounded by dolls and more dolls bearing names such as Madame Alexander, Middleton, Hibel and Pauline, Beatrice Potter books, animals, lamps and bath accessories, as well as an entire line of Brambly Hedge by Royal Doulton, provide an opportunity for pure delight! An extensive selection of puppets - rod, finger,hand and body puppets, a variety of people puppets, as well as stages set for creative performances will tickle your imagination! Unusual baby gifts, adorable stuffed animals and furry forest creatures by Folktails are cunningly displayed. Quite popular, also, is the Three Wishes Ambidextrous line of assorted items that may be personalized for school, room decorations and teachers' gifts.

Nao figurines by Lladro', Pimpernel trays, trivets, mats and coasters in wonderful designs, Hibel-framed lithographs and prints, plates, books and soap stone boxes are all perfect candidates for wedding, shower, special day and take-home gifts. Whether browsing, selecting elegant costume jewelry or a piece of Whimsy (jewelry made from unique buttons!), the experience is totally enchanting!

AMERICA 201 King Street, Alexandria, VA 22341. Tel: (703) 836-1491 Hrs: Monday - Sunday: 10:00 a.m. - 9:00 p.m.; Sunday: noon - 6:00 p.m. Visa, MasterCard, American Express, Discover and Diners Club are accepted. A delightful, fun store that offers flags, banners, patriotic gifts and apparel. Everything sold here is made in the United States.

jewelry

AUSTIN & ELKINS OF OLD TOWN
GALLERY OF FINE JEWELRY
115 North Fairfax Street
Alexandria, VA 22314
Tel: (703) 684-5555
Hrs: Tuesday - Friday 11:00 a.m. - 5:30 p.m.
Saturday 10:00 a.m. - 5:00 p.m.
Hours are extended for special appointments.
Visa, MasterCard and American Express are accepted.

It is a rare and one-of-a-kind opportunity! The chance to choose or create your statement in fine jewelry. You may find the ring you have always looked for, the perfect brooch, a heavy gold bracelet or the classic earring, all designed in 18 karat gold. All of this is possible when you visit this charming jewelry gallery that is nestled into a 200-year-old Federal townhouse (between King and Cameron Streets) in historic Old Town Alexandria.

Its energetic, innovative, and experienced owner, Robin Austin Elkins, offers, as she refers to it, "Contemporary Classic" jewelry composed of diamonds, vibrantly colored stones and pearls all mounted in 18 karat gold or platinum. Her reputation for personalized service, which includes custom design and redesign, repair and appraisal services and house or office visits, has developed from her special ability to anticipate each customer's needs. The gallery is known for its high quality and award winning designer jewelry.

AUSTIN & ELKINS also carry a lovely selection of Mikimoto pearls, watches by Baume & Mercier and a special selection of men's cuff links and tuxedo shirt studs. Heirloom quality jewelry, that blends the best of classic into fresh perspectives, abounds in this elegantly comfortable and appealing shop. If you are not looking to continue a tradition, why not start your own? In this exciting gallery, you can choose or create family heirlooms. Your dreams can be made or they can come true!

pet hotels

FOR PET'S SAKE HOTEL
3208 Colvin Street
Alexandria, VA 22314
Tel: (703) 823-DOGS
(703) 823-3647

Hrs

Monday, Tuesday, Thursday, Friday	8:00 a.m. - Noon 2:00 p.m. - 6:00 p.m.
Saturday	8:00 a.m. - Noon
Sunday	5:00 p.m. - 7:00 p.m.
Wednesday	9:00 a.m. - Noon

Visa and MasterCard are accepted.

Upscale clientele deserve the ultimate in catering! And FOR PET'S SAKE HOTEL offers exactly that! Favored pets are apt to feel devalued, dejected and deserted when left behind. The next best thing to having mistresses and masters present is seeing to it that pets are treated as well as if they were. For six years, FOR PET'S SAKE HOTEL has been extending home away from home comfort and care in Alexandria, Virginia. Attention is lavished on each boarder and diets and routines are carefully maintained according to each owner's specification.

The large, spotless facilities are temperature controlled with fresh air circulating continuously. Since a city ordinance requires that animals be boarded indoors, five different dimensions of enclosures are available to suit any size. A regular exercise period is programmed for each one every day. Cats, safely separated in the cattery, are free to roam or be contained as each owner chooses.

Arrangements can be made for pick-up and delivery within Alexandria and, to and from, the National Airport. Before signing in, proof of current immunization is required and provisions for treatment and medication may be made. As members of the American Boarding Kennels Association, FOR PET'S SAKE HOTEL takes pride in considering every detail to ensure the contentment of their guests. Owners are encouraged to bring along clearly marked, favorite toys, blankets or bedding. And, if a pet prefers hamburgers and ice cream for dinner, at this hotel, they can have it!

restaurants

TERRAZZA
710 King Street
Alexandria, Va. 22314
Tel: (703) 683-6900

Hrs:	Lunch	
	Monday- Friday	11:30 a.m. - 3:00 p.m.
	Dinner	
	Sunday - Friday	6:00 p.m.- 10:30 p.m.
	Saturday	6:00 p.m. - 11:00 p.m.

Closed on Christmas Day.
Visa, MasterCard, American Express, Diners Club, and Carte Blanche are accepted.

An enormous vase of deep red roses--dozens of them-- dominate the large, classically Mediterranean foyer and emphasize an ambiance of grandeur. In contrast, there is stark simplicity...in the marble, the white textured walls, and the rugged, wooden banister of the open staircase leading to a spacious, skylighted room above with softly draped windows overlooking the streets below...and, more roses! Through the arcade, roses preside over desserts-on-display and bouquets of pink roses are centered on each table. At dinner, the owner, Giulio Santillo, and Umberto Giannori, the manager, present each lady with a single rose. A charming touch!

Having gained experience in the family restaurant business in Europe, the Santillos came to America in 1974. They opened TIBERIO on K Street in downtown Washington and TRAGARA in Bethesda. They now own five restaurants in this country and specialize in fine Northern Italian cooking. The elegant TERRAZZA, in Old Town, Alexandria is one that should not be missed.

The TERRAZZA boasts an extensive, yet moderately priced wine list. The Daily Specials, changed three times weekly, include homemade pasta, fresh fish, and wonderful zuppe (soups). Sword fish is very popular and the veal scaloppine--either thick with red peppers, tomato and garlic or thinly sliced in delicious butter sauce--is unsurpassed. The antipasti, linguine with clam sauce, spinach-filled fresh pastas, and poached salmon are favorites. But! One MUST leave room for the fantastic dessert. Perhaps, Chocolate Mousse or Cheesecake?

FISH MARKET, corner of King and Union streets, Alexandria VA, 22134; Tel: (703) 683-1135. The building has been renovated to appear as it did during the mercantile trade boom of the 19th century. Serves an abundance of Seafood and has sing-along entertainment, upstairs, every night at 8:00 p.m..

river cruises

THE CRUISE SHIP DANDY
Zero Prince Street
Alexandria, VA 22314
Tel: (703) 683-6090
Hrs:

Lunch cruises	12:15 p.m. boarding.
Friday dinner cruises	7:30 p.m. boarding.
Saturday and Sunday dinner cruises	7:15 p.m. boarding.

Visa, MasterCard and American Express are accepted.

Leave the dock from Old Town Alexandria and see the spectacular sights of the Washington's skyline on board the CRUISE SHIP DANDY. At the same time enjoy a romantically intimate atmosphere while dining on Prime Rib, Salmon or Cornish Game Hen. The food is prepared fresh in the ship's galley and everything is served piping hot. The side dishes are cooked to perfection, especially the new potatoes. The service is excellent. The waiters and waitresses behave courteously and perform efficiently. It is personal service with a smile.

After dinner the mood changes and it's dancing or dreaming to the sounds of pre-recorded music piped throughout the ship. The music selection is carefully orchestrated according to what is most popular with the dinner guests. The Dandy is the only cruise ship that can pass effortlessly under the bridges, affording a magnificent view of the Kennedy Center, Lincoln Memorial and Washington Monument.

The owner is Nina Wilson, who is a charming lady and a wonderful hostess. She is constantly and unobtrusively paying attention to every detail of the trip and the ship's operation. Any time of the year is a perfect time for a cruise and any special occasion can be made even more special with memories on the Dandy.

ANNANDALE

Up until the last 30 years, Annandale was nothing more than a sleepy, country crossroad whose only real landmark was a rather inconsequential railroad flagstop. Originally one of four small villages located on the Ravensworth Plantation, Annandale was the property of the Fitzhugh family of Virginia, whose relatives included George Washington and Robert E. Lee.

Today, the Annandale's original owners would be shocked to see the town, one of Northern Virginia's most bustling areas. Since the beauracratic boom of the 1940s and 1950s, Annandale has grown by enormous proportions. Annandale is now the home of 85,000 Fairfax County residents, and its once-sleepy country roads are now some of the busiest in the area.

gift shops

ANNSANDRA
4417 John Marr Drive
Annandale, VA 22003
Tel: (703) 354-2110
Hrs:
Monday - Saturday 10:00 a.m. - 5:30 p.m.
Holiday Hrs:
Monday and Thursday 10:00 a.m. - 8:00 p.m.
Sunday Noon - 5:00 p.m.
Visa, MasterCard, American Express are accepted.
Customers may ship by UPS daily, throughout the country.

See it with your own eyes! Take beltway exit 6-E and follow Little River Turnpike for a mile-and-a-half to John Marr Drive. Turn right, look left! There's ANNSANDRA! This unusual gift shop burst into Annandale, Virginia out of the dream of its owner, Sandra Davidson, whose "grand new concept" dared to provide the very latest in elegant dinnerware and giftware at very special prices! And, everything is absolutely first quality merchandise!

Beautifully organized spacing, soft lighting, and deep pile carpeting furnish a rich background for artistic arrangements of exceptional selections of (just to name a few) Wedgewood, Kosta Boda, Waterford, Royal Dalton, Haviland Limoges, Lenox and Orrefors china and crystal stemware, dinnerware and giftware. There is an enticing selection of trays, picture frames, clocks, vases, and bowls, as well as an extremely lovely collection of Lladro' figurines that are delightfully displayed in a large, walk-around glass cabinet!

This distinctive shop is a perfect "one-stop" for hostess gifts, thank-you presents, showers, wedding and anniversary gifts. It even boasts a bridal registry and is proud to offer, classic to quite fancy, gift wrapping! Gift Baskets can be custom made with gourmet foods that include salad dressings, unique mustards, specialty nuts, chocolate covered potato chips, and dessert toppings. One can also find children's gifts, bath articles, and unusual items in Lucite, pewter and leather. Elegance, variety and choice! Big names and latest designs! All at 20- to 60-percent savings! A grand concept--for any reason!

ARLINGTON

Steeped in history, Arlington County is now one of the country's most sought-after business locations. The area, with its many monuments to the past, is also a modern day high-tech center, providing valuable information locally and to the world.

Arlington sits on the banks of the mighty Potomac River. It covers over 25-square miles, of which nearly 25-percent is Federal property. With a population of well over 150,000, and only a five-minute Metro ride into center city Washington, the county is a melding of dozens of ethnic groups, making for a rich and diverse community.

The second smallest county in the U.S., and the only one with no cities, Arlington is the site of the world's largest office building, the Pentagon. Home to the U.S. Department of Defense, this five-sided building contains three times more office space than New York City's towering Empire State Building. But the massive size is utilized efficiently. Even though the Pentagon has 17.5 miles of corridors, no office is more than a seven-minute walk from any other office.

Another major landmark in Arlington is the Marine Corps War Memorial, better known as the Iwo Jima Memorial. The statue, dedicated to all Marines who died in battle, is based on a Pulitzer Prize-winning photograph by Joseph Rosenthal. This 78-foot-high statue is the largest piece of cast bronze in the world and contains a real flag that flies day and night by Executive Order.

No trip to this Washington, D.C. suburb would be complete without a trip to Arlington National Cemetery. The neat rows of stark, white grave markers are an awesome sight unto themselves; along with the Tomb of the Unknown Soldier, and the graves of Presidents John F. Kennedy, Robert F. Kennedy, and many other truly great Americans, an afternoon at the cemetery is a trip that is both moving and unforgettable.

But history isn't Arlington's only attraction. A plethora of rooftop restaurants provide tantalizing views of Washington's skyline and incredible cuisine, and some of the best shopping in Northern Virginia can be found here.

Arlington is also home to 79 parks and 67 miles of hiking and biking trails, making for a truly comprehensive community. This small-but-mighty county has been called a tourists' paradise, and its many fine facilities are proof of this statement.

limosine services

CAREY LIMOUSINE DC INC.
768 S 23rd Street
Arlington, VA 22202
Tel: (703) 892-2000 Direct Reservations
(800) 336-4646 world wide reservations
Hrs: Open 24 hours a day, seven days.
Visa, MasterCard, American Express, Diners Club, and JCB cards are accepted.

Elegance is one thing! Function and dependability, along with continuity and longevity are quite another! The world knows this; CAREY LIMOUSINES prove it!

CAREY has been a leader in luxury and service in the field of transportation for well over 70 years! There are CAREY offices in more than 300 cities throughout the world. One of the finest and most reliable is available right here in the District area. They not only take care of all your needs in this area, but they delight in making or adjusting advance reservations for the rest of your itinerary. They have every right to be proud of their service, both in and outside the office. And they are.

Their experienced drivers know every inch of this city! Their interviewers are meticulous in developing an understanding of customers' wishes and tailoring service to suit each client's needs and desires. They offer a large choice of Lincoln Towncars, Formal Limousines, Stretches and Vans in which the hassle of driving can be left to their experts. Visitors and Corporate customers, alike, can relax, or entertain, with personalized dinner, theater and sightseeing service. They are ready with a wide range of immediate and complete service suggestions. They specialize in meeting planes and trains. For a spectacular welcome into the finest capital city in the world, give CAREY a call!

restaurants

BANGKOK GOURMET RESTAURANT
523 South 23rd Street
Crystal City
Arlington, VA 22202
Tel: (703) 521-1305/06

Hrs:	Tuesday - Friday	11:00 a.m. - 3:00 p.m.
	Monday - Friday	5:30 p.m. - 10:00 p.m.
	Saturday & Sunday	5:00 p.m. - 10:00 p.m.

Closed on most major holidays.
Reservations are suggested.
Visa, MasterCard, Choice and Diners Club are accepted.

It's worth looking for! On 23rd Street, the block beyond the Metro--opposite Route 1 from Crystal City--there's a narrow building with a green awning and a sign high up in block letters, BANGKOK GOURMET! It's nestled in the midst of small shops and eating places fronted with outside tables. At BANGKOK GOURMET, streetside dining is offered when the weather is pleasant, but in the winter the area is enclosed and heated, providing a quaint, inviting, anteroom for overflow dining. Inside, a lovely bay window in the front presides over all. A mirrored wall reflects the fresh flowers on the double line of tables extending the length of the room and lends an air of openness to the small space. The ambiance imperceptibly develops from early evening, quiet dignity to later on, controlled, bustling activity.

Suvicha Phatiphong (Pat), amiable owner and chef, zealously presides over his kitchen, constantly creating extraordinary combinations which he is proud to describe as "Thai Nouvelle Cuisine." His regular customers admit to coming, particularly, for these innovative "specials" which are as delicious as they are beautiful. Flawlessly prepared filet mignon, for instance, is presented under a crown of fanned out asparagus spears with green peppercorn sauce, and warm, crisp vegetables are arranged as on an artist's palate. Startling combinations delight even the most jaded connoisseur: steamed salmon with ginger and black bean; rabbit in mustard sauce; eggplant stuffed with seafood; and lobster dumplings in won ton soup!

Charming and intimate with friendly, attentive service, BANGKOK GOURMET is a perfect choice for unusually exciting and deliciously tasty Thai food served superbly!

NAM-VIET
1127 North Hudson Street
Arlington, VA 22201
Tel: (703) 522-7110 or (703) 276-7110
Hrs: Open seven days.
Sunday - Thursday 10:00 a.m. - 10:00 p.m.
Friday and Saturday 10:00 a.m. - 11:00 p.m.
Reservations suggested on weekends.
Carry-out available.
Visa, MasterCard, and American Express are accepted

Not one, but two--two restaurants since arriving as "boat-people" from Vietnam! Nguyen Van Thoi and his wife, Ngocanh Tran, have transported the tastes of their homeland to the heart of Northern Virginia. Hard work and family involvement have helped them to provide the finest of culinary dishes from the family restaurant in Can Tho.

First, it was MY AN 2 in Falls Church. Then, they opened NAM-VIET in Arlington--a restaurant which whispers serenity with its mirrored capiz chandeliers and its beige linens complementing the soft beige walls. NAM-VIET provides an ideal setting for the delicately spiced and freshly prepared traditional favorites of Vietnam. Wonderfully tender beef is expertly sauteed in orange juice and combined with hot peppers, wrapped in bacon or simply marinated, then grilled on skewers and served with "funny noodles." Hearty soups, including the Vietnamese favorite, Pho; light and tasty seafood combinations, stir-fried or grilled; and a special shredded salad with shrimp and chicken are delicious choices. The super-crisp spring rolls, plump with ground meat and bits of seasoned vegetables, are lightly fried and not the least bit greasy.

This restaurant was selected as one of 15 in the area to be listed in the 100 Top Values in the country, and it continues to be praised in local journals and newspapers. It's been a long journey for Van Thoi, who had to bribe his way out of prison a short decade ago. Each year on the Tet New Year, he remembers. He celebrates. And he honors P.O.W.'s at his Nam-Viet Restaurant.

PINES OF ITALY
237 North Glebe Road
Arlington, VA 22203
Tel: (703) 524-4969
Hrs:
Sunday and Monday 11:00 a.m. - 10:00 p.m.
Tuesday, Wednesday, Thursday 11:00 a.m. - 11:00 p.m.
Visa, MasterCard, American Express, Diners Club, and Carte Blanche are accepted.

Everyone calls him "Kahn," everyone! His customers, his employees, even the kids, whom he considers very important people, and who like to cluster around him as he hurries about the restaurant! He loves Arlington, his restaurant, and above all, his customers--95% of whom are "regulars." All are his friends. He personally greets each one at the door and continues to look out for them at the tables. And the food ... well, the food IS wonderful! The best of Southern Italian cooking.

White pizza--a small, thin crusted, crispy edged, soft centered, blending of spices and Fontina cheese--is definitely the appetizer of choice! But, then, there are those who would swear by the sauteed, garlicky Fagioli bianchi (white beans). Any of the "Homemade Pastas" listed on the menu would please a discriminating palate. However, for an excellent main course, choices of either the Shrimp Fra Diavalo with spaghetti, the Sausage and Eggplant, or the Veal Scaloppine with tomato sauce would certainly make you want to return another time to enjoy the others!
For delightful neighborhood dining, the PINES OF ITALY is listed in the" Washingtonian" magazine--and has been for three years! A poll of 1500 readers for their 1989 People's Choice Award, declared the PINES OF ITALY one of five "Best Italian" restaurants in the area. When it's time for a break from shopping and sightseeing, see for yourself! Drop

in on the friendly Kahn. You will find him waiting to greet you ... personally.

BALLSTON

Originally called Ball's Crossroads, Ballston was literally an intersection at the crossing of Glebe Road and Wilson Boulevard. It now serves as Arlington's downtown area.

A focal point of Ballston is the Ballston Common, a four-story shopping mall, filled with wonderful places to shop and dine.

CRYSTAL CITY

Perhaps one of the finest points about Crystal City is its strategic location. Set between the Pentagon and the National Airport, the area has grown and prospered over the years.

Located in Crystal City are the U.S. Patent Office and the Naval Systems Command. These prestigious Federal offices have drawn dozens of Federal contractors into Crystal City.

COLUMBIA PIKE CORRIDOR

cinemas/draft houses

ARLINGTON CINEMA 'N' DRAFT HOUSE
2903 Columbia Pike
Arlington, MD 22204
Tel: (703) 486-2345
Hrs: Friday and Saturday 6:00 p.m.
Sunday - Thursday 7:00 p.m.

Eat, drink and watch a movie with Mary. The total social entertainment experience has got to be at the ARLINGTON CINEMA 'N' DRAFT HOUSE. There, people can gather with friends, dine on pizza and beer, and watch a good movie. Watching the big screen, while sitting in a large Art Deco theater, has got to be what movie-going is all about! Why, then, are we reduced to 200-seat theaters that show several films at once? One thing for sure, it isn't done with the customer in mind. Toni Fisher bucks the system to provide old style dining pleasure and entertainment. He sports a really big movie screen with room enough to move around. If you like, there are love seats for two. There are tables for dinner and eager, attentive waiters and waitresses to take your order as soon as the movie begins. Smoke in the right section, but most of all, enjoy the movie.

The menu is a movie goers' and couch potato's dream. They have great sandwiches, chicken, beef, ham and cheese and dogs. Buffalo Chicken Wings, Nachos Deluxe and MunchSkins are among the super appetizers. The most remarkable entree is the fresh dough pizza. A Tony Fisher inspired special sauce creates the perfect pizza to share or hoard to ones self. A good selection of beer and wine is available complete with wine coolers or spritzers.

The movie screen doubles as the largest sports screen in the D.C. area. Space is also provided for cooperate teleconferencing and presentations. Tony has tried to preserve the feel of the original 1930s Art Deco theater and highlight what is still there. There is a lovely Tarrazzo floor in the lobby and the color theme is blue, green and mauve. The movies are current, not first-run, but with all the amenities, its worth a little wait.

restaurants

ATLACATL I
2716 Washington Boulevard
Arlington, VA 22201
Tel: (703) 524-9032

ATLACATL II
2602 Columbia Pike
Arlington, VA 22204
Tel: (703) 920-3680

Hrs:	Sunday - Thursday	11:00 a.m. - 11:00 p.m.
	Friday and Saturday	11:00 a.m. - Midnight

Visa, MasterCard, American Express, Diners Club, and Discover are accepted at both restaurants.

Atla is Aztec for "son of the leader." Atonal refers to a Salvadorian leader. The name says it! Salvador Mejia and his son, Jorge, have created two restaurants that lead the field in Salvadorian Cuisine. They don't follow trends. They stick to their own instincts and provide a simple and tasty meal for a very reasonable price. The walls are covered with posters and other Salvadorian decorations.

The atmosphere is colorful and comfortable, nothing fancy, just pleasant surroundings with cheerful waiters! ATLACATL I has a back dining room that is more intimate and is reminiscent of a small restaurant in old Mexico.

I usually recommend the Combination #2 to get a feel for Salvadorian food. It includes a pupusa (heavy tortilla with pork and cheese on the inside), a Pastelito (deliciously light pastry with meat inside) and a Tamal De Elote (a little log of cream corn). Refried beans and marinated cole slaw round out the dish. Beef, chicken, shrimp and fish are available, all with the unmistakable taste of El Salvador. They will fix a vegetarian platter, if asked. Every meal starts with Yucca, a root vegetable called casawa by the Incas. It is similar to a lightly fried potato. Fruit drinks are particularly special, like Tamarindo or the Ensalada Refresco which is a bit like having a delicious fruit salad in a glass.

If you are looking for a good meal, that is fun and reasonably priced, ATLACATL I & II are the places.

PENTAGON CITY

Located centrally among Virginia's most affluent suburbs, the Fashion Centre offers 150 fine specialty stores and two anchor stores in which to shop. Incorporating the Jeffersonian-style of architecture and making it totally modern, this multi-use complex also includes a nine-story office building, and a 360-room Ritz Carlton Hotel, a multi-level parking facility and residential units.

The Fashion centre is located directly across the Potomac River from the Pentagon, the world's largest office building, and is easily accessible from Georgetown, Alexandria, McLean, Arlington, Falls Church, Rosslyn and Crystal City.

kitchen supplies

KITCHEN BAZAAR, Pentagon City, 1100 South Hayes St., Arlington, VA 22202 Tel: (703) 415-5545. See their story under Uptown.

leather

GEORGETOWN LEATHER DESIGN, Pentagon City; Tel: (703) 418-6702. For fine Leather goods. See their story under Georgetown.

SHIRLINGTON

Visitors to Shirlington are delighted by the old-fashioned, Main Street atmosphere of the area, but shopping can only be described as totally up-to-date.

The focal point of the region is a newly-renovated retail center, which houses 40 stores, movie theaters, restaurants, and cafes.

billiards & games

CHAMPION BILLIARD SUPPLY, INC.
2620 S Shirlington Road
Arlington, VA 22206
Tel: (703) 521-4670
Hrs: Showroom:

Monday - Friday	9:00 a.m. - 9:00 p.m.
Saturday	9:00 a.m. - 6:00 p.m.
Sun0day	11:00 a.m. - 6:00 p.m.

CHAMPION BILLIARDS
Tel: (703) 521-3800
Hrs: Open 24 hours.

OFF THE RACK BAR & GRILL
Hrs: Open 24 hours.

Pool halls have moved up-scale and up-town, and dark, dank and dingy have given way to family fun fare! CHAMPION BILLIARDS is a classic example of the latest concept in Billiard Parlors! Housed on the second floor of its own newly completed building, which curves around a corner in Shirlington, it's conveniently located just off Route 395. The large lower level provides ample parking, handicapped access and an elevator to the upstairs entrance.

On the right, at the top of the rounded stair, a wide glass door opens into CHAMPION BILLIARD SUPPLY, INC., the largest, most completely stocked show room on the East Coast! It's pool heaven with every kind of big name table on the market. Designed in a variety of wood finishes, chrome, marble and molded plastic, topped with different color felts, they easily fit into any style of decorating. Custom cues are sized and balanced to perfection. Tiffany to modern stylized lights hang from every inch of ceiling, and walls are colorful with pool pictures and accessories.

The large game room is top of the stairs, bear left! High chairs of lightly varnished, natural wood line the walls of deep green wainscoting topped with buff and hung with large, attractive pool and people pictures. Eighteen tables, under shadowless and glare free lighting, beckon the novice and professional alike! For a break, OFF THE RACK BAR & GRILL offers delicious, well prepared food at any time--day or night--in a raised, neon framed vantage point that oversees the action or provides a quiet corner!

caterers

DESIGN CUISINE
2659 South Shirlington Road
Arlington, VA 22206
Tel: (703) 979-9400
Hrs: Open seven days.
Arrangements can be made for any time desired.
Office Monday - Saturday 9:00 a.m. - 6:00 p.m.

A dream can come true! An intimate moment for two. An elegant dinner for a few close friends. The perfect party for 5,000. Host/hostess of the hour! Every detail in place and not a glitch in sight. The table set, food prepared, drinks ready to be served. It's all possible with DESIGN CUISINE!

The choices are endless! Since 1981, when they began on a small scale to "do" parties in the home, Horst Klein, Bill Homan and Steve Veletsis have engineered their business from small scale to the most completely versatile and visionary catering service in the area. No idea is too insignificant or too grand for them to tackle with gusto. And they will perform as many or as few services as are needed or desired. Completely flexible, they stand ready for cocktail parties, dinners, receptions and picnics for any number of guests. Never is their food warmed over! All dishes are prepared at the site, with equipment being provided--even a stove, if necessary! Tables, cloths, chairs, serving dishes and utensils, ranging from luxurious to casual, are available for the asking. They will help with the planning or do it all.

Orders can be handled entirely by phone. However, a visit to the office will provide an opportunity to sample the food or preview an entirely set table! Though they employ a large full-time staff and have access to others on a temporary basis, it is usually necessary to give them two to three weeks notice. So, dream a fantasy! Then, call DESIGN CUISINE.

the nation's capital

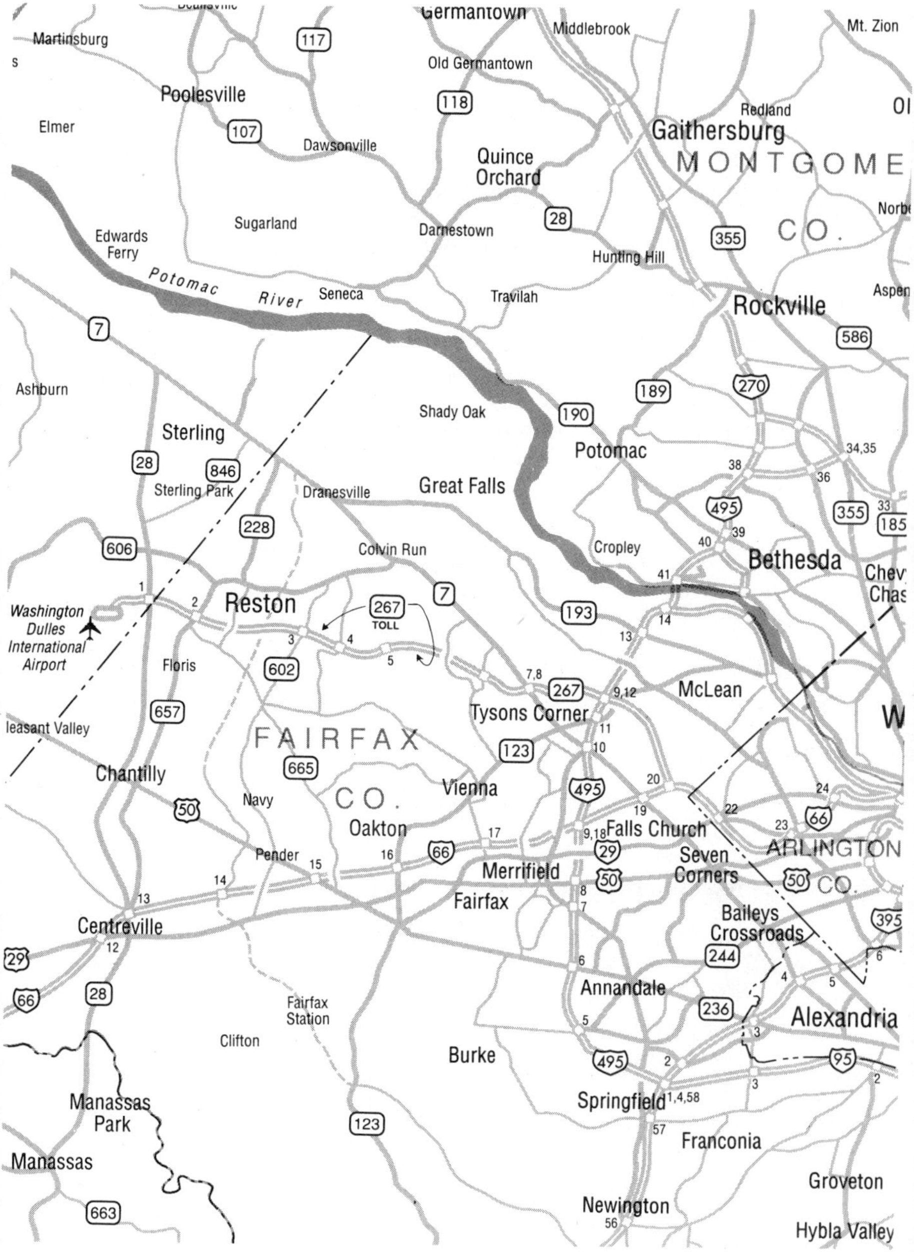

FAIRFAX COUNTY

Fairfax County, by far the largest county in Virginia, was established in 1742 by a vote of the Virginia House of Burgesses. At that time, it included what are now Arlington and Loudoun Counties, as well as the cities of Alexandria, Fairfax, and Falls Church. In 1791, a portion of Fairfax County, including Arlington and Alexandria, was ceded to the federal government for the establishment of the national capital.

Today, with a network of interconnecting highways, Fairfax County has become part of the Washington, D.C. Metropolitan area. Historic communities like Tysons Corner, the site of Fairfax County's first Courthouse, and Annandale and Seven Corners, once trading centers for Indians and colonists, have become major residential and shopping districts. Home to thousands of federal workers, Fairfax County is today known as the capital city's "Bedroom Community".

attractions

Nature lovers, camping enthusiasts, and picnickers will enjoy **BULL RUN REGIONAL PARK.** (Route 29, Centerville) In addition to featuring one of the East coast's largest swimming pools, this pleasant park offers miles of hiking and bridle trails, large playing fields, camping and picnic facilities, and a rifle and archery range.

A spectacular view of Bull Run, and 200-year-old hemlocks are the features of **HEMLOCK OVERLOOK REGIONAL PARK** (13220 Yates Ford Road). Opererated jointly with George Mason University, the park serves as an outdoor education center for the school.

Downstream from the Bull Run Marina, the 2,150 acre **FOUNTAINHEAD REGIONAL PARK** (Interstate 95 at the Lorton Exit) offers nature hikes of the Fairfax county shore, boat rental and launching, and backpack camping.

Boating enthusiasts will enjoy **SANDY RUN REGIONAL PARK** (Van Thompson Road), which features individual and group rowing and crew facilities, as well as one of the finest rowing courses in the country.

Reminiscent of the Potomic shoreline before development, **POTOMAC OVERLOOK REGIONAL PARK** features a nature center with archeological and wildlife displays, as well as nature trails over hills and rock outcoppings that lead to an overlook with a spectacular view of of the Washington Monument.

Built in 1785 on the Washington family's River Farm as a home for an overseer, **THE COLLINGWOOD LIBRARY AND MUSEUM ON AMERICANISM** (8301 E. Boulevard Drive) possesses an interesting collections of artifacts, as well as a library containing, among other things, a genealogy section loaned by The Mayflower Society of Washington.

Built in 1755 by George Mason, author of the U. S. Constitution and father of the Bill of Rights, **GUNSTON HALL** (off Interstate 95 at Lorton exit) is known for its Chinese Chippendale dining room and intricate wood wark in the Palladian room.

Children can pet, walk, or even talk with animals from all over the world at the **PET-A-PET FARM** (Route 606, at the Hunter Mill Road intersection). This unique attraction also features a giant tortoise that will take kids for a ride on its back.

Originally built for Irish Catholic railroad workers, **SAINT MARY'S CHURCH** (Ox Road at Fairfax Station) was used by Clara Barton, founder of the American Red Cross, as a hospital for Union and Confederate Soldiers wounded in the Battles of Second Manassas and Chantilly.

Built in 1794 by Richard Bland Lee, Virginia's first congressman, **SULLY PLANTATION** (on Sully Road in Chatilly) has been beautifully preserved. A tour of the main house, filled with antiques from the Federal period, along with the kitchen/laundry, smokehouse, stone dairy, and other outbuildings will help familiarize you with Southern plantation life.

events

Held each June on the campus of George Mason University, **THE FAIRFAX FAIR** is one of the county's major community events. The fair's major attractions include food, rides, crafts, county and trade exhibits, and the Virginia State Chili And BBQ Cookoffs.

More than 250 juried crafspersons display their wares at the **OCCOQUAN CRAFT SHOW** held at the Occoquan town center in late September.

BAILEYS CROSSROADS

In 1809, the Columbia Pike was built across the Leesburgh Pike, and Bailey's Crossroads was created. Named for its owner, Hachaliah Bailey, Bailey's Crossroads became the center for the pastoral communities of Vienna, McLean, and Herndon. Today, the crossroad is an overpass on the Leesburgh Pike, and the surrounding area is teeming with residential and commercial developments. Bailey's Crossroads encompasses a scant six square mile, but is home to 31,00 of Northern Virginia's one million people. Almost a third of these people live in Skyline Towers, a magnificent complex of 20-story condominiums.

health clubs

THE SKYLINE CLUBS AT SKYLINE CITY
5115 Leesburg Pike
Falls Church, VA 22041
Tel: (703) 820-4100
Hrs:
Fitness Center/Pool

Monday - Friday	6:00 a.m. - 10:00 p.m.
Saturday	7:00 a.m. - 7:00 p.m.
Sunday	7:00 a.m. - 9:00 p.m.

Racquet/Locker Rooms:
Open one hour later than fitness center.
June - September:

Sun.	7:00 a.m. - 8:30 p.m.

Racquet/Locker Rooms:

Open seven days	7:00 a.m. - 9:00 p.m.

Nursery:

Monday - Thursday	8:30 a.m. - 8:00 p.m.
Friday	8:30 a.m. - 7:00 p.m.
Saturday and Sunday	9:00 a.m. - 3:00 p.m.

SKYLINE CITY is big, bright, clean and beautiful! Settled solidly above the Skyline Center Mall, it's not simply glitz and glitter! Not all stretch and sweat either! It's a hard mix of hope, grit, incentive, determination and reward! It's a blend of superior service, various machines, courts, a pool and a track with warm smiles, friendliness, supervision, training, and encouragement! It's a network of possibilities for all ages and all sizes and shapes! There's a Seniors fit group, Junior campers, the Masters swimmers, a kiddie swim bunch, tennis, basketball and racquetball players, yoga enthusiasts, aerobicisers, machine devotees, and an evening group mastering old and new dance steps! Something for everyone! And shinning through it all, there's the gleam of hope for discovering the wondrous-self-within! For reward, recreation, and rest, there are steam rooms, saunas, and a Jacuzzi. And, THE FAN CLUB CAFE & SPORTS BAR stands ready, on the premises, to serve healthy drinks, snacks and meals.

The club is committed to excellence! The staff is committed to caring. Three locations are available. CRYSTAL PARK and CRYSTAL GATEWAY in Crystal City and SKYLINE CITY, on Route 7 just off of Shirley Highway (US 395), can be "on the way home" from anywhere!

A matter of taste, a matter of choice! Healthy heart? Fabulous fitness? Beautiful body? Stunning slimness? Ordinary maintenance? Fun? Whatever. Go for it!

FAIRFAX CITY

Situated on the West Side of Washington D.C., Fairfax City is a residential community teeming with history. With the exception of the Civil War, when Union troops occupied the city and used the building as a stable, Fairfax City's original courthouse has been used continuously since it was first built in 1800. Standing on its grounds is a memorial to the first Confederate officer killed in the Civil War .

attractions

An important stagecoach stop in the 1820's for travelers along the Little River Turnpike, **EARP'S ORDINARY** (Main Street, between University

Drive and and Route 123) was built according to building specifications set by the Virginia Assembly in 1805.

events

A parade, Family Fun Fair, evening shows and fireworks highlight Fairfax City's **ANNUAL DAY-LONG FOURTH OF JULY CELEBRATION**. Events take place in various locations around the city, including the historic district, City Hall, and Fairfax High School.

computer services

COMPUTER TECH SERVICES
Fairfax, VA
Tel: (703) 591-7101
Hrs: Monday - Friday 9:00 a.m. - 5:00 p.m.

Conducting a seminar, giving a presentation, working a special project? Do you need a computer? Now? The place to go for a convenient, no-hassle solution to a short term computer need is COMPUTER TECH SERVICES. They are a computer rental and support company serving the Washington Metropolitan business community, and they are absolutely committed to satisfying their customers needs with rapid response, excellent service and top quality products.

If specific hardware is required, Computer Tech Services carry the best. They provide names like IBM, AST, MACINTOSH, GRID, HP, EPSON and DICONIX. If there's a problem evading a solution, just explain what it is that you are trying to achieve, and they will recommend an equipment configuration that will accomplish the job for you. Then, when you decide what you want, their service technicians are dedicated to providing timely delivery and quick installation. In the unlikely event that the equipment should not function as expected, a technician will quickly investigate the situation and, if necessary, promptly repair or replace it within four hours! COMPUTER TECH SERVICES also provide classroom and personalized consultation on Aldus Pagemaker and Harvard Graphics. They have one-on-one instructors that can assist in familiarization or brush up on software, such as, PC fundamentals,

DOS, Lotus 1-2-3 and WordPerfect. For on-the-spot training, instant upgrading, temporary and long term leasing or friendly, expert guidance, simply call on the company that considers you and your needs the basis for their business!

FALLS CHURCH

Falls Church is one of the most pleasant residential communities in Northern Virginia. Founded in the 1700's as Truro Parish, the name of the town was changed to Falls Church in 1769, after the church that still stands in the center of the city. Located in the middle of the United States' highest growth area, Falls Church has gone from being a suburban "Bedroom Community", to a thriving urban center.

Although it covers only two square mile, Falls Church is one of the country's most diverse areas. Many points of interest, ranging from historical landmarks, to shopping centers, are scattered in and around Falls Church. And, while it has definitely benefited from the tremendous growth of the Northern Virginia and Washington areas, Falls Church has managed to retain the unique character that has made it such a pleasant place to live and visit.

attractions

Known for the Foutain of Faith, which contains 38 figures and was designed by Swedish sculptor Carle Milles, **NATIONAL MEMORIAL PARK** (U.S. Route 29) is dedicated to four Army chaplains, two Protestant ministers, a Catholic priest, and a Jewish Rabbi who gave their lifejackets to sailors aboard the Dorchestor when it was torpedoed in 1943.

Built in 1733, one of the oldest surviving structures in Virginia, **THE FALLS CHURCH** (East Fairfax Street) gave the city of Falls Church its name. The present brick structure was actually built in 1769, and served as a recruiting station during the Revolutionary War, and as a hospital and stable during the Civil War.

Described as excellent in the cities Architectural Inventory, the **300 BLOCK OF EAST BROAD STREET** features four buildings that provide a glimpse of Falls Church in the 1850's.

Part of the defences of Fort Buffalo, **THE TAYLOR BATTERY** (Roosevelt Street at East Broad Street) reveals the remains of earthworks that were occupied alternately by Conferdate and Union Troops in the Civil War.

A farm in the city, **CHERRY HILL** (312 Park Avenue) is being restored by the Falls Church Village Preservation and Improvement Society. Built in the 1840's, the farms Greek Rvival house, barn and other farm buildings are still largely in tact.

catering services

PIES ON THE RUN
Barcroft Plaza
6347 Columbia Pike
Falls Church, Va. 22041
Tel: (703) 941-A PIE or (941-2743)
Hrs: Open seven days Noon - 8:00 p.m.
Closed Sundays in July and August.

Fast, good and healthy are no longer mutually exclusive! You can have it all with one phone call to PIES ON THE RUN! If you live or work within three miles of the shop, they will deliver to your home or business within 45 minutes to an hour. Or, you can stop in, and within 15 minutes, be on your way with one of the flaky crust goodies for slicing and feasting.

They call it "A hot new idea" that is "Great taste delivered in haste!" That's true, but, choosing might take time. From chicken and turkey pies, Shepherd's pie, Tamale and Seafood to Key Lime and Chocolate Mousse, each is freshly made with low fat, low cholesterol, choice ingredients with no preservatives. They are perfectly seasoned and the portions are so generous that a two person pie can easily serve three! There are lunchbox specials, which include an individual pie, a fresh salad and a large homemade cookie. The dinner for two doubles it all, except the price, which becomes even more of a bargain.

The founder of this innovative idea is Linda Ambrus who has been chosen by the Chamber of Commerce to receive the coveted Small Business Product of the Year Award for 1990. With 48 hours notice, this lady will even branch out to cater anywhere in the D.C. area for a minimum of twenty people. She says she offers convenience. We see her offering the healthiest, best tasting, quickie food to be enjoyed anywhere in this area! We're both right.

restaurants

MY AN 2
6785 Wilson Boulevard
Falls Church, VA 22042
Tel: (703) 538-7110
Hrs: Open seven days 10:00 a.m. - 10:00 p.m.
Carry-out available.
Reservations suggested on weekends.

At first, it's the wonderful aroma of stir-fry and spices, but then, it's the smiling man who hurries to greet you. Then, you realize you're glad you came. Later, you discover that it is Nguyen Van Thoi's wife Ngocanh Tran, as head chef, who, with numerous family members team work to prepare the dishes that their customers consider the best Vietnamese food outside of Saigon.

In 1978, this man, who had hoped to "study" in the United States, found himself and his family fleeing for their lives and arriving in this country, finally, as "boat people." They settled, eventually, in a worn down section of Arlington where they, with their Vietnamese neighbors, set to injecting new life into the declining community. My An is their tribute to hard work and courage.

It takes several visits to even taste the specialties. The Saigon Pork & Shrimp Noodle Soup, the Stir-fried Beef with "Funny" Noodles, Grilled Pork & Broken Rice (authentically Vietnamese) all vie for your attention when you look at the menu. How is one to know where to begin? Thoi, himself, patiently explains that the spring rolls flake in your hands so you can roll them in lettuce and add special fish sauce and capture every morsel. No one wants to miss the Special My An Muffins. All Vietnamese love them; few can make such delicious ones.

GREAT FALLS

attractions

Once the site of America's first canal, **GREAT FALLS PARK** (Old Dominion Drive, north of Georgetown Pike) is now a popular spot for rock climbing, picknicking, and hiking.

Restored and fully operating, **THE COLVIN RUN MILL** (Capital Beltway, exit 10W) is made entirely out of wood. The grounds include a dairy barn, blacksmith shop, millers house, and a general store where you may purchase grains ground in the mill, as well as a variety of homemade items.

restaurants

SERBIAN CROWN RESTAURANT
1141 Walker Road
Great Falls, VA. 22066
Tel: (703)759-4150
Hrs: Lunch Monday - Friday 11:30 a.m.- 2:30 p.m.
Dinner Open seven days 5:30 p.m.- 10:00 p.m.
Closed for lunch on Saturday & Sunday
American Express, Visa and MasterCard are accepted.

For an important occasion demanding elegance and grandeur, the perfect choice can be found tucked away in Great Falls, Virginia--a whisk away from the District of Columbia. The SERBIAN CROWN RESTAURANT bespeaks royalty with its deep, rich red carpeting and draperies, its crystal chandeliers, rococo walls, classic, old-world paintings,and live Gypsy music Wednesday through Sunday during dinner. The only restaurant in the area known for its outstanding, Russian specialties, as well as the Serbian and French selections on its unique and extensive menu, is owned and operated by Rene Bertagna and Zlatan Stamenitch. It is competently managed in a courtly, European manner by the ever-attentive Francois, who will explain that out of eight choices of Vodkas, Raspberry and Pepper are favorites, served in chilled, custom designed, hand blown glasses.

A recommended way to begin the evening is with Russian Hors d'Oeuvres--Zakuska, a variety of dried fish. Other popular choices among many tempting delicacies include Canadian Salmon Roe Caviar and Oysters "Moscow Style." Borscht is served hot or cold and Ribarska Corba is THE soup selection of fish lovers! Outstanding entrees that are broiled, baked, or grilled on skewers include fresh fish, the most tender of beef, lamb, pork and game--wild boar, venison, rabbit and bear--depending on availability.

Kulebiaka, the epitome of excellence, is Russian-style Salmon served with lobster sauce, and is a feast for two that can be followed by Crepes Suzettes or Banana Flambe--if one does not succumb to other temptations on the dessert menu or the passing cart of fruit and tarts! All in all...an experience to celebrate. And to remember!

HERNDON

While this area was first settled in 1728, Herndon did not enjoy any real prosperity until 100 years later when New England farmers came to Virginia to escape the Northern winters. Herndon is home to many historic buildings which include a renovated railroad station, and more than 25 homes dating from the 1870's. While Herndon is, for the most part, a residential district, several high-technology businesses have located here.

attractions

A working model of a 1920's farm, **FRYING PAN PARK** will give you a good idea of what farming was like prior to mechanization. Complete with barnyard animals, growing crops, a blacksmith shop, and an activities/equestrian center, Frying Pan Park is an ideal place to take the family.
Built in 1857, **HERNDON TRAIN DEPOT AND MUSEUM** (??) contains memorabilia for the town of Herndon.

A spectacular example of modern architecture, **THE WASHINGTON DULLES INTERNATIONAL AIRPORT** (Dulles Access Road) features a terminal designed by architect Eero Saarinen that echoes the idea of flight. A bronze panel showing the relationship between human beings and space highlights this wonderful building.

events

Herndon celebrates the Fourth of July with a **BIRTHDAY PARTY IN TWO PARTS** . Morning events at Bruin Park include games, entertainment, free hot dogs and lemonade, and a birthday cake. Concerts and fireworks mark the evening program at Herndon High School Stadium.

accommodations

COURTYARD BY MARRIOTT, 533 Herndon Parkway, Herndon, VA, 22070; Tel: (703) 478-9400. A beautiful new Courtyard by Marriott. They have an indoor pool.

MCLEAN

Built upon land that once belonged to the famous Lee family., McLean is more an area of smaller communities, than a town. McLean's first community was Mathildaville, which was to be part of George Washington's failed Potowmack Company. In the years that followed, various other communities sprang up in the area, among them Langly, which began as the residence of Benjamin Mackall, and Chesterbrook. Eventually, all of these small communities were linked by the building of the Old Dominion Railway, and the name of the area was changed to McLean in honor of the railroads builder, "Washington Post" publisher John R. McLean.

Today, McLean is an area of tremendous growth, much of which has occurred in the Tysons Corner area where many high-technology firms have located. Despite all of this growth, McLean still possess the characteristics of a small town. The citizenry of McLean deserve a good deal of the credit for this, as they have taken a great role in preserving the beauty of the area.

attractions

An old tenant tobacco farm comes to life at **THE CLAUDE MOORE COLONIAL FARM AT TURKEY RUN** (Langly exit of Georgetown Pike). Visitors to this restoration will be able to visit the farm family, who, dressed in 18th century garb, will demonstrate such colonial living skills as open hearth cookery and hoe agriculture.

florists

FLOWERS AND PLANTS ETC.
1378 Chain Bridge Road
McLean, VA 22101
Tel: Dial F-L-O-W-E-R-S (703) 356-9377 or (800) 878ROSE
Hrs: Monday- Friday 9:00 a.m. - 6:00 p.m.
Saturday 9:00 a.m. - 5:00 p.m.
Closed on Sundays.
Visa, MasterCard, American Express, Diners Club, Discover and Carte Blanche are accepted.

For the very latest in floral get-well, thank-you or hostess gifts, turn into Langly Shopping Center, just off Route 123 in McLean, Virginia. There, you will discover FLOWERS AND PLANTS ETC. with numerous silk and dried flowers, colorful balloons, varieties of blooming and green plants, and lovely fresh-cut flowers, including iris and lilies, tulips, freesia, and other unique flowers from all over the world. One may choose simple or innovative designs to carry out, wire out of town, or have delivered anywhere in the area.

For 14 years, family members Bev and Arnold Krauss and son, Chip Frederick, have had able help from a most capable and professional staff - under the supervision of manager, Scott Heisler, and canine approval of Beggar and Max! They have surpassed the ordinary in achieving their motto: The Total Concept in Flowers and Plants. Conveying age-old messages in intriguing new ways such as adding humor to a 40th birthday with 'Forty carrots' or sending 'a rose-a-day for thirty days' are only two of many possibilities offered. Brass, ceramic, terra cotta and basketry provide a wide choice of containers which can be arranged with dried, silk or fresh flowers. They also have a selection of gourmet foods to include in fruit baskets!

Custom, creative arrangements, personalized service and commitment to satisfying individual tastes give true meaning to the "etcetera" in their name!

gift shops

APPLE PIE COUNTRY DESIGN
1382 Chain Bridge Road
McLean, VA 22101
Tel: (703) 734-0044
Hrs: Monday - Saturday 10:00 a.m.- 6:00 p.m.
Visa, MasterCard, American Express are accepted.

Elegant, charming, and tastefully decorated, APPLE PIE COUNTRY DESIGN is a pleasant respite from the ordinary. It's a lovely surprise tucked into the Langly Shopping Center in McLean, Virginia. Eve Carrow-Barnett, the owner, blends her love of custom-made quilts with over 700 bolts of fabulous cotton fabrics, antique wicker furniture and a distinctive variety of unique, handmade gift items into a fascinating and delightful place to shop!

Quilts definitely dominate the scene--with an incredible choice of made-to-order and readymade; new and antique; from Amish country, New England and Kentucky; to use on the bed, a couch, the table, a wall; to love, to treasure and to pass on to the next generation! But, if you have always wanted to quilt your own, there are supplies and lessons available, as well!

And that's not all! You will find a collection of charming animals and wonderful pillows made of antique quilts. There are handmade pillowcases, shams, tablecloths and baby clothes. Perfect for wedding gifts,
showers and birthdays! You will love the hand crafted wooden lamps, pottery and stoneware for yourself or for a friend. And just touch one of

the downy soft, handmade throws...practical, washable, and purely luxurious.

There is another APPLE PIE COUNTRY DESIGN at 4524 Lee Highway in Arlington and one at 1146 Walker Road in Great Falls. Each is unique. There is superb quality at all three!

SQUIRE CHASE LTD.
1319 Chainbridge Road
McLean, VA 22101
Tel: (703) 790-5649
Hrs: Summer and winter
Monday - Friday 10:00 a.m. - 5:30 p.m.
Saturday 10:00 a.m. - 5:00 p.m.
Visa, MasterCard and American Express are accepted.

"A very fine gift to match almost any price" awaits the shopper at Squire Chase Ltd! This is the promise made by two gentlemen who own and run this extraordinary gift shop located in the oldest shopping center in McLean, Virginia. Sparkling crystal chandeliers accent the wonderfully crafted and unusually displayed art and gifts. But, first you notice Nicholas, the impeccably groomed poodle who delights customers with a greeting.

The shop boasts of a connoisseur collection of Boehm birds and flowers in finest porcelain, and the largest retail assortment of beautifully hand-painted Herend porcelain in the United States, including china, lamps and figurines. The shopper is also treated to a choice of dinnerware designs adapted from rare, antique originals by the renowned Mottahedeh Company.

Dwight E. Bryant, who had been a buyer for a well known chain, realized his dream when he convinced Stanhope Chase to come out of retirement to open their elegant gift shop. Since the pair maintain close contact with representatives of the most prestigious firms throughout Europe, they are able to offer an unusually fine selection of choices for the most discriminating shopper.

ice cream parlours

THE CUSTARD SHOPPE
6653-A Old Dominion Drive
McLean, VA 22101
Tel: (703) 790-1165
Hrs: Open seven days

Monday - Thursday	10:00 a.m. - 10:00 p.m.
Friday & Saturday	10:00 a.m. - 11:00 p.m.
Sunday	11:00 a.m. - 10:00 p.m.

What's red and white and delicious inside? No need to guess! It's Sam and Mauvette Malizia's CUSTARD SHOPPE on Old Dominion Drive in McLean Square, Virginia--a lick and a gulp from the center of Washington, DC! Under its awning sign, a large white, ruffled window with red flowers on the sill, frames a red and white checkered floor, red and white booths, and a very long, red and white counter (with computerized check-outs that move almost too quickly for time to choose among all the tempting suggestions)! It's a cheerful place to be and it's fun!

THE CUSTARD SHOPPE - the only place within 150 miles that sells authentic custard (a never-to-be-forgotten frozen-confection-taste-experience which must contain at least 10% egg and 10% butterfat)--is the realization of a man's dream and a family's effort! Sam recognized the compatibility between his love of ice cream and his desire to own a business and decided to combine the two. Every family member in the area offered strong support and solid help, with Uncle Russ Kiel of Kiel Construction Company supervising the building effort. The Malizias became parents the day before the store opened and celebrated their son by naming their mouth-watering cookies, Joey's Cookies! Uncle Pat Kiel is manager of cookies and custard by night while Jo-Ann Seger is in charge during the day.

To any bon vivant of goodies: visit THE CUSTARD SHOPPE! Savor the choosing! Twenty flavors of old fashioned ice cream parlor goodness; rich and smooth Gourmet Yogurt; endless varieties of mixes, toppings, splits, floats, and dips; freshly baked cookies, fudge and brownies; or Skinny Dip (the latest in no cholesterol, no fat deliciousness!). And would you believe? They also serve freshly baked bagels and authentic Hoagies on real Italian rolls.

restaurants

KAZAN
6813 Redmond Drive
McLean, VA 22101
Tel: (703) 734-1960
Hrs: Lunch
Monday - Friday 11:00 - 2:30 p.m.
Dinner
Monday - Saturday 5:00 - 10:00
Closed on Mondays.
Visa, MasterCard, American Express and Diners Club are accepted.

Behind the door are two hidden jewels! Choose One! Step into the Turkish tent elegance of yesteryear with its heavily-beamed, fabric-domed ceiling set sparkling with cut-out brass, hanging lamps and a colorful Turkish chandelier--the Blue Room. OR - go with modern grandeur in the Pink Room with pink tablecloths, and pink and mauve walls rising from wine carpet, hung with lovely Turkish prints, and highlighted by a magnificent crystal Turkish chandelier. Either is the perfect choice for enjoying soft, Turkish instrumental music, impeccable service, and the very finest of Turkish cuisine.

Lamb and eggplant are key components in Turkish recipes with absolute freshness a prime requirement for all ingredients. KAZAN'S specialty is the famous National Turkish dish, Doner Kebab, which is available on Wednesdays and Fridays and for dinner on Saturdays. Swordfish Kebab is in daily demand. Borek (small puff pastries) and Cerkez Tavuk (chicken with walnut sauce) are two among delectable appetizers. A "must" for dessert is Zeynel's own creation of Orange Baklava a la Kazan!

In 1980, Zeynel Uzun carefully tucked KAZAN into the heart of McLean at the junction of Old Dominion Drive and Old Chain Bridge Road--just ten minutes from Washington, DC. There are, now, three chefs in the kitchen who are carrying on the tradition that Zenyel's father passed to him. This gifted chef/restaurateur was selected to prepare for and serve the Queen of England when she visited Turkey as well as the President of Turkey when he came to the White House. Zenyel has a son. We can hope the tradition continues!

THE ITALIAN OVEN RESTAURANT
6852 Old Dominion Drive
McLean, VA 22101
Tel: (703) 893-7777
Hrs: Summer and winter

Monday - Thursday	11:30 a.m. - 11:00 p.m.
Friday	11:30 a.m. - Midnight
Sunday	Noon - 10:00 p.m.

Closed on Thanksgiving and Christmas.
Other holidays: closed for lunch, open for dinner
Visa, MasterCard and American Express are accepted.
Reservations are suggested for groups of six or more.
Carry-out and banquet rooms are available.

In 1985, Salvatore and Joan Esposito brought a touch of Italy into the heart of McLean, Virginia! They had previously introduced the first wood-burning pizza oven to the Washington, D.C. area, and it has been "Buon Appetito" at The Italian Oven ever since! Sal, who was born and raised in Naples, Italy, insists on authenticity in every detail from the "trattoria" style atmosphere to the savory perfection of each dish that is served. The traditional Naples clown solemnly presides over red and white checkered tablecloths, imported Italian chandeliers, soft Italian music, and animated diners enjoying homemade pasta, freshly baked Italian bread, and imported Italian candies.

Local favorites on the reliably consistent and decorative menu are Ravioli, Linguine with fresh clams and red or white sauce, and Pollo Cardinale (chicken breasts stuffed with ham, cheese and garlic). Seafood aficionados return again and again for the Festa del Mare (a heavenly blending of shrimp, mussels, clams and squid in red or white sauce over linguine)--always served with a salad. And the pizza! It is still precisely prepared and cooked to unequalled excellence in a wood-fired oven.

Whether to try a Naples-style Margherita Pizza or to enjoy a full Italian meal, one must visit The Italian Oven to experience a thoroughly satisfying "taste of Italy" in the Metropolitan Capital Area of the U.S.A.

restaurants & pubs

McKEEVER'S PUB
6641 Old Dominion Drive
McLean,VA 22101
Tel: (703) 790-9453

Hrs:	Summer and winter	
	Monday -Thursday	11:00 a.m. - Midnight
	Friday	11:00 a.m. - 1:00 a.m.
	Sat.urday	Noon - Midnight

McKeever's provides Old English warmth and merriment in a neighborhood-style Pub where one can find sustenance and camaraderie after a day of work, sightseeing or play. Located in McLean Square, a short breathing space from downtown Washington, its Tiffany lamps and cozy, dark wood tables draw regulars and visitors into a family-like atmosphere. Amid pictures of Shirley Temple, mounted game animals, and a completely decorated Christmas tree hanging from the ceiling, all feel equally at home whether enjoying the hearty, homemade soup, a specialty sandwich, one of the wide variety of hamburgers offered, or drinking draft beer from a 13 ounce chilled mug.

Lori McKeever, who began to build her loyal clientele when she started as a waitress there, is now the owner and zealous supervisor of the daily specials, tasty deserts, and ample bar which includes hot and cold cider. Alyson Ehat, the all around manager/waitress and Mo, the chef, know, by name, many of the patrons who sometimes wander back to the kitchen to visit, fill their own coffee cups and, often, pitch in to clean up at closing time.

For a meal, a snack or just a moment of respite, McKeever's is the place to visit for a friendly break and excellent refreshments.

OAKTON

gift shops

THE MOLE HOLE OF OAKTON
2952-G Chain Bridge Road
Oakton, VA 22124
Tel: (703) 281-0025
Hrs:
Monday, Tuesday, Wednesday, Saturday: 10:00 a.m. - 6:00 p.m.
Thursday and Friday 10:00 a.m. - 9:00 p.m.
Extended hours from Thanksgiving until Christmas.
Visa, MasterCard, American Express, Discover and personal checks are accepted.

The best of all worlds! Some of the finest decorative art from the Orient, enchanting cards from Denmark and France, exquisite Russian crystal; from Italy, an elegant, inlaid, music box which provides a variety of classic and popular music for shoppers--tunes to enjoy and browse by or even...to own! And from American artisans, there are many unique items, some of which are created especially for the MOLE HOLE. All this, and more, are located a short, pleasant ride into Northern Virginia from the Nation's Capital. In Hunter Mill Plaza on Route 123 (Chain Bridge Road), THE MOLE HOLE OF OAKTON, is easily accessible from Route 66, Route 7, and Route 50!

The shop, itself, is an appropriate setting for its remarkable inventory of collectibles and gifts. Charming, artistically decorated in mauves and gray, and highlighted by Tiffany lamps, it boasts an uncommon air of comfortable spaciousness where one can savor the fascination of the Tom Clark gnomes, the Wee Forest Folk, Edna Hibel prints and lithographs, designer jewelry, and a large assortment of Kaleidoscopes. A family affair, with a mother/daughter team as owner/manager and family members pitching in as the need arises, they offer many personal touches such as gift wrapping, shipping, layaways and special ordering. After only three years in operation, this exceptional boutique has built an enviable reputation for drawing customers from many miles--sometimes to simply look and listen to the Porter music box!

Anne Groff, with her daughter, Kathleen, are justifiably proud of the wide variety of distinctive items they provide--something for everyone and for every occasion.

RESTON

The first residents moved into Reston in 1964, making it Northern Virginia's newest community As the prototype for planned communities in this country, Reston was designed with an emphasis on walkways, bike trails, and neighborhood conveniences in an attempt to maximize energy efficiency, Residents of this modern-day Utopia have access to 16 swimming pools, 42 tennis courts, a public golf course, 44 ballfields, a health and fitness club, and a private country club. Four lakes, a nature center, playgrounds, 50 miles of walkways, three libraries, and 35 restaurants make Reston one of the most convenient places to live, as well as an interesting place to visit in Fairfax County

apparel

HARVEST TRADING COMPANY, 11160-C Southlakes Drive, Reston, VA, 22091. This store carries clothes with a comfortable air and a casual flair. They offer many one-of-a-kind garments, imported and domestic. They provide uniforms for the national "Pologator" team.

SEVEN CORNERS

kitchen supplies

KITCHEN BAZAAR, Seven Corners Shopping Center, Falls Church, VA 22044 VA. Tel: (703) 534-0220. See their story under Uptown.

SPRINGFIELD

In Colonial times, Springfield was one of four small villages within the enormous Revensworth Plantation. It was not until 1854, when a railroad station was built, that Springfield got its name, and it was nearly 57 years later that the first school was built. Looking at this bustling community today, it is hard to believe that as late as 1940, Springfield's population had never exceeded 150 people. Today, Springfield is home to the worlds largest warehouse and numerous industrial firms.

leather

GEORGETOWN LEATHER DESIGN, Springfield Mall; Tel: (703) 971-8151. For fine leather goods. See their story under Georgetown.

TYSONS CORNER

One of the most prosperous suburbs in the United States, Tysons Corner is a paradise for any shopper. Because it is home to two gigantic shopping malls, visitors to Tysons Corner are able to shop in eight of the country's finest department stores, including Nordstroms and Bloomingdales.. A third mall, slated to be completed by 1991, will house such famous names as Tiffany & Co., Hermes, Fendi and others.

accommodations

THE McLEAN HILTON AT TYSONS CORNER
7920 Jones Branch Drive
McLean, VA 22102
Tel: (703) 847-5000
1-800/HILTONS (Reservations)

Restaurant Hours:	Martinique's: 6 p.m. - 11 p.m.
	Flamingo's: 4:30 p.m. - 11 p.m.
Lounges:	The Cafe': 6 a.m. - 11 p.m.
	Atrium Lounge: 4 p.m. - 2 a.m.

How magnificent it is! A glass dome arches in elegance over the Atrium Lobby. Splendid foliage softens the expansive areas of rich green and peach marble as it reflects the gleam of glass and brass. Enchanting, oversized statuary preside over cozy corners and larger, beautifully furnished groupings that are perfect for relaxing or conversation. But much more than elegant beauty can be found at THE McLEAN HILTON AT TYSONS CORNER! Whether visiting or living in the Washington area, vacationing or on business, for overnight or longer, alone or with a family, as guest or host of superb in-house catering, you will delight in discovering service, concern and friendliness blended into the very finest of Virginia hospitality.

The HILTON hospitality extends to the local community and the international scene as well. Under the leadership of General Manager C. Arnie Quirion, named "Citizen of the Year" by the Fairfax County Chamber of Commerce, the hotel hosts a no-alcohol after-prom party for the area high school, raises money annually for Big Brothers, Leukemia Society, and various other charities, has been designated the official hotel for Wolf Trap, is sponsor of the International Children's Festival, and has even arranged a parade for the U.S. Olympic team.

In addition to a health club, pool, and jogging maps, bicycles are provided with no extra charge. Frequent guests are invited to become "Honor" members with many attending benefits. Children are welcomed, at no charge, to stay in their parents' room. The famous rub-a-dub-duck in every bath is NOT just for them! The Governor of Virginia, himself, enjoyed getting one when he visited this exceptional, AAA Four-Diamond award winning hotel--The McLEAN HILTON AT TYSONS CORNER.

SHERATON PREMIERE AT TYSONS CORNER
8861 Leesburg Pike
Tysons Corner, Vienna, VA 22180
Tel: (703) 448-1234
(800) 325-3535
FAX: (703) 893-8193
Dining and entertainment:

Ashgroves	Serving breakfast, lunch & dinner.
First Impressions	Seafood Raw Bar featuring piano music in the Lobby Lounge.
Baron's Lounge:	Small, intimate & relaxing.
Baron's Restaurant:	Elegant dining, dinner only.
Capital Club:	Nightclub with dancing.

Superlatives! Only superlatives fit the SHERATON PREMIERE AT TYSONS CORNER! Number one--it's larger than large! The tallest building in the area, it has two Penthouse, Presidential Suites, 455 splendid, extra-sized guest rooms with a view, 20 elegant suites, 35,000 square feet of space for meetings--apportioned in generous sizes and shapes, an Amphitheater, an attractive gift shop, a hair salon which boasts Washington's best stylist and a Grand Ballroom! There are also five uniquely different environments for a choice of dining, cocktails, entertainment and/or dancing, as well as extensive recreational facilities to challenge the most dedicated health enthusiast!

The lobby is breathtaking with its extravagant and spacious entrance beneath a vaulted, atrium ceiling and its glazed marble floors which lead into cozy, comfortable and carpeted areas, all of which are flawlessly appointed for working, waiting or relaxing. In the background, from the glitzy lounge, a piano softly accompanies the pleasant, harmonizing sounds of a nearby waterfall. Lavish trees, in oversized, terra cotta containers, and fresh flowers, in beautifully stylized arrangements, both accent and define the thoughtfulness given to the comfort and pleasure of guests.

The stars of the story, however, are the incredible members of a most congenial and accommodating staff! All are extraordinarily committed to providing a "home away from home" experience in the midst of splendor and magnificence!

fashion specialty retail

NORDSTROM
TYSONS CORNER CENTER
1961 Chain Bridge Road
McLean, VA 22102
Tel: (703) 761-1121
Hrs: Monday - Saturday 10:00 a.m. - 9:30 p.m.
Sunday: 11:00 a.m. - 6:00 p.m.
Hours are extended during the holidays.
Visa, MasterCard, American Express, and Nordstrom are accepted.

Family fashion with quality, variety and flair, took hold with vigor in the Washington Capital area when NORDSTROM leapt across the United

States to settle in Virginia--for the first time on the East Coast, at Tysons Corner and a year later at Pentagon City. Specializing in contemporary apparel, shoes, accessories and gifts, this giant of the fashion industry has captured the astute, upscale shoppers' market of this nation with 49 stores built on the principles of "service, selection, quality and value" espoused by its founder, John W. Nordstrom, in opening a small shoe store in 1901 in Seattle, Washington.

His descendents continue to live out that original commitment to the customer and to quality merchandise. In emphasizing service, "Personal Touch" offers group or individual shopping assistance in the store or at home. Friendly, experienced personnel stand by to assist with wardrobe planning, selecting or updating; gift buying, wrapping and mailing; and an "At Your Service" desk is prepared to check coats and packages; provide account and directory information; sell Metro passes or stamps; and provide strollers or baby accessories--all designed to ease and enhance your shopping experience!

From the company's own private-label merchandise to ready-to-wear lines from Anne Klein II, Donna Karan New York and Ellen Tracy, to exclusive couture by Caroline Herrera and Carolyne Roehm, with an extensive selection of shoes in sizes ranging from women's 2 AAAA to men's 14 D, NORDSTROM provides fashion at its very finest at Tysons Corner or Pentagon City (easily reached by Metro!)--where a customer is pampered with service, quality and elegance!

health and fitness

SPORTING CLUB AT TYSONS CORNER
8250 Greensboro Drive
McLean, VA 22102
Tel: (703) 442-9150
Hrs: Mon. - Fri. 6:00 a.m. - 10:00 p.m.
Sat., Sun. 8:00 a.m. - 8:00 p.m.
Not open on Christmas or New Years Day.
Visa and MasterCard are accepted.

Total fitness is like perfection! The closer we get the better we feel. And, the more aware we become of how much farther there is to go! It's tough to keep trying without adequate support and feedback. That's why health clubs are not a luxury and have continued in existence through history. They are the system that enables possibility to become a reality! Many different kinds, shapes and sizes of fitness centers have proliferated during the last decade. They have become available and convenient and they offer a variety of amenities! It's a matter of suitability and choice! A matter of what works for YOU.

THE TYSONS CORNER SPORTING CLUB has, for eleven successful years, lived the philosophy of pioneering in the field of fitness by offering a dynamically developing facility with services, programs, and amenities which are continually intriguing and challenging. There is a choice in types of memberships available, but each begins with a personal fitness evaluation of strength, flexibility and aerobic capacity leading to an individual fitness plan developed by the exercise physiologist. One-on-one training is available for those interested in a personally supervised system that can achieve maximum benefit in minimal time.

Cross training is encouraged with 75,000 square feet of an eclectic mix of weight training; jogging track; a seven lane Olympic pool; a cardiovascular center of Lifecycles, Stairmasters, bikes and treadmills; courts for squash, racquetball, basketball, and volleyball; seminars; aerobic classes; separate saunas, jacuzzis and steam rooms. Then, there are adventure trips to exotic places that furnish a fitting reward for the effort. This club offers a vibrant setting in which to work-out your life and enjoy it!

leather

GEORGETOWN LEATHER DESIGN, Tysons Corner; Tel: (703) 893-1620. For fine leather goods. See their story under Georgetown.

shopping

One of the newest, most sophisticated malls in Northern Virginia is the GALLERIA AT TYSONS TWO. Anchored by some of the most prestigious retail outlets in the country, Tyson's Two is fast becoming one of the area's most popular shopping complexes. Exclusive shops, charming restaurants, and a Concierge service that includes coat and bag check, gift wrapping and a courier service makes shopping at the Galleria at Tysons Two a very special event.

fashion specialty retail

NEIMAN MARCUS
2255 International Drive
McLean, Virginia 22102
Tel: (703) 761-1600

Mazza Gallerie
5300 Wisconsin NW
Washington, DC
Tel: (202) 966-9700

Hrs:	Monday . - Friday:	10:00 a.m. - 9:00 p.m.
	Saturday:	10:00 a.m. - 7:00 p.m.
	Sunday	12:00 noon - 6:00 p.m.

Special appointments with special arrangements.
American Express and Neiman Marcus credit cards are accepted.

For more than 80 years, NEIMAN MARCUS has held true to its original concept of offering the finest, most carefully selected merchandise in the world. Rare, imaginative pieces (many of which are exclusive), world renowned designer collections, and an unsurpassed dedication to quality, service and style have made NEIMAN MARCUS one of the most successful specialty stores in the United States.

The NEIMAN MARCUS stores at Mazza Gallerie and Tysons II take shopping to a new level of ease and elegance. Service is attentive and efficient, with expert sales associates alerting customers to new merchandise and special events. Neiman Marcus's unique customer recognition program, InCircle, awards points for every dollar spent in the store; enrollment begins with the customer's first Neiman Marcus Charge Card purchase, and points can be redeemed for prizes at year's end.

Of course, the NEIMAN MARCUS reputation is founded in fashion, Couture collections include Ungaro, Oscar de la Renta, Adolfo, Caroline Herrera, Louis Feraud, Anne Klein, Valentino and Mary McFadden. Escada, Laurel, Armani, Sonia Rykiel and Donna Karan are among the major names represented in designer sportswear. The Man's Store features finely tailored men's clothing, including the superb quality of Oxford suits and ready-to-wear options ranging from traditional to cutting edge.

kitchen supplies

KITCHEN BAZAAR, The Galleria at Tysons II; 1795M International Dr, McLean, VA 22102. Tel: (703) 883-1313. See their story under Uptown.

specialty retail

TIFFANY & COMPANY
Fairfax Square
8045 Leesburg Pike
Vienna, VA 22182
Tel: (703) 893-7700
Hrs: Monday - Saturday: 10:00 a.m. - 5:30 p.m.
Holidays hours are extended.
Visa, MasterCard, American Express, Diners Club, and JCB are accepted.

President Abraham Lincoln bought his wife, Mary, a beautiful pearl suite. With that purchase, the long standing relationship between Tiffany & Co. and the Washington, D.C. community began. In 1988 Tiffany designed the Blair House China for the presidential guest house. Now, Tiffany & Co. has placed its largest branch in the United States at Tysons Corner.

The exterior of the store has been designed in pink granite mirroring the Art Deco style of the New York Flagship. Inside, stately wood columns lead the way from the rotunda into three salons which house Tiffany's exclusive collections of jewelry, tableware and luxury accessories. The Jewelry salon is spectacular, furnished in cherrywood, with streamlined vitrines, elegantly appointed. Two private showing rooms are available for customers who wish to make their selections discreetly. Tiffany offers exclusive jewelry designs including collections by Elsa Peretti, Paloma Picasso and Jean Schlumberger. They also have exquisite china, crystal, silver, stationery, timepieces, fragrance, scarves and leather.

More than a century ago the Tiffany setting was created, raising the diamond on six prongs, to best reveal its quality and brilliance. For over 150 years Tiffany designers and craftsmen have inventively shaped and skillfully endowed every creation with inherent quality and enduring value. That is Tiffany Taste! From a key to an engagement ring, there is always special magic in the Tiffany blue box.

VIENNA

Incorporated into a town in 1890, Vienna was a rural community until the 1940's. Since then, rapid growth has transformed it into one of Northern Virginia's most prosperous communities. However, in spite of this enormous growth, Vienna still maintains a rich sense of community and history. Its recently restored Freeman House, once used as a Civil War hospital, and the 18th Century homestead of Jeremiah Moore are just two of Vienna's attractions that must be seen.

attractions

Seventy-five acres of wood, meadow, and scenic overlooks highlight the **MEADOWLARK GARDENS REGIONAL PARK** (1624 Beulah Road). The landscaped park gardens feature a spectacular assortment of trees, shrubs, and flowers that blend beautifully into natural surroundings.

events

A flea market, games, musical entertainment mark the **TOWN OF VIENNA CELEBRATION** on the Fourth of July.

Wolf Trap Farm Park is the site of Vienna's annual **CAROL SINGING.** Held in early December, this event features the Yultide sounds of the U.S. Marine Band and local choirs.

gift shops

THE CHANTICLEER SHOP
127 Maple Avenue, West
Vienna, VA 22180
Tel: (703) 281-1091
Hrs: Mon. - Sat. 10:00 a.m. - 6:00 p.m.
Thu. 10:00 a.m. - 9:00 p.m.
Sun. 1:00 p.m. - 5:00 p.m.
Closed on Sundays in August.
Visa, MasterCard, and American Express are accepted.

It's the "finishing touch" that counts! Like putting a bow on a package or adding ambiance to a home. Accents and accessories focus, underline and complete the house! And these people are the experts in accessorizing! THE CHANTICLEER SHOP in Vienna, Virginia, provide the ultimate in choice and variety for the home. The selection of decorative items includes framed pictures, lamps, mirrors, table and wall decorations.

With its matching carriage lamps and brown-awninged entrance, the shop is classic and comfortable, and possess an extraordinary inventory--including Swarovski, Department 56, Lladro, Hummel, Kaiser porcelain, David Winter, Royal Doulton and Lenox giftware, collector plates, pewter, Williamsburg brass reproductions, silver, enamel and limoges boxes, and a well-priced line of small upholstered furniture. Owner Ann McNeish hand picks everything that she brings into her shop from many trips over the United States. She also carries children's accessories, lace pillows and fancy soaps, as well as an impressive selection of large serving pieces, unique planters and elegant giftware.

From September to December, the highly popular Christmas room abounds in nutcrackers, decorated trees, Dickens Village Houses, Duncan Royale, Byer's Choice carolers and many other exquisite decorations. For any day, every day or Christmas day, unusual and striking gifts and collectibles await your choice.

theater

WOLF TRAP FARM PARK, Filene Center, 1624 Wolf Trap Road, Vienna. VA; Tel: (703) 703-255-1860. The only National Park for the performing arts. From Opera to Folk music, Wolf Trap offers an extremely diverse schedule of performances throughout the summer. A beautiful covered section affords protection from the elements, but the open lawn seating provides a good stage view and room to stretch out and have a picnic. Wolf Trap comes highly recommended for a really new and different theater experience. Shuttle buses are available from the Falls Church Metro stop beginning two hours before performances.

SECTION FOUR: CIVIL WAR IN RETROSPECT

BALL'S BLUFF BATTLEFIELD

In Loudoun County, one of the scenic areas of rolling hills and green pastures near Washington, D.C., there are farms with golden corn ready for harvest near expansive estates with horses in grass-covered pastures. Sometimes, cows can be seen grazing with wild deer that have ventured from the forest.

Cutting through the County is the majestic Potomac River, making its way from West Virginia past Harper's Ferry, on to Hancock, Maryland and the Virginia shoreline. In many places, the old C & O Canal, which was used to bypass the many rocks and rapids dotting the river, can be seen. There are only traces visible upstream, but the lower section is now restored and is part of the National Park Service.

The Potomac splits the earth into a series of islands as it passes through Loudoun County, where the shore remains a mixture of pastures and high bluffs. Near one of the bluffs is a small military cemetery, seemingly out of place amid the trees, rocks and open fields near the river. The cemetery is unique in being the smallest National Military Cemetery in the nation. Despite its size, it is as carefully monitored by the U.S. Park Service as if it were one of the larger, more well-known ones.

To understand how the cemetery came to be in this wild, unusual setting, the pages of history must be turned back to the early stages of the Civil War in 1861 and the Bull Run Battlefield near Manassas Junction, Virginia, roughly 25 miles from the banks of the Potomac and the Bluffs. Bull Run, also known as the First Battle of Manassas, was the first major battle of the War Between the States and would test the new, untried Confederate Army against a well-equipped Union Army.

The War had begun in April, and in July, many people still believed that it would only last for several months. When the gentry of Washington, D.C. learned that something was going on in the country, they quickly assembled their picnic baskets and hitched up their carriages for the trip to Manassas. They expected to enjoy an interesting outing, have a good time, and enjoy a colorful show.They arrived, spread blankets on the hillside, and settled in to watch the excitement.

The Confederate Army was inexperienced, untrained, and undisciplined. The various units didn't wear the same uniforms, and, it was said, there were many volunteers without uniforms at all. The Union regiments, better-equipped and better-trained, began to form on the open battlefield. Each arriving unit was cheered by those already there. The regimental bands played; their young drummers helping to keep the marchers in step. It was quite a show for the city folks. And they, too, joined in the cheering.

The bugles sounded and bands echoed the signals for formation as they were called out by the commanders. The grey-dressed Confederates, holding high their own battle flag, marched in from the other direction. The enemies paraded before each other. Cannons from both sides began to raise the dust and smoke. As some said later, the ranks of the blue started to melt like candles as they attacked, and the Confederates started to fall back. A line of Confederates that held were from Virginia. Their Commander was William Jackson, a young teacher at Virginia Military Academy. One of the confederate officers shouted "rally round the Virginians, there stands Jackson like a Stonewall!"

The Confederates regrouped and began to "yell like dogs from hell itself", wrote one Union soldier later. The battle blurred to civilians until blue-coated soldiers came into focus, in full route. Panic struck both soldiers and civilians alike, as the grim reality of pain and death shattered complacency and all rushed for the few roads going back to Washington.

The entire Union Army fell into retreat and scattered among the civilians. Death came to those in the rear because their escape had been hampered by the clogged road. Everyone was certain that the wild men, now called Rebels, would put them to death by the worst possible means. For days after the battle, soldiers slowly streamed into Washington. It was agreed that only God had spared their city, since the Confederates had chosen not to press their advantage.

As a result of the victory, only Arlington and Alexandria stayed out of the hands of the Confederate Army. The Confederates controlled Northern Virginia, with their headquarters in Fairfax and the main body of the Rebel troops camped near Centreville. Units were spread out along the Potomac River on the Virginia shoreline, including the Bluffs. Ball's Bluff was of keen interest to both armies, since upstream, there was a crossing near White's Ferry where many horses and wagons could ford the river. This unique area could dictate which army could make the next move.

At this time, there was somewhat of a lull in the War. The area of Ball's Bluff was a difficult place for a battle because of its high cliffs and heavy undergrowth. However, Harrison's Island could be reached by boat and an assault could be launched to the other side. Pressure mounted from Washington for something to be done about the Rebels across the river. Usually, when a mission is planned under pressure, the results can be disastrous. This was the case with the attack on the Bluffs. Ill-advised and unplanned, the commanders, who had not been chosen well, had little or no information about the the enemy in the area. All of this came to light in a Congressional investigation of the battle and concluded that The Battle of Ball's Bluff was "the most atrocious military blunder of the war".

As most of the trees stood bare of leaves in the late fall, the Union Army made their move. The Union commander, Colonel Baker, and his men crossed in boats on that October day, full of hope that a short and sharp battle would remove the enemy from the area. The troops in crossing the river went almost without fault. Equipped with poor information, the commanders dispatched their men into the wooded area. It was considered a frontal charge.

Meanwhile, the Confederate Regiments in the area were well-aware of the Union position and waited for the right moment to attack. The Confederate Commander, Colonel Evans and his men knew every path and rock in the area. The Union forces were split and caught like animals in a net. They broke and ran. Many of the officers were killed or wounded, and many soldiers were captured or drowned while trying to return to the island. The battle was lost. The Union Army suffered heavy losses.

In any conflict, some names are frozen in history. This battle brought out the heros and cowards alike. A young soldier wrote his mother about his first experience in battle. He was Oliver Wendell Holmes, Jr., later, a famous lawyer and Supreme Court Justice .

There was also a local resident of the area who became a hero in that battle. His name was Eliza White. He helped a Confederate unit work its way around enemy lines to capture over 388 Union troops near the beach along the river banks. Later, he was given his own command in the Confederate Army. He survived the war .

This battle, which became only a footnote among many battles of the war, left many dead and wounded. The Ball's Bluff cemetery was created to hold the remains of unknown soldiers. Only one was identified by a grave stone. The others were known only to their Maker. Those who survived from both sides would one day walk these cliffs, look down on the graves, and wonder if they had met or had known them in the course of the fight. Outside the cemetery walls another grave site holds the remains of the single Confederate soldier buried in that area. Not far from him is a larger stone identifying the location of the remains of the Union Commander, Colonel Edward Baker, who was killed leading his men near the Bluffs.

Veterans return year after year to this place. One group of Union veterans, as a gesture to heal the wounds of a nation, donated the head stone for the lone Confederate soldier near the cemetery wall. Another year, a reunion of Union regiments toured the whole area and remembered how they had looked death in the eye and survived. Some felt guilty because they had been left alive while others lay buried in this simple but beautiful cemetery. They walked the cliffs and strolled along the beach, recalling the horror of escaping in the water to the island. Their local guide pointed out the Confederate positions and the small Fort site, now overgrown.

One of the visitors recounted the story of his horror as the Union soldiers were suddenly attacked by a swarm of gray uniforms springing out of the bushes surrounding them. He added that he had had his gun barrel trained on a Confederate officer who, astride a white horse, was shouting orders and rallying his troops. The man continued to tell how he had fired but in the smoke and confusion he had not known the effect of that shot. He told them that he had always wondered if that officer had survived the war. The guide looked deeply into his eyes and slowly said, "Yes, he survived. I am that man." The visitor was elated and told the guide how happy he was to know that that he had been spared.

The group ended their visit, glad that they had come. Certainly, their children would always remember what had happened there. They all said fond-good byes to their guide, Eliza White.

Ball's Bluff Military Cemetery Site is located at the end of a long country lane that passes open fields on one side and heavily wooded areas on the other. It is located on Route 15, nine tenths of a mile, north of the Leesburg city limits. Take I-66 to the Leesburg (Rt. 7) exit to Tysons Corner. Continue west on Rt. 7 to the intersection of Rt. 15, near Leesburg, VA. A small, simple sign on the side of the road marks the way.

Fairfax Courthouse, Fairfax, Virginia

The original Courthouse still exists and is in use with portions that were added after the Civil War. The Courthouse was used as headquarters by both Confederate and Federal Armies. It was here that the first soldier died in the Civil War. His name was John Marr, an officer assigned to the Confederate outpost. He was killed when the outpost was attacked by a Federal raiding party.

Later in the war, Federal troops occupied the town and built a series of fortifications near the Courthouse. These were outer defenses to the main defense network, such as Fort Ward in Alexandria.

Near the Courthouse, across the street, is a church rectory that was used during the war to house visiting officers and their staffs. One visitor was General Stoughton. One night, the famous Confederate Raider, John Mosby, and his men came into the town on Ox Road, from the South, and captured the General, some of his men and a number of horses. This action prompted President Lincoln to remark that he regretted losing all of those good horses.

Directions: Proceed west on I-66. Take the exit at Rt. 123 South. Travel about two miles and the Courthouse is on the right.

Fort Ward Park, Alexandria, Virginia.

Fort Ward was one of the many outposts that protected the city of Washington from invasion by the Confederate Army. The fort was never attacked during the Civil War. However, one of the forts to the north of Washington near Silver Spring, MD. was attacked by the Confederate Army, led by General Early in 1864. All of the forts guarding the city were built to almost the same design. With the exception of Fort Ward, none of the forts were preserved as part of the Military Park System.

The city of Alexandria decided to rebuild a portion of Fort Ward to be part of its park program. A section of the fortifications with gun positions were reconstructed on the western side of the site. A museum on the site was built following the original specifications designed by the Corps of Engineers during that period.

Directions: Proceed south on I-395, across the 14th Street Bridge. Take the King Street exit to Alexandria. Follow King Street to Braddock Boulevard. Turn right on Braddock. Fort Ward Park is on the right, less than a mile after turning on Braddock.

The Manassas Battlefield Park

The Manassas Battlefield Park is the largest preserved Civil War site in Northern Virginia. This was the site of two important battles that took place about a year apart. The first battle was known as the Battle of Bull Run and the later battle was called the Second Battle of Manassas. The site is located near the town of Manassas, Virginia.

The Battlefield Park has a Visitors Center that houses a museum and a short slide and light show about both battles. Maps of the battlefield are available for both walking and driving tours. Points of interest includes the Henry Farm House, the Stone House, Bull Run Creek Stone Bridge and the famous unfinished railroad site. The battlefield has gun positions marked by detailed cannons, reconstructed to the exact specifications of those used during the battle .

Directions: Take I-66 west and turn right at the exit marked Rt. 234 North, Sudley Rd. The entrance is about a mile on the right.

bed & breakfast inns

SUNRISE HILL FARM
5605 Sudley Road
Manassas, VA 22110
Tel: (703) 754-8309
Check-in: 3:00 p.m.
Check-out: 11:00 a.m.
Arrangements required for rooms held after 6:00 p.m.
Reservations require a 50% deposit Visa or MasterCard.

the nation's capital

Steeped in history and natural beauty, the lovely, Federal period, home on SUNRISE HILL FARM, presides in stately elegance over the rolling countryside and its winding Bull Run Creek. Standing in the midst of the site of the First and Second Battles of Manassas, it offers its own unique grandeur and peacefulness for guests to enjoy overnight or longer as a Bed and Breakfast accommodation. Along with the farm animals, there are nearby facilities for renting horses and many intriguing trails to enjoy. The attractive, comfortable, period rooms, which are furnished beautifully with European and Early American antiques, are a wonderfully relaxing home-base for visiting in the busy, spread-out, Washington, D.C. area. It's a chance to not be stuck in the city!

Middleburg, Leesburg and the famous "hunt country" of Virginia offer sights, sounds and shopping not always available to the downtown visitor. And, within an hour from Manassas, one can be thrilled to the seasonally changing beauty of the Skyline Drive, the Blue Ridge Mountains and historic Harpers Ferry and other Civil War Battlefields. Virginia wineries are encouraging visitors to come to taste, and the breathtaking wonder of Luray Caverns is beckoning from near by.

Beautiful and near the Nation's capital, with historic surroundings, city advantages and country pleasures, SUNRISE HILL FARM is an ideal place for history zealots, artists, and peace seekers to stay! It's quite perfect for the rest of us, as well!

SECTION FIVE: DAY TRIPS

ANNAPOLIS

Annapolis is rich in history, its roots going back three-and-a-half centuries. In 1649, a group of Puritans from Virginia ventured to this area and established a settlement, naming it Providence. Annapolis, originally called Anne Arundel Town, was established across the river from Providence as part of the rapid expansion of the area. The growth was so quick that in 1694, Annapolis was named the capital of the United States and remained so for nine months.

These days, Annapolis is the capital of Maryland and the county seat of Anne Arundel County. It is perhaps one of the loveliest cities in the United States with more than 80 buildings that predate the American Revolution still standing. An architectural jewel, the William Paca House on George Street underwent 15 years of restorations. This 37-room Palladian-style mansion was built in 1765 by William Paca, a signer of the Declaration of Independence.

The United States Naval academy is a favorite attraction in Annapolis. Visitor can enjoy viewing the Naval Academy Chapel, where stained glass windows by Louis Tiffany bathe the interior with a gem-like glow. Below, the tomb of Revolutionary War hero John Paul Jones rests in a massive marble sarcophagus supported by four carved dolphins. Visitors are also welcome to tour the facility at any time on their own.

The historical sights and tour, along with a beautiful harbor, makes Annapolis a wonderful place to spend a day. Situated at the confluence of the Chesapeake Bay and the Severn River, Annapolis has a totally unique flavor and ambiance, and is a haven for seafood lovers. Once visitors have entered the town, they find it very easy to park their cars and walk to all the attractions.

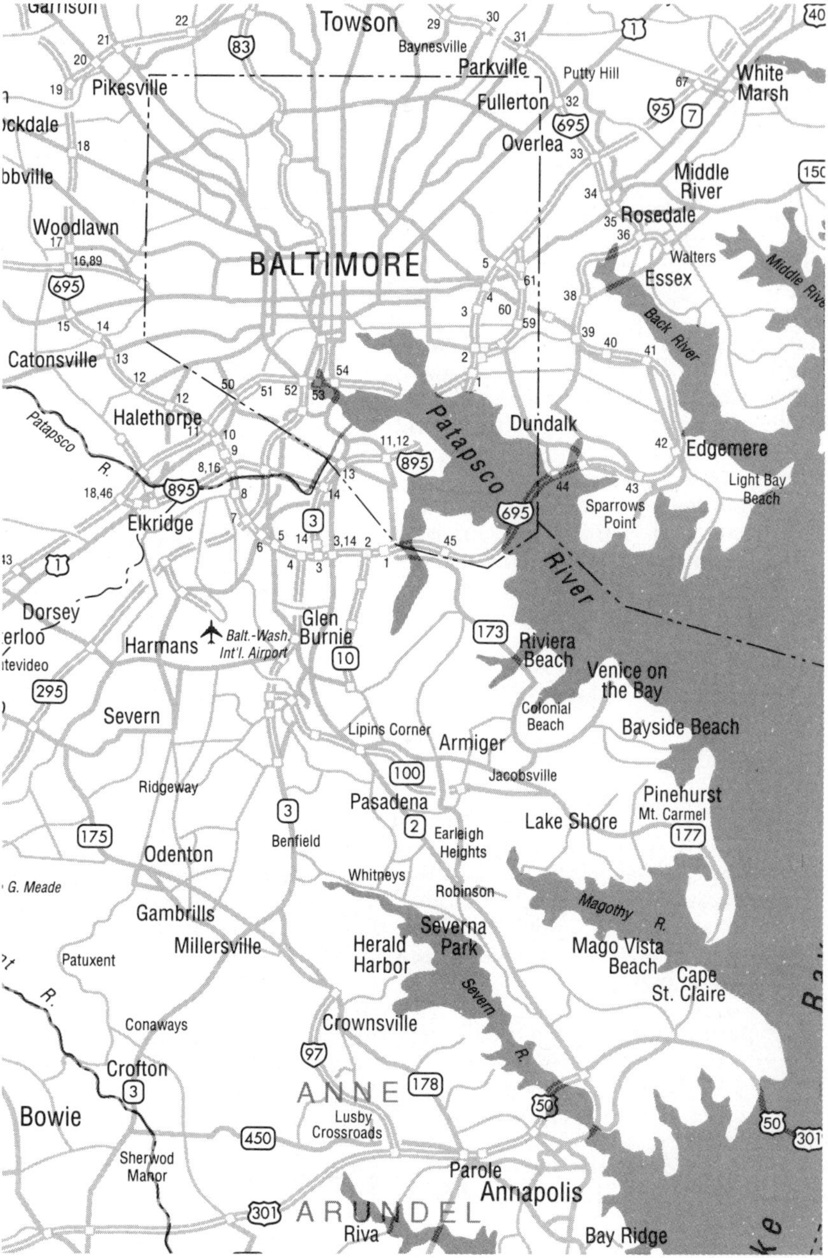
Towson
Baynesville
Parkville
Putty Hill
White Marsh
Pikesville
Fullerton
Overlea
Middle River
Rosedale
Woodlawn
BALTIMORE
Walters
Essex
Middle River
Back River
Catonsville
Patapsco R.
Halethorpe
Patapsco
Dundalk
Edgemere
Light Bay Beach
Sparrows Point
Elkridge
River
Dorsey
Harmans
Balt.-Wash. Int'l. Airport
Glen Burnie
Riviera Beach
Venice on the Bay
Colonial Beach
Bayside Beach
Severn
Lipins Corner
Armiger
Jacobsville
Ridgeway
Pasadena
Pinehurst
Mt. Carmel
Lake Shore
Benfield
Earleigh Heights
Odenton
Whitneys
Robinson
G. Meade
Gambrills
Magothy R.
Severna Park
Millersville
Herald Harbor
Mago Vista Beach
Patuxent
Severn R.
Cape St. Claire
Conaways
Crownsville
Crofton
ANNE ARUNDEL
Bowie
Lusby Crossroads
Sherwod Manor
Parole
Annapolis
Riva
Bay Ridge

BALTIMORE

Baltimore is a thriving and exciting city, located only about 20 miles away from Washington, D.C., but with a spirit all its own.

Baltimore instituted an urban renewal program years ago and it has proved to be one of the most successful in the country.

Today, visitors can enjoying viewing the city's carefully-renovated, marble-stooped rowhouses, along with the modern structures that dominated the downtown area. Charles Center is a striking sight, with its many overhead walkways, plazas and fountains.

No visit to Baltimore would be complete without a trip to Inner Harbor. Once dominated by decaying warehouses, Inner Harbor is now a vibrant and exciting area filled with great shopping, restaurants, nightlife, and other attractions. The National Aquarium is also located in Inner Harbor, and the U.S. Frigate *Constellation* calls the harbor home.

FREDERICKSBURG

History buffs would be wise not to miss Fredricksburg, Va.

Located 50 miles south of Washington, D.C., the city is most well known for the Battle of Fredericksburg, fought Dec. 13, 1862. The armies of both the North and the South in the Civil War experienced more than 100,000 casualties in the four battles that took place in what is now ,the **Fredericksburg and Spotsylvania National Military Park**. This land was desired greatly by both sides because it was located halfway between the opposing capital cities.

Four battlefields, located within 17 miles of Fredericksburg, may be toured. Five miles of Confederate entrenchments have been preserved. and the Fredericksburg National Cemetery, located on top of Marye's Heights, contains the graves of more than 15,000 Union soldiers. Fredericksburg was the final home of George Washington's mother, Mary Washington, and the only home his sister, Betty Washington Lewis, ever knew. Today, bus tours offer visitors first-hand looks at such sights as the **George Washington Birthplace Monument** in Northern Neck, Washington's mother's birthplace in Lancaster, and Robert E. Lee's birthplace in Stratford.

Visitors should also be sure to take in the **Mary Washington House** (Charles and Lewis streets) where an English garden featuring boxwoods that Mary planted herself; the Mary Washington Monument and Grave (Washington Ave.), which Andrew Jackson laid the cornerstone; and **St. George's Episcopal Church**, built in 1732. William Paul Jones, brother of John Paul Jones is buried there, as is John Dandridge, father of Martha Washington.

HARPERS FERRY

Harpers Ferry, W. Va., was named after Robert Harper, who began a ferry service there in 1747. Up until the time of the Civil War, Harper's Ferry was part of Virginia. It now sits in Jefferson County, named after Thomas Jefferson, who stated that this area was one of the most beautiful he had ever seen.

Harpers Ferry is located at the confluence of the Potomac and Shenandoah rivers. It is for this strategic location that George Washington recommended a federal arsenal and armory be built here in 1796. These facilities manufactured much of the artillery used in the War of 1812 and the Civil War, and was the target of John Brown's attack on Oct. 16, 1859, which he waged in order to incite the slaves to insurrection. Brown was captured and hanged by the U.S. Marines, under the leadership of Robert E. Lee.

In 1861 the town was abandoned by the Federals, but they destroyed the arsenal and armory before leaving. Shortly thereafter, in 1862, Stonewall Jackson captured the town, taking more than 12,000 citizens prisoner.

These events are all memorialized at **Harpers Ferry National Historical Park**. This 2,500-acre park rests in both West Virginia and Virginia and contains John Brown's fort, Civil War gun emplacements, the Stone Steps, Jefferson Rock, and Earthworks. Guided tours of the park are available.

Since it is located so close to the river, Harpers Ferry is also a popular spot for anglers, boaters, and white water rafters, and the nearby Appalachian Trail is a haven for backpackers.
The **Visitors Center** (Shenandoah St.) consists of five restored buildings, including a museum, and an exhibit on Store College, one of the first schools created for freed slaves at the end of the Civil War.

HILLSBORO

Nestled in the gap of the Short Hills Mountains on the western fringe of Northern Virginia lies the historic town of Hillsboro. With only two retail stores, one Bed and Breakfast, several antique shops and a few artists'galleries, it is the smallest incorporated town in the state. It's a great place to stop on the way to Harpers Ferry.

One of the two retail stores is Hunt Country Jewelers, owned and run by two Hillsboro residents, Ed and Claire Cutshall. Their store is as unusual as its setting. Ed Cutshall is both a highly skilled artistic goldsmith and a worthy gemologist. He focuses much of his time making original and commissioned platinum, 10K gold and gem pieces for his clientele, which ranges across the United States as well as Europe and Japan. He frequently uses unusual shapes, cuts, and exotic gems in his work. When time permits, Ed teaches occasional gem courses at George Mason University, where he's been an adjunct professor in the Geology Department.

His work is on display in their store (Thursday - Saturday from Noon - 7:00 p.m., Sunday from 1:00-5:00 p.m. or by appointment), which served as Hillsboro's Post Office for over 70 years. The preserved two-story clapboard building is on the StateRegister of Historic Buildings (as is the whole town) and proudly displays a locally-made sign complete with 24K gold-leaf hunting horn. Inside, it is restored to a charming Victorian country feeling, using the original oak frame Post Office boxes as a functional motif.

KINGS DOMINION

Visitors to the Capital City will find that Kings Dominion, just 75 miles south of Washington, is an ideal destination for a day trip. Rides, games, live entertainment, and scores of restaurants make Kings Dominion a perfect spot for the entire family.
Kings Dominion is divided up into four areas, and each has its own distinct atmosphere. International Street features restaurants like the Alpine Cafe, which specializes in German food, and Tower of Pizza, as well as rides like the Scrambler, Cinema 180, and the Eiffel Tower. You may want to catch a show at the Mason-Dixon Music Hall in Old Virginia, or take a ride on the Shockwave. In Safari Village, you can take a ride on a Monorail, where you will see live jungle animals. Scooby's Play Park and Yogi's Cave are just two of the attractions that make Hanna Barbera Land a favorite among children.

For those who would like to spend more than one day in Kings Dominion, the park offers some of the areas most attractive accommodations. Kings Quarters, located adjacent to the park boasts 248 guest rooms, a restaurant and lounge, as well as tennis and shuffle board courts and a swimming pool. The Kings Dominion Campground offers modern hook-ups, a swimming pool, showers, and a camp store. Both facilities provide their guests with free shuttles to the park.

A day at Kings Dominion is guaranteed to be fun for the whole family. Less than two hours from Washington, it is a perfect way to round out your Washington, D.C or Virginia vacation.

BUSCH GARDENS

If you can't afford a trip to Europe, consider driving down to Busch Gardens, one of Virginia's most popular amusement parks. Here, the unique ambiance of the Old Country has been faithfully recreated. Eight countries are represented here, and the authenticity of each will make you feel as though you have been on a Grand Tour.

Banbury Cross, with its Globe Theater, and Hastings, where the attractions include King Arthur's Chamber and Wizard Works, brings medieval England to life. At Her Majesty's Fancy in Banbury, you can buy English soaps, scents, and other gifts; or, you can research your family coat of arms at the Heraldry. Rides are a primary attraction at Hastings, with the most popular being the Questor, a ride that uses special effects to take you on a journey through the earth and air, as well as under water.

Heatherdowns, a recreation of Scotland, offers some of the parks most popular attractions. Foremost among them is The Loch Ness Monster, a double-looping steel roller coaster, and small children will be thrilled with Li'l Clydes, a delightful ride for small equestrians. While you're in Heatherdowns, be sure to stop at Highland Stables, were you will be able to see the world-famous Clydesdales.

France is well represented in the Aquitaine and New France areas, two of Busch Garden's most popular places for shows and shopping. Big name talent is usually on the bill at La Palais Royal Concert Theater in Aquitaine, while shopping Caribou Pottery Shop in New France specializes in handcrafted pottery gifts. Rides in these areas include the Le Mans Raceway in Aquitaine, and Le Scoot, a flume ride, in New France.

Rhinefeld and Oktoberfest have brought Germany to Virginia. In Oktoberfest's Das Feshaus, one of the largest restaurants in the country, you will experience a real German beer hall and sample traditional German Cooking. In Rhinefeld, you may purchase imported German gifts, including Hummels, clocks, and steins at German Gifts.

Finally, end your tour of the Old Country with stops in San Marco and Festa Italia, where you will experience the finest Italy has to offer. Sample authentic Italian pizza and sausage at Festa Italia's La Cucina, or shop for fine Italian imports at Bella Casa in San Marco.

Whether you enjoy the thrills of double loop roller coasters, or if shows and shopping are more your pace, you are guaranteed to find something you will enjoy at Busch Gardens. Europe is only a few hours south of Washington, so after you're through seeing the sights of this country, why not stop and sample some of the Old Country's at Busch Gardens.

COLONIAL WILLIAMSBURG

Step back in time, and visit one of the most cosmopolitan cities of 18th-century America. Set on over 173 acres, Colonial Williamsburg is one of this country's most accurate reconstructions of a colonial city. Historic buildings, museums and galleries, and people who live their lives as the city's original residents had, make Colonial Williamsburg an ideal place to learn about life in early America.

There are scores of things for a family to do in Colonial Williamsburg. Start off by visiting the homes of the people who lived here; nearly every social class from planters to slaves is represented here. Watch craftspeople at work as they create furniture, wigs, shoes, and clothing using the same tools and techniques as artisans did in the 18th century. Sample colonial cooking at one of Williamsburg's many restaurants and taverns, or shop at the many fine stores that line Duke of Gloucester Street or Merchants Square.

Don't leave as soon as the sun sets over Williamsburg, as that is perhaps the city's most magical time. Attend a ball or a less formal dance, watch an 18th century play, or stop at Gambol's tavern and enjoy some games or entertainment.

If you're going to be in the area for a while, you may want to stop at historic Jamestown, the first English Colony in the New World. Jamestown is as rustic as Williamsburg is sophisticated, and it will give you a good idea of how difficult life was for the first colonists. You'll visit the glasshouse, where artisans demonstrate the art of 17th century glassblowing; Jamestown Festival Park, where you will find reconstructions of Jamestown's first fort, ship, and Powhatan Village; and New Towne, a section of the village where residents, having grown prosperous due to the tobacco trade, built more substantial homes.

While you are visiting Washington, D.C, you'll learn a lot about the history of the United States. Visit Williamsburg, and, if you have time, Jamestown, and you'll discover what life was like when this nation was only a colony.

MIDDLEBURG

West of Washington, in the heart of Virginia's wine country on the Piedmont Plateau, lies the little town of Middleburg. Home of two of Virginia's best wineries, a drive through the scenic countryside to Middleburg is a perfect way to spend a day.

Wineries and vineyards are the biggest attractions in this tranquil section of Virginia. When you are visiting Middleburg, be sure to stop at Meredyth Vineyards. This world-class vineyard is famous for its French-American hybrid and European vinifera wines. Another place you might be interested in visiting is the Piedmont Vineyards. Located on a picturesque 18th-century estate, Piedmont produces fine white varietal wines. A tour and tasting session at either vineyard is guaranteed to make you a connoisseur of Virginia's wines.

A visit to Middleburg and Virginia's wine country is a perfect addition to a Washington holiday. If you need to escape the hustle and bustle of the Capitol City, consider spending a day in Middleburg; the drive to this picturesque area alone will make it worth the trip.

HUNT COUNTRY

The beautiful town of Middleburg is located in Loudoun County, Virginia and is considered the unofficial capital of the Hunt Country. Throughout the county we find people involved with horses and hounds in steeplechase and point-to-point horse racing and the traditional Virginia Foxhunt. Why the chase?

Foxhunting means many different things to many different people and there is much more to the sport than meets the eye. Hunting the fox is a cold November morning with a faint, hazy mist beginning to fade as the sun reaches to warm the land and dissipate the shadow. Anticipation fills the air and the fox prepares to elude. A dozen or so horseback riders are uncertain where the day will take them, but they are confident that the never ending chase, fraught with exhilaration and danger, will be its own reward.

Foxhunting takes many forms, from the man silently perched on a hilltop listening for the sound of horns and hounds to the handsomely dressed riders on their well-turned-out mounts flying across field, fence and stream in hot pursuit of the hounds. Caravans of cars carry supporters and onlookers who enjoy the thrill vicariously, with each glimpse of the hunt riders and maybe, the fox. It is often said that "people first hunted to live, but now many live to hunt."

It is interesting to note that the red and grey fox exist, today, in significant numbers because the hunt itself does everything possible to protect the species.

As in any sport, foxhunting consists of rules and skills developed over the course of hundreds of years. Rules are a product of good manners and they are observed among the insiders, toward landowners and the society that surrounds them. Endless pains are taken by the Master of Fox Hounds and the entire hunt to assure good relationships with landowners. Numerous do's and don'ts reflect the respect that the hunt has for their hosts, such as not blocking the road, not galloping over any seeded or growing fields, shutting all gates and not breaking fences. Entertainment and good will are promoted by special invitations for landowners, farmers and followers to hunt-sponsored parties, picnics, point-to-points and hunt balls.

The Master of Hounds is the director of the carefully orchestrated event. He or she requires punctuality, skill and strict observance of decorum. The Master has absolute authority over behavior in the field. The Master's ultimate responsibility is providing sport for some neighbors without annoying others.

When the morning ritual begins, it's a "Good morning" to the master and a proper turn- out (horses and riders suitably dressed and looking smart). The scarlet coat is a product of an ambitious tailor, named Pink, with an overabundance of material for British Soldiers' uniforms after the American Revolution. The color, of course, was red and he touted it as more easily seen than the standard green. Stocks around the neck double as bandages for damage to horse or rider and are held fast with a straight gold pin. Each rider requires a horse with heart, stamina, good training, and conditioning. A few of the in-terms must be mastered such as: a hound feathering with his stern (wagging his tail), giving tongue (barking), carrying a great head (hounds working in good order), marking a fox to ground (fox in his hole), draw a blank (not finding a fox), rat catcher (less formal dress for cub hunting which is foxhunting early in the season for the purpose of training young hounds), butcher boots (plain black riding boots), and the brush (tail of a fox).

Then, it's on to draw at the cover (look for the fox in a wooded area) and coax the fox from the woods. A series of double toots on the horn and they are gone away (the hounds are in hot pursuit of the fox), "All on sir" (the message to the Master that all hounds made it from the cover) "the hounds are sounding good voice" (barking with purpose). The idea is to keep the hounds in view while surmounting difficult terrain, fences, coops (jumps over fences resembling chicken coops), rivers, and ditches. As each obstacle is tackled with a "will we or won't we?", a rider may unwittingly separate from his horse. Others must do their utmost to catch and return the horse to its owner. This is considered fair play. When the fox is accounted for, is lost or, more usually, put to ground. The hunt is over.

At the conclusion of the hunt, concern shifts to the horse. The last two miles must be at a walk to cool down and relax. The riders' responsibility is to make sure the horse is properly groomed, fed, and put up for the night. Every good rider knows that when a horse has worked long and hard in the hunt field, he deserves the riders respect, care, and perhaps a special treat.

Though the hunt country is shrinking with development, rising costs, and civilization closing in on small towns and counties, the hunts struggle to protect their right to a sport, which is as old as time itself and as new and fresh as the dawn of each new day.

LEESBURG

One of Northern Virginia's oldest and most historic towns is just a short drive from the District of Columbia. Anyone vaguely interested in the history of the United States and Virginia would be wise to visit historic Leesburg in Loudon County. Rich in history, this little town has played a vital role in many of the most important episodes in the life of the United States.

Leesburg, originally known as Georgetown, was founded in the early 1700's, and several of the towns earliest buildings, including a log cabin and George Washington's headquarters, are still standing. Leesburg residents were important players in the events leading up to the Revolutionary War. In 1774, a group of them drafted the "Loudon Resolves" in protest of The Stamp Act. When the British invaded Washington in the War of 1812, Leesburg became a refuge for many of the city's fleeing residents. During the Civil War, Leesburg hosted the

Confederate army after its victory at Manassas, and the Battle of Balls Bluff took place here in 1862.

Today, Leesburg has been beautifully restored and evokes an atmosphere of a past era. While you are there, be sure to visit Oatlands, a prime example of a classic Virginia plantation. The center of the area's thriving agricultural economy in the 1800's, Oatlands once covered over 3,000 acres and had its own sawmill, gristmill, brick foundry, blacksmith shop, school, church, and store.

Another popular attraction is Morven Park, one of the area's most beautiful mansions. Located in Virginia's hunt country, Morvan Park is a beautiful example of turn-of-the-century architecture. Highlights of a tour of Morvan Park include the Museum of Hounds and Hunting and the Carriage Museum. Morvan Park offers something for everyone, including picnic facilities and hiking trails.

A day in Leesburg is the perfect remedy for those who may be feeling burned out by a fast-paced Washington vacation. Just an hour from the capitol, the historic atmosphere and many attractions found in Leesburg make it a wonderful day-trip destination.

POTOMAC MILLS

Potomac Mills is a bargain hunters' dream come true and one of Washington's leading attractions.

Located 30 minutes from downtown Washington in Prince William, Va., the mall is huge complex of manufacturers' outlets. Over 200 manufacturers are represented here, offering nearly any type of merchandise imaginable. Discounts are generally 20- to 60-percent off, and feature everything, from the best in home furnishings and decor to designer clothing.

Also located within Potomac Mills is more than 20 of the finest restaurants, giant video screens that provide information and entertainment, ten movie theaters, and special events all year long.

Special incentives are offered to tour groups, bus drivers and tour leaders. Those new to the facility may stop by the special kiosk to pick up mall and tourist information.

SECTION SIX: BIKE AND HIKE

For the biking enthusiast, the nation's capital offers an abundance of bike trails. Whether you plan to make a day of it, or just want to spend a couple of hours in the fresh air, taking in the sites, a capital bike ride is guaranteed to be a memorable experience.

the nation's capital

Memorial Bridge is a central location and can be the starting point for many different rides. Riding down the left hand side of Memorial Bridge toward the Lincoln Memorial, bear left at the end and follow the bike path down by the Potomac River. Follow the trail past the Kennedy Center, and before long you will find yourself on the Rock Creek Park Trail. The trail meanders under historic bridges, through small, green parks, and up to the National Zoological Park. Bike riding is not allowed in the Zoo, but bike lock-ups are available, and many exhibits can be enjoyed while walking through the Zoo with bike in hand. Continuing past the Zoo, there are many picnic areas next to Rock Creek, and you will surely be tempted to take a break and enjoy the scenery. The path comes to an end at Beach Drive, which is closed to traffic on weekends and holidays, providing an excellent surface for biking. A word of caution though, the bike trails are also used by walkers, joggers, and families with small children, so please be observant and considerate of others.

For another interesting ride beginning at Memorial Bridge, go on a "monumental" bike trip. Facing the Lincoln Memorial from Memorial Bridge, take the path to the right and follow Ohio Drive toward West and East Potomac Parks. Pedal through West Potomac Park, with the Potomac on the right side and the Tidal Basin on the left. After crossing the bridge, you will see a lovely flower garden straight ahead of you which is especially beautiful in the spring. From there, bear left by the Japanese Cherry Trees, and you will soon see the Jefferson Memorial. Back-track to Ohio Drive and continue to East Potomac Park, which is surrounded on three sides by water. When you are pedaling around the tip of this small peninsula, don't be startled by the sculpture The Awakening at Hain's Point. Follow the loop around as far as Buckeye Drive, and to avoid heavy traffic, make a left to return to Ohio Drive, then make a right, and you'll be heading back to the Lincoln Memorial. When you arrive at the Lincoln Memorial, bear right toward the Mall. The Mall is approximately two and one half miles in length, has a wide gravel surface perfect for biking. Pedaling past the Reflecting Pool, the Washington Monument, and the magnificent Smithsonians with their various sculptures and gardens, is truly a "monumental" way to see Washington, D.C.'s historic sights.

If that's not strenuous enough, an eighteen mile ride begins just north of Memorial Bridge at Roosevelt Island. Named the Mount Vernon Trail, this lovely path winds its way next to the Potomac River to the historic home of George Washington. Look out on your right for a beautiful sculpture " Gulls and Waves"; it's between the Parkway and the Potomac, just past Lady Bird Johnson Park. The memorial is dedicated to the Navy and Merchant Marines. Continue past National Airport (watch out for cars!) and the Washington Marina, and soon you'll be on Union Street, entering Old Town Alexandria. You may be ready for a snack or refreshment by now, and the smell of freshly baked bread at Deli on the Strand will surely entice you to enjoy a fresh muffin or fruit juice. Once you've left Old Town, the trail winds its way on to Mount Vernon. But don't go too fast! You'll want to savor the sights along the way. Standing at the edge of the Potomac, imagine that you're seeing it as George Washington saw it two hundred years ago. After you've climbed that final hill and arrived at Mount Vernon, you'll surely agree that the scenery was worth the ride. While there, lock up your bike and take a tour of Mount Vernon, or simply relax at the picnic area. If an eighteen-mile, one-way bike ride is too much for you, try parking your car at Belleview Park, just south of Alexandria on the George Washington Parkway, and pedaling the rest of the way. You won't miss any of the marshes, trees and other scenery that make the Mount Vernon Trail one to be remembered.

One of the first places visitors to Washington, D.C. want to visit is Georgetown. For "fat tire" bike fans, it is especially worth a visit because the Chesapeake and Ohio Canal, better known as the C & O Canal, starts there. Under the supervision of the National Park Service, the Canal is kept in excellent repair and the scenery is splendid. From time to time, you'll want to park your bike and hike up to where you can get a breathtaking view of the Potomac River. The Canal continues for 184 1/2 miles, all the way to Cumberland, Maryland, so you can pedal to your heart's content. The gravely, and sometimes rocky surface make the towpath more suitable to mountain bikes than racing bikes.

One of the most well known bike trails to area bicyclists is the Washington and Old Dominion trail. It originates in Shirlington, Virginia and follows the old W & OD train route, continuing 45 miles north to Purcellville, Virginia. There are several places to begin your exploration of the W & OD Trail; so you'll want to contact the Northern Virginia Regional Park Authority for a guidebook. (703) 352 5900.

If you'd rather go on foot, you can still see many of Washington's points of interest. Many parts of the city avail themselves to hikers, but two of the most thrilling tours are of the East and the West Mall.

The biggest attraction in the East Mall is the Smithsonian Buildings, but there are many other places to see. If you start at Constitution and Pennsylvania, head west on Constitution where you will be able to see The National Gallery of Art, The Mellon Fountain, The Federal Trade

Commission, The U.S. Capitol Gatepost, The National Archives Building, The Department of Justice, The National Museum of Natural History, and The Internal Revenue Building. At this point you will want to turn left just short of 14th Street and make a left onto Jefferson Drive. Heading East on Jefferson, you will see The Department of Commerce, The National Museum of History and Technology, The Freer Gallery of Art, The Smithsonian Castle, The Air and Space Building, The Arts and Industries Building, The Hirshhorn Museum and Sculpture Garden, The National Air and Space Museum, and the Botanical Gardens. You can end your tour with a walk around the Capitol.

The West Mall is beautiful and inspirational. Start at the Washington Monument and proceed south where you will find the outdoor Sylvan Theater and The Bureau of Printing and Engraving. When you find yourself at the Tidal Basin, bear right and head towards the Jefferson Monument. Enjoy the Japanese Cherry Trees which, beautiful anytime, are magnificent while in bloom. Walk around the Tidal Basin until you reach the Reflection pool, then turn left and follow it to the Lincoln Memorial. Facing the Reflection Pool from the Lincoln Memorial, head toward the left and you will come to the Vietnam Memorial. Keep following the side walk and you will come to Constitution Gardens, where you can rest on the grass and make friends with the ducks.

No matter what you want to see in Washington, you will find plenty of hiking trails and bike paths to see them. It's good exercise and a real thrill the first time you take any of these trips, but the exhilaration and well-being you gain will stay with you long after your holiday has ended.

SECTION SEVEN: KIDDIE KAPERS

As the author, it was my pleasure to enlist the able assistance of budding young writers at All Saints School. It was suggested at the beginning of this project that the best people to talk to children are children themselves. Kids read and believe these kids just like you, because they have some very definite ideas and some pretty sound advice. And parents,... Ahhhhhh,... go ahead and read what the kids had to say. They might just have some good advice for you too.

kid's best choices

First Grade, All Saints School

I like

the Washington Monument because:

I have never been in it, but I want to see whats inside.

Shaun Gar

I got to go on top. I saw people and the Lincoln Memorial.

Jennifer Buckley

I want to see it.

Eric Salsberg

I want to go to the top and look out.

Courtney Waksmunski

I want to go up to the top.

Mathew Carroll

Out of the windows you can see planes, and I saw the President.

Dana Fitzwater

There is an elevator that goes up high.

Richard Bowen

When I go there, there's a lot of people around it.

Brooke Sefchick

the Lincoln Memorial because:

I saw President Lincoln. It was neat.

Danny Rosinski

There was lots of people inside.
Nicole Bergeron

the park (Mall) in Washington DC, because you can climb trees.
Evan Chicoine

the church (Cathedral). They had lots of people in it.
Gerald

the White House. George Bush lives there.
Meghan Leonard

the Smithsonian because it has dinosaurs.
Octavia Schramm

the park (Mall) in Washington DC, because you can climb trees.
Evan Chicoine

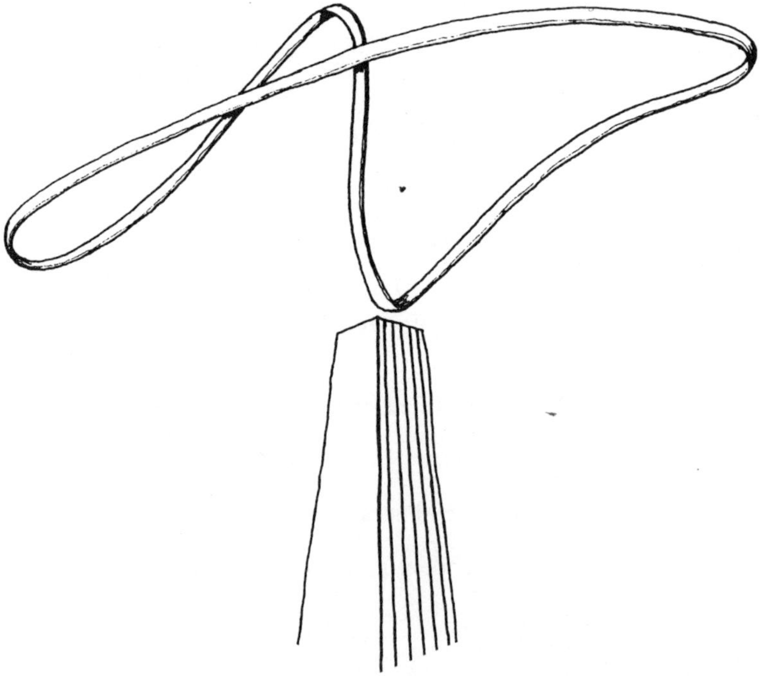

Third Grade, All Saints School

Smithsonian Museum

At the Smithsonion you can look at very neat stuf. You can lean more about things. Or see things you have not seen befor.

Megan M.

Smithsonian National Zoological Gardens

Washton zoo is a fun place because the animales do funny things. It is allso fun because you get good food and you can pet the sheep. You can eat ice cream and wacth the animales get feed food.

Matt

At the zoo there are funny animals. And some of the animals you would see are lions, tigers and bears and when you go there you will learn all about them.

Suzanne

Smithsonian Museum of Natural History

When you walk in you will see a giant elifent. It has tellifons arand it. Thay tell about them. There are big and little things. I can't tell you anymore but this. There are lots of floors. "Go in all of Them!"

Jamie Rudzenski

National Aquarium

Kids would like to go there because you can see sharks, school fish and dollfins and there is a little pool and in it is little star fish and snails that you can pick up. And there is a little birds thing and in the birds thing all kinds of birds. And if you go out of the birds thing is a laser thing that you can walk through. And there is a bar and if you look down there is the very beautiful thing.

Rose Wall

Baltamore Aqarium is a nice place because there is beautiful creatures. Ones who fly some who swim and some that crawl. There are people that water ski on dolfins. They have food stands and nature walks.

Joe

Baltamore Aquarium is a good place to go to because it has alot of beutiful creatures. It also a manmade rain forest. The baltamore aquarium has fish, sharks, frogs, eels and it has 3 beluga whales. It is 20 stories tall. So why don't you visit there I now you'll have a lot of fun.

Nathan

Manassas Battle Field Museum

You can look at interesting stuff like different bullets or clothes that might have been worn by important people from the past or canones from the past.

Anisa A.

They have the Heney house, Stonewall Jackson, pathes, Rodinson house, canons. When you go there you would see all of the things that they wore, bullets, the stone house, in a building they have guns, clothes that the ladies wore.

Meghan

Fourth Grade, All Saints School

Smithsonian Institution Museum

Museums are fun & exciting places to go while your in Washington D.C.In most museums you would probably have to pay, but not in Washington D.C! Here's a an exciting museum to visit:

The Smithsonian Institution is the biggest museum in Washington D.C., it's suprisingly big & is actually many different buildings combined. It has 100 million historical pieces that many people enjoy, while visiting. There's a huge object that might catch your eye, it's a eight ton stuffed elephent, the largest stuffed animal in the world!

Other than that you will see dinosaur skeletons, other stuffed animals, air & space exibits, a giant blue whale, & more!

My impresion of the Smithsonian Institution is it's an exciting place to go because there's so many impressive things to see!

Jessie Tamer

My favorite place in Wasington D.C. is the Smithsonian. The Smithsonian has lots of museum. Some of my favorites are The Museum of Natural History and The Air and Space Museum.

You should go there because it is fun and you can look at lots of things. There is an Insect Zoo for children too. Perants and children would like it.

Hagan B.

One of my favorite places is the Smithsonian Associates restaurant located under the Museum of Natural History. The types of food are: a full range of non-alcoholic drinks, a buffet and different plates from the menu. They have seafood, steak. and fancy cakes: Double Death by CHOCOLATE. This is a sit down restaurant with wooden tables and chairs and a table cloth. It costs only what an ORDINARY cafeteria costs, if you are a Smithsonian Associate. My Grandfather and I go there all the time. Sometimes we invite others we love to go with us.

Brian Clark

Wait until you come to this zoo they have all kinds of animals. I liked the monkeys, bears and other animials. The Bald eagle was my favorite. It's in Washington D.C. and its free.

Lisa Haulsey

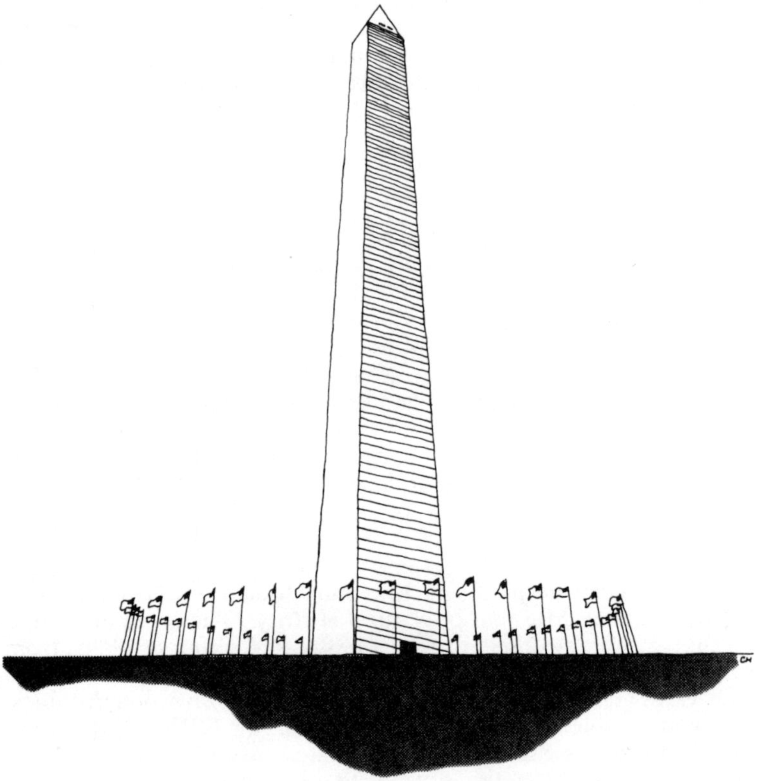

the nation's capital

The Washington Monument

I like the Washington Monument because I think that it is nice to learn about. It is shaped like a pencil. The Washington Monument is very huge and wonderfull to look at. You can go up an elevator and you can see the whole city of Washington D.C.

There are two different kinds of stones on the Washington Monument. The bottom stones were laid before the Civil War. The top stones were laid after the Civil War. When you look at it you can see the difference between the stones.

You can see the Washington Monument from a long way away.

The Washington Monument is a very nice place that honors the first president of the United States. He was George Washington.

Catherine Martin

I think peopl would like the George Washington Monument because it honers our first presdent. The flags that suround it are colorful. Going up alot of stairs is very tiring I'd much rather take the elevator. Looking down from the top of the George Washington Monument is a great vew.

I think it would be interesting to see what it's like inside.

I wouldn't like going up the stiars.

Joshua Young

National Aquarium

National Aquarium - It's a nice place to go. It has big fish tanks. Their are lots of different kinds of fish. They have sharks.

Beth

A good place to go when you're visiting Washington D.C. is The national aquarium. It was fun because there was so much to see like: fish, turtles, & a portrayal of a rainforest. It was fun for me because I went to the shark tank & it looked like they would come up & bite you, but if they tried they would hit the wall.

Kristen Rooney

Cox's Farm

One of my favorite places to visit is Cox's farm. I remember this trip well, because it was a time when my whole family got together -- aunts, uncles, and cousins -- for a day of hay rides and pumpkin picking. Once we met, we set off to see the animal exhibits. My favorite animal was the pig because he got slop on my sister. Next, we went on the hay ride. My cousins and I had a hay fight until mom told us to stop. I especially liked the cut-out pilgrims, ghosts, and witches that we passed. During the hayride, we made a stop at the pumpkin patch, in search of the perfect pumpkin. Then after we each found the pumpkin we each wanted, we walked to the edge of the road to await the next wagon. Once we got on the hayride again we set back off to where we started. Then my cousins and I looked at the crafts, while eating warm applebutter. They had almost everything imaginable. There were jams, jellies, dried corn, and little dolls made of hay--and pumpkins with silly faces painted on them. After looking at the crafts, we set off to the pumpkin fort, with tunnels and secret hiding places, except for one thing, it was covered with pumpkins! Big ones, little ones, and medium sized ones covered the entire place! Well after we had our fill of climbing a mountain of pumpkins, we were getting hungry. So, tired but happy, we set off for the car, carrying our pumpkins, and looking forward to a picnic lunch. Once we were full and sipped all of our Hot Coaco, we packed up and got into the car. I don't think I made it 15 minutes before I fell asleep. Even though I was tired, I will never forget the day at Cox's farm!

Sean Van Vleet

Pet Farm

Pet A farm - It's a fun place to go. It has real big turtles that you can ride on. It has pigs, rabbits, cows, sheep, monkeys, and much more. They have horse rides and you can feed the animals.

Beth

Washington Cathedral

My favaorite place to visit is the Washington Cathedral. This is the largest Chirch in the United States. One of the presidents was baried here. He was Woodrow Wilson.

There are lots of meaterals in the workshop of the Washington Cathedral. You usualy make a Brass rubbing of nights and armers with speaseal kinds of crayons and paper.

This gothic-style cathedral, started in 1907 and was just compleated. They have a childrens chapel, a room scaled down to our size, stain glass and other cathedral crafts.

I rote about this because it is neat and fun to visit in Washington D.C.

Jenny S.

Lake Manassas

Is located in Nokesville around 30 miles from D. C. It is reservour for Manassas. Theare is a golf course being bilt by it. You can rent rowboats or electric boats too.

You can fish but not swim. You can enter in a bass tournament. It is a large lake with lots of coves. If you don't have fishing suplies there is a store calledMayhughes 1. They sell fishing license too.

Children's Museum

The best place to go is the Children's Museum. The Children's Museum is super, when you invite a couple of friends for your child. The kids can eat forien food, play in a maze, make paper hats, and even pretend your a firefighter!

I choose this place because when I was only 7 years old and had the best of fun.

Stephanie Gibson

National Airport

National Airport - You can go and wach the planes land. The noise is very loud. It has a river, and a place where you can have a picnic there.

Beth

Library

I like the library you will too. It has so many books in the library and when you can't find a book their are computers that tell you where to find that book.

The nice thing about the library you can get own library card when your a kid. And when you need to copy something there is a copy-machine.

Marrissa Carta

Occoquan

I wrote about Occoquan because it is a very interesting place to visit. I like the arts and crafts stores, the marina, the Christmas shops, the toy stores, the dollhouse shops, and the restaurants. I always have fun in Occoquan. I hope you will, too.

Occoquan is authentic 18-century mill town on the bank of the Occoquan River. It was made a Virginia historic landmark in 1983. Occoquan offers everything from antiques and arts to crafts and dining in its many shops.

Here are some handy tips for visiting Occoquan. You might enjoy a picnic on the banks of the river. Don't miss the Occoquan Craft Shows in June and September. In December there is a Christmas House tour, and Santa Claus arrives by boat. You might enjoy staying at the old Rockledge Mansion on the hill which has been opened as an inn.

Chris Baronavski

Kilroy's
5250 AB Port Royal Road, Ravensworth Plaza
Springfield, Va 321-7734

Kilroy's takes all major credit cards. The house specialty is prime rib. Kilroy's is a family restaurant that does birthday parties and sponsors baseball and soccer. Fargo Wells is an employee there who creates and dresses up in his own holiday costumes to delight the customers.

Hours: Children's menu
11:30 A.M. - 2 A.M.

Chris Baronavski

Center For The Arts
8959 Center Street in Old Town Manassas 368-FINE

The Center offers classes in music, dance, drawing, painting, pottery, creative writing, and drama. It also serves as a recital hall and gallery.

I choose The Center for the Arts because I take violin lessons there.

Chris Baronavski

Patomac Mills Mall
I-95 Exit 52 at Dale City 643-1770 or 490-5448

One of the world's largest outlet malls. There are over twenty eateries. Bus tours are available.

Hours:
10 A.M. - 9:30 P.M. Monday - Saturday
11 A.M. - 6 P.M. Sunday

Chris Baronavski

Washington D.C. Parks

Parks in the city are beautiful. I like them because they have interesting sculptures, flowers and nice people. Its a good place to read, walk and take pictures.

Lisa Haulsey

Great Falls Park

Great Falls is a nice park to climb rocks and take pictures. There are mules pulling the boats up the channels. You can climb rocks to see waterfalls. The best part is it's free and fun!

Lisa Haulsey

Tips For Trips (Tips for kids and grownups)

1. Bring a firsst aid kit. Make sure you have change for emergency phone calls!

2. Listen to the weather. If cold bring coats, if hot bring or buy cold drinks.

3. Bring money for a sovenier.

David

1. Bring snacks like crackers, cookies, and pickles.

2. Take things to do like crayons, writing tablets, colored pencils, and games.

3. Take a map with you in case you forget where you are going.

Craig Eckert

Tips for trips bring cookies, crackers, chips, sandwiches, drinks, games, sweaters, money, map.

Beth

Seventh Grade, All Saints School

Old Town Alexandria

In old town Alexandria there is a cute little shop called Unique. The things in there are nice and have reasonable prices. They have stationary, buttons, stickers, cards, little toys and more. It's a great place to buy things for young children. The service is excellent. So if you're looking for a place to shop when touring Colonial Alexandria, Unique is the place. I highly recommend this little shop because of its location near other shops, and the wide selection of items.

La Ree Pallone

the nation's capital

Not so long ago, my class went to Alexandria. I was amazed at all of the wonderful stores there. First we went on a tour called, "Doorways to Old Virginia." The tour lasted about one hour. It was not only fun, but we also learned about the colonial times, the schooner, "Alexandria", and the structure and architecture of the buildings. Then we went to the Torpedo Factory, where they actually made torpedoes for World War II. It is presently a center for the arts full of vibrant colors, spectacular shapes, and unbelievable paintings. Outside of the Torpedo Factory is a marina. The shops in Alexandria ranged from quaint little flower shops to splendid ice cream shops and toy stores. One store, Unique, is very much different than any store I've ever been in. It has little gadgets and toys on the second floor and postcards and souvenirs on the first. I recommend Alexandria for a trip that is amusing and full of pleasure.

David

I think Alexandria is a very enjoyable place to visit. It has variety of ice cream shops. We went to one ice cream shop that had not only excellent ice cream but scrumptious looking cookies and pastries. We also went to the Torpedo factory, where they didn't make torpedo's but they did make pottery. The lady's that were making the pottery did a good job. One lady was making pitchers the other lady was making bowls. In addition to the pottery, we also saw other kinds of arts, paintings, sculptures, clothing, and jewelry. We also went on to the Doorways to Old VA Tour, that was really great, we saw a lot of Shops on the tour. During our tour we saw a ship called the Alexandria it was long, we also saw a chunk of sugar shaped as a cone covered with blue paper.

Tasha Cisler

Inner Harbor

The Harbor at Baltimore is a very exciting place to go. You can go shopping at three indoor malls. The malls have everything from food to china. You could also go to one of the best aquariums on the east cost, visit some beautiful ships, go to a very interesting science museum. You can also have dinner in a restaurant that has a live band. The restaurant also serves delicious seafood & while your waiting for your food you can dance or just watch the beautiful Harbor. Sometimes you'll see a boat from a foreign shore.

Moira Lozzi

My family and I visited the Baltimore Harbor. We started at the Aquarium. When you walk in there is a big pool with dolphins. There is also a little aquariums all around with varieties of fish. There is also a place for little kids its a touching aquarium. Where you can feel, and look at different kind of fish. Then you walk upstairs and see a version of a rain forest with rare birds, waterfalls, streams and trees. (Its very humid) After the rain forest you walk down a ramp of a big aquarium of different kinds of Sharks and rare fish.

When you finished the aquarium. I would recommend the submarine right outside the aquarium. When you walk in you see where the captain and the crew, ate, slept, and
cooked the food. You can also see the control room and were they shot the torpedoes. Theres a lot more stuff you can see at the Baltimore Harbor like the Spice factory and
Water works.

Lauren Conde

K.C.'s Restaurant

I'm going to tell you about K.C.'s restaurant in Old Town Manassas. My favorite food is the chicken tenders all the other food is terrific too. The waiters & waitresses are very kind to you & if you have kids there are video games & candy machines. I really like this restaurant, I go there all the time.

Kimmie

Hard Rock Cafe

When action is where you want to be, consider the Hard Rock Cafe. The Hard Rock Cafe is a restaurant complete with a bar and loud music. From the second floor you can't help but notice that the bar is shaped like a piano. It's a great place to bring a few friends on a night on the town. The walls of course, are another thing. They're covered with everything from gold Elvis Presley records to a pink cadillac hanging from the ceiling. You can sit at a table or booth, upstairs or downstairs. The food is magnificent. They have a variety of sandwiches, subs, soups, drinks, and many other things. The lettuce is crisp and fresh, while the tomatoes are red and juicy. While you wait for your number to be called, you might want to take a look in the shop next door. It's filled with a variety of hats, t-shirts, and other memorabilia of the Rock and Roll era.

Oakton

Boy have I got a place for you! There is this little park in Oakton, Virginia. This place is a quaint scenic park. It has picnic tables right on the waterfront. At this park they have a batting cage, golf course, running and cycling path, and places where you can play volleyball, and football, and basketball. Whenever I go I pack a big lunch. We load in our bikes, running shoes, baseball and bat, volleyball and football. We don't usually play golf but if you do you will be accommodated to the best of their ability. When we are done exercising and doing our sports we sit down and eat by the waterfront. When we are done eating we watch the sun go down, and we feed the ducks our food if we have any left.

Joy Outten

Occoquan

One of my favorite places to go is Occoquan. Why? It's a very peaceful place because it's located right on the Occoquan River. You can walk across the Occoquan Bridge, or you can go into the Occoquan Museum to learn about the river, the storms there and the way it used to look. It is also famous for its shops like the bakery. The cakes and cookies taste as if you were eating at your own personal gourmet baker's. The town also has a doll shop, a Christmas shop, many antiques shops, and hand-made crafts shops. If you are looking for an enjoyable day this is the place to go. There are, of course, many enjoyable places to have dinner or lunch, especially CC's on the water. This restaurant offers dancing in the upstairs lounge, and outdoor dining in season.

Liz Williams

Westgate Shoppomg Center

I know a great place at Westgate Shopping Center in Manassas. It is called the China Jade and they have a great buffet from twelve o'clock to three o'clock. The ervice is excellent and the Chinese food is wonderful.

The people are very kind and the buffet is very inexpensive. It is not a huge place but it's just the right size.

I go there every chance I get. The light is dim and that makes it pleasant for eating. Plus after you are finished eating, you can go shopping in Marshall's, Evans, Super Crown, or The Added Touch, a gourmet shop. You only have to get into your car and drive across Sudley Road to the great Manassas Mall!

Francis Whitfield

Redskin Game

Every year we go to a preseason Redskin game at R.F.K. stadium in Washington D.C. After the game, my whole family goes to Mario's Pizza. Mario's Pizza has the best square pan-pizza you'll ever taste. It's an old place and it doesn't have many parking spaces but once you get through the long line and get up to the counter, you'll know by just the smell that the long wait was worth it. Take my advice, just go.

Mike Harar

Western Sizzlin'

Western Sizzlin' is located in Arlington. It has not only the largest salad bar I've ever seen, but it has a separate sundae bar. It is the perfect place to have a formal dinner, a delicious afternoon snack, or a wonderful lunch. Their immortal steak is mouth-watering and they even have convenient seafood in the salad bar. This huge restaurant is in Arlington but there is also a new one in Manassas where the Chesapeake Bay Seafood House was, near the Manassas Mall. All you dieters, Western Sizzling has a deLIGHTful salad bar.

Bernard Loveless

La Chappelle

La Chappelle is an exquisite formal restaurant. It is located across the street from Grace United Methodist Church in Old Town Manassas, Va. The food is excellent. The price is fairly high but it's worth it. La

Chappelle is a good place to go when you want to relax and enjoy a good meal.

Grand Pause Attic

Have I got a place for you if you like baseball cards. It has millions of cards, cases, pennants, and other collectors' items. The prices are very good there. It is not that far away. Some of the cards are worth more than $1,000.00 dollars so they are fun to see. If you want fun for the whole family come to the Grand-Pause-Attic. It is located off 66. You drive in towards Manassas and at the first Shell gas station you turn right. Take the first right on that road. Go down past all the big stores and there is a small mall. It is the fourth shop on the left.

Michael Brocki

Hunan East

There is a place just off Bristow Rd. called Hunan East. I believe it is the greatest Chinese food restaurant in all of Manassas, and I have been to almost every one! They have two statues of lions in front of the restaurant, so it makes you feel like you're going to the most exotic restaurant you've ever been to, and you probably are!

The food there is the most tasty and scrumptious food that just makes you want to eat more and more. While you're eating all that great food, take a look around you, and you'll feel like you're in China! They have a carry-out menu with the same great food in heat-consealable packages.

The wide selection ranges from an egg roll to the great Kuang-Pow beef. Try Hunan East and eat the best food. Hunan East, just off Bristow Rd. -- go ahead and eat in style.

Robert Kurian

Smithsonian National Zoological Park

The Washington Zoo is fun for all ages. It is also very educational. Children can learn a lot about animals. There is a pleasant fast-food restaurant. The Washington zoo has many species of animals that are nowhere else in the United States. The zoo also has the only pair konnotto-dragon in the western hemisphere. They also have a very large gorilla house. It may not smell good, but for people who love gorilla its a treat. They are still adding on. Soon the zoo will be larger than ever. For hildren there are many activities to keep them from getting bored. There is even a petting zoo where children can meet and greet some animals.

Union Station

When I go to Washington D.C. I always ask to go to Union Station. It is actuary a very large railroad station that has recently been renovated. You can watch trains come and go, and there is also a shop that sells model trains, which is appropriate for the setting.

There are so many shops and restaurants its as close to heaven as you can come. Inside Union Station you will find whatever kind of food you like from Chines to Italian, even good old American hotdogs and hamburgers. I don't know about you but this is the kind of place that will keep me coming back.

Brendan Hilleary

Lazy Susan Dinner Theater

The Lazy Susan Dinner Theater is fabulous place in Woodbridge, V.A. I enjoyed a fabulous play and a wonderful dinner that included roast beef, mashed potatoes w/gravy, salad, and biscuits. When I walked out side of the theater I saw an old wagon that my aunt and I were fooling around on, we also, were playing around with a carousal.

Anita Scowcroft

Torpedo Factory

I would recommend the Torpedo Factory because the building is big and exciting. It has paintings that are very original and stand out. It also has a staircase the statues all over the railings not only that is has miniature dolls built into one of the steps underneath that look so realistic.

Outside there is a dock where you can see lots of boats and just relax it a beautiful place.

Catherine Kapur

These were the suggestions of the 1st, 3rd, 4th and 7th grades at All Saints School in Manassas and excellent suggestions they were. Here are a few more suggestions and some more information on some of the attractions mentioned above.

aquariums

BALTIMORE AQUARIUM
Pier 3, 501 E Pratt Street
Baltimore, Maryland
Tel: (301) 576-3810
Hrs: Monday - Thursday 9:00 a.m. - 5:00 p.m.
Friday - Sunday 9:00 a.m. - 8:00 p.m.

Explore a South American rain forest or see the sharks in a large tank of the National Aquarium in Baltimore. A large collection of fresh water and marine life is available for viewing. Admission. Discount for Children, Military, and Senior Citizens.

NATIONAL AQUARIUM
Department of Commerce Building
14th and Constitution, NW
Washington, DC
Accessible from Federal Triangle Metro Rail.
Tel: (202) 377-2825
Hrs: Open seven days 9:00 a.m. - 5:00 p.m.
Piranha feeding
Tuesay, Thursday, and Sunday 2:00 p.m.
Accessible from Federal Triangle Metro Rail.

See over 1,000 specimens of aquatic life, including a shark tank and alligator exhibit. Hands-on exhibits include a touch-tank, where children can hold horseshoe crabs and other harmless beach creatures. Another popular activity is public piranha feeding. Admission. Discount for Children and Senior Citizens.

attractions

DINOSAUR LAND
Intersection of Routes 277, 522 and 340
Between Winchester and Front Royal, Virginia
Tel: (703) 869-2222
Hrs: Open seven days 9:30 a.m. - 6:30 p.m.
Fall and Winter 9:30 a.m. - 5:00 p.m.

Go back in time to Dinosaur Land, where 37 models of prehistoric creatures live in a small wooded park. Onlookers can stroll through the tree lined pathways and see a stegosaurus, tyrannosaurus, pteronodon and even King Kong! Each model is labeled with a bit of the creature's historical background.

Shady spots for picnicking are abundant through Dinosaur Land. A gift shop is also located on the premises.

LAND OF LITTLE HORSES
125 Glenwood Drive
Gettysburg, Pennsylvania
Tel: (717) 334-7259
Hrs: April - October 11:30, 2:30,and 4.40.
Barn Displays 10:30, 12:30, and 3:00 p.m.
Sulky races 1:30 p.m.

While visiting Gettysburg Battlefield, wander over to the nearby Land of Little Horses where toddlers and young children will be fascinated by the country's largest herd of Falabella miniature horses. Three daily half-hourshows, wagon and saddle rides, nature trails, and sulky races will delight young and old alike. Admission. Discounts for Children and Senior Citizens.

NOYES CHILDREN'S LIBRARY
10237 Carrol Place
Kensington, Maryland
Tel: (301) 949-3780
Hrs:Tuesday, Thursday, and Saturda 1:00 a.m. - 5:00 p.m.
Summer: 9:00 a.m. - 1:00 p.m.

Just for children, the Noye's Library is filled with children's literature and picture books along with furnishings just their size. It is a part of the Montgomery County Library System.

historic sites

CLAUDE MOORE COLONIAL FARM
6310 Old Georgetown Pike
McLean, Virginia
Tel: (703) 442-7557
Hrs: Wednesday. - Thursday 10:00 a.m. - 4:30 p.m.

Visitors can tour the recreation of a lower-income Colonial homestead. See the colonial family at work on the farm. Admission. Discount for children and Senior Citizens.

FRYING PAN PARK
2709 West Ox Road
Herndon, Virginia
Tel: (703) 437-9101
Hrs: Open seven days 8:30 a.m. - 5:00 p.m.
Closed Thanksgiving, Christmas and New Year's Day.

This park is a model farm of the 1920's with lots of appeal to the school-aged child. Children can observe farm life, and tour farm buildings and fields. Picnic areas are available.

MOUNT VERNON
Route 235
Mount Vernon, VA
Tel: (703) 780-2000
Hrs: November - February 9:00 a.m. - 4:00 p.m.
March. - October: 9:00 a.m. - 5:00 p.m.

Tour the home of George Washington while learning about life in the 18th century. There are features of the mansion for all ages to enjoy. A very popular tourist attraction, visitors are encouraged to visit Mount Vernon during the mornings on weekdays to avoid large crowds.

A snack bar and restaurant are located on the premises, however picnicking is not allowed on plantation grounds.Admission. Discount for Children and Senior Citizens.Children, under six are free.

NATIONAL COLONIAL FARM
3400 Bryan Point Road
Accokeek, MD
Tel: (301) 283-2113
Hrs: Tuesday - Sunday 10:00 - 5:00 a.m.
Closed on Thanksgiving, Christmas and New Years.

Located on the Potomac River across from Mount Vernon, visitors can explore the re-creation of a mid-18th century tobacco plantation. Children can observe farming methods and learn about family life during this period in history by touring the farm. Children are free.

OXON HILL FARM
6411 Oxon Hill Road
Oxon Hill, Maryland
(Beltway Exit 3A)
Tel: (301) 839-1177
Hrs: Open seven days 8:30 a.m. - 5:00 p.m.
Closed Thanksgiving, Christmas and New Year's Day.
(Beltway Exit 3A)

Oxon Hill is a turn-of-the-century working farm. Toddlers and young children will enjoy petting the animals. Older children can learn more about animal care and farming techniques.

SULLY HISTORIC PLANTATION
Fairfax County Park Authority
3701 Pender Drive, Fairfax Drive
Fairfax, VA
Tel: (703) 437-1794
Hrs: Wednesday - Monday 11:00 a.m. - 4:30 p.m.

Visitors can visualize living in the 18th century during a tour of this restored 1794 mansion. Slip back in time when you visit Richard Bland Lee's colonial home. Nooks and crannies are stocked with curious items that were vital to gracious living in the 18th century. Candle rimmers, sugar cones, bed warmers, fine china, and boot jacks are just a few of the items.

The staff is always eager to share points of interest that serve to enliven historical facts and flesh-out our forebearers. For instance, some Colonial households such as Sully plantation had an access to the roof with a bucket of water close by, which was an early form of fire prevention. Many mysteries of early American living unfold as these new insights are revealed. Small charge for admission.

museums

CAPITAL CHILDREN'S MUSEUM
800 Third Street, NE
Washington, D C
(Metro Red Line - Union Station)
Tel: (202) 543-8600
Hrs: Tuesday - Sunday 10:00 a.m. - 5:00 p.m.

Hands-on exhibits allow children opportunities to work with computers and puzzles, experiment with machines, and learn about sound and cultures. Interesting exhibits for all ages. Children under two are admitted free. Discount for Senior Citizens.

CLOISTERS CHILDREN'S MUSEUM
10440 Fall Road
Brooklandville, MD (Baltimore County)
Tel: (301) 823-2500
Hrs: Wednesday - Friday 10:00 a.m. - 4:00 p.m.
Saturday and Sunday Noon - 4:00 p.m.

Children ages two to 12 will delight in the hands-on exhibits and demonstrations. Admission. Discount for children and Senior Citizens.

DOLL'S HOUSE AND TOY MUSEUM
5236 4th Street, NW
Chevy Chase, MD
Tel: (301) 244-0024
Hrs: Tuesday - Saturday 10:00 a.m. - 5:00 p.m.
Sunday Noon - 5:00 p.m.
Closed on Thanksgiving, Christmas and New Year's.

Displays of antique dolls, doll houses, toys and games are beautifully arranged in this museum for all ages. Christmas, Halloween, Easter and other holidays, exhibits are always eye-catching. Special arrangements for birthday parties can be made. Doll supplies are available and there is consignment shop for antique dolls and toys. Admission. Discount for children and Senior Citizens.

NAVAL MUSEUM
Ninth and M Streets
Washington, DC
Tel: (703) 433-4882
Hrs: Monday - Friday 9:00 a.m. - 5: 00 p.m.
Saturday, Sunday, and holidays 10:00 a.m. - 5:00 p.m.
June - August
Wednesday 9:00 a.m. - 8:30 p.m.

Youngsters will enjoy the playground type museum with hands-on exhibits. Children can board a ship, climb on a cannon and play with actual weaponry. Breakfast and lunch can be purchased at the Snack Bar.

RAILROAD STATION MUSEUM
Main Street and Maryland Avenue
Ellicott City, MD
Tel: (301) 461-1944
Hrs: Wednesday - Saturday 11:00 a.m. - 5:00 p.m
Sunday Noon - 5:00 p.m.

A diorama depicting the trip of Tom Thumb is included in the exhibits of the Railroad Station Museum. Weekend excursions are available from September 1 through October 15 on a variety of vintage trains. Prices vary, depending on the length of the trip, and children under four are free.

TROLLEY MUSEUM
Northwest Branch Regional Park
Bonipart Road between Layhill Road and New Hampshire Ave.
North of Wheaton, MD
Tel: (301) 384-6088
Hrs: Saturday and Sunday 12:00 noon - 5:00 p.m.

European and American trolleys are featured in this museum. Rides are available. Children under two are free. A model trolley is displayed, which children can operate.

parks

BEN LOMOND PARK
7500 Ben Lomond Park Drive
Manassas, VA
Tel: (703) 361-7126 Metro 690-3878

Watch your children's eyes sparkle as morning's studies are rewarded by shooting down the Hydrotube and Hydrowhip at Ben Lomond Park! The cool down may continue with a dip in the 50-meter pool, followed by a few rounds at the mini-golf course. Youngsters may also unwind at the well-equipped playground. Tennis and racquetball courts are also available,

Other public parks within easy driving distance of Washington, D.C. are:

GLEN ECHO PARK
MacArthur Boulevard at Goldsboro Road
Glen Echo, MD
Tel: (301) 492-6663
Hrs: May - September 30
Wednesday and Thursday 10:00 a.m. - 2:00 p.m.
Saturday and Sunday Noon - 6:00 p.m.

Children can ride bunnies, ostriches, a tiger, and horses, or any of the other animals that can be found spinning on the carousel in Glen Echo Park. Home of one of twenty-seven Dentzel Carousels in the United States, Glen Echo Park also is home for Puppet Company Playhouse

(301) 20-6668 and Adventure Theater (301) 320-5331, where performances of children's shows are staged.

LAKE RIDGE PARK
12350 Cotton Mill Drive
Woodbridge, VA 22192
Tel: (703) 494-528

Lake Ridge Park features a marina with a variety of boats for rent. There is a ramp for launching private boats as well. The fishing is more relaxing than challenging, the nature trails are long and winding, and miniature golf is, as always, intriguing for old and young alike.

Choose from a variety of different boats to rent from Lake Ridge Park Marina or launch your own craft using their ramp. Both recreational boating and fishing are available. Cool lake breezes gently ease tensions while waiting for fish to nibble.

Explore the long, winding nature trails with family and friends or commune with nature on your own.

LOCUST SHADE REGIONAL PARK
4701 Locust Shade Drive
Triangle, VA 22172
Tel: (703) 221-2158 or 221-8579

High points of the park include: a golf driving range, a batting cage, a marina, week-end fishing, miniature golf, tennis courts, pavilions, a volleyball court, playgrounds and over six miles of fitness trails.

Enhance golf and baseball skills at Locust Shade's driving range and batting cage. Enjoy other sports such as miniature golf, tennis, volleyball.

Pavilions, some which include electricity, provide a dry area for picnics. Youngsters may frolic at the nearby playgrounds as the adults may socialize or barbecue.

In keeping with our national interest in health, Locust Shade Park also has over six miles of fitness trails.

ROCK CREEK PARK AND NATURE CENTER
5200 Glover Road NW
Washington, DC
Tel. (202) 426-6833
Hrs: Shows

Saturday and Sunday	1:00 p.m., 4:00 p.m.
Nature Walk	
Saturday and Sunday	3:00 p.m.

Golf, bike trails, horseback riding, as well as picnic groves with tables are available. Fireplaces and shelters are also available for pleasurable outings in the Rock Creek Park. The Rock Creek Nature Center, open daily except Mondays, boasts outstanding exhibits for children including nature walks, bird feeding workshops, and planetarium shows. Tickets are free and are distributed 30 minutes prior to the show.

VETERANS MEMORIAL PARK
14300 Featherstone Road
Woodbridge, VA 22191
Tel: (703) 491-2183

Facilities to be enjoyed are: a 50-meter pool, a 400-foot AguaLuge waterslide, a weight room, tennis courts, pavilions, a gymnasium, a 34-mile wooded nature trail, a playground, outdoor basketball courts, as well as areas for softball and soccer.

If you relish cool, wet speed on a blistering day, try Veterans Memorial Park's 400 foot AguaLuge waterslide. Others may appreciate a leisurely dip in the 50-meter pool.

Young and old may ramble this natural, peaceful escape from hectic daily life. Playgrounds absorb the excess energy of children with sturdily built, stimulating play equipment.

zoological parks

PET FARM PARK
2338 Hunter Mill Road
Vienna, VA
Tel: (703) 759-3636
Open seven days from April to October.
Hrs: Weekends 10:00 a.m. - 6:00 p.m.
Weekdays 10:00 a.m. - 5:00 p.m.

Spend the day at the farm, feeding and petting exotic and domestic animals. Enjoy elephant rides, pony rides, and hayrides.

NATIONAL ZOO
3001 Connecticut Avenue, NW
Washington, DC
(Metro Red Line - National Zoo)
Tel: (202) 673-4800
Hrs: Open seven days, weather permitting, except Christmas.
May 1 - September 15:
Grounds 8:00 a.m. - 8:30 p.m.
Animal buildings9:00 a.m. - 6:00 p.m.
September 16 - April 30:
Grounds 8:00 a.m. - 6:00 p.m.
Animal buildings 9:00 a.m. - 4:30 p.m.

Visit white tigers, panda bears, giraffes, monkeys, hippos-- a few of the animals living in the National Zoo. Three family learning centers are available. Zoo Lab, Bird Lab, and Herb Lab, provide opportunities for children and adults to learn more about the zoo. Public transportation is available by Metro Rail and is recommended, as parking areas fill quickly. Food and light concessions are available as well as picnic areas. Admission is free.

the nation's capital

SECTION EIGHT: SENIOR SIFTINGS

Many discounts are available to Senior Citizens (in addition to seats on the Metro) who can, and want to, show proof of being over age 60. The GOLD MINE is a free directory published by the District government. Ask at any information desk, the place where you are staying or call the Visitor Information Center at (202) 789-7000.

Be sure to take your AARP membership card when you travel. There are discounts for you, especially at hotels and motels.

Senior Centers throughout the area are active and offer many scheduled events and If contacted may be able to give you some information on senior events.

Senior Center Listings

Baley's Senior Center
Woodrow Willson Library
Falls Church, VA 22041
Tel: (703) 820-2131

Devonshire Senior Center
2831 Grahm Road
Falls Church, VA 22042
Tel: (703) 698-5799

Groveton Senior Center
Groveton Elementary School
6900 Harrison Lane
Alexandria, VA 22306
Tel: (703) 765-7011

Hollin Hall Senior Center
1500 Shenandoah Road
Alexandria, VA 22308
Tel: (703) 765-4573

Lewinsville Senior Cente
1609 Great Falls Street
McLean, VA 22101
Tel: (703) 442-9075

Lincolnia Senior Center
4710 North Chambliss Street
Alexandria, VA 22312
Tel: (703) 914-0223

Reston-Herndon Senior Center
1850 Cameron Glen Drive
Reston ,VA 22091
Tel: (703) 481-4200

Springfield Senior Center
Springfield Estates
6200 Charles C. Goff Drive
Springfield, VA 22150
Tel: (703) 971-5248

Viena-McLean Senior Center
Pimmit Hills Center
7510 Lisle Avenue
Falls Church, VA 22043
Tel: (703) 743-3338

Wakefield Senior Center
8100 Braddock Road
Annandale, VA 22003
Tel: (703) 321-3000

SECTION NINE: FREE FUN

The Nation's Capital is a place for marvelous entertainment and a great deal of it is yours for the asking. No matter how much research is done, things change and information becomes dated. Every effort has been made to assure the correctness of phone numbers at time of publication so please use these numbers to do a little advance planning of you own to make sure you are able to enjoy the Free Fun.

Take in free summer concerts every other Sunday 1:30 p.m. - 4:00 p.m. at **30th and Jefferson Streets.**

Hike, bike, or canoe along the towpath of the **Chesapeake & Ohio Canal**. The Canal was built between 1828 and 1850 and provided barge traffic between Georgetown and Cumberland, Maryland (202) 472-4376.

Beautiful flowers and flowering trees grace **Columbia Island** and make it a beautiful place for a picnic. Located on the island is **Lady Bird Johnson Park**, dedicated to the former First Lady for her efforts to increase the beauty of America. An unadorned red granite monument is there, dedicated to her husband, Lyndon B. Johnson. A little known memorial to the Navy and Marine Corps can also be found in the park. Open daylight hours.

A peaceful respite can be found between the Washington Monument and the Lincoln Memorial at the **Constitution Gardens** (Constitution Ave. and 18th St., N.W.). Fifty acres of rolling grass and wooded park has replaced the "temporary" government buildings from the post World War II era. On an island in the six-acre lake is a memorial to the signers of the Declaration of Independence. It's a favorite spot for ducks and people. This relatively new park is a welcome addition to the myriad of city parks available for a quick lunch and a moment of nature or people watching amid the hustle and bustle of city life.

Found directly above the Smithsonian's underground portion, you will find the **Enid A. Haupt Garden** (1000 Independence Ave., S.W.). Complete with flowers, shrubs and trees, the Victorian setting is highlighted by tea roses and magnolias.

In April of each year, Shakespeare's birthday is celebrated in fitting tradition at the **Folger Shakespeare Library** (Union Square or Capitol

South Metro stops, 201 E. Capitol St.,). In the spring, there are elementary and high school festivals to delight children of all ages. April 15 through Labor Day, Sunday 10:00 a.m. - 4:00 p.m.; Monday. - Saturday 10:00 a.m. - 4:00 p.m. Not open on holidays. Volunteers are available to answer questions in the exhibit hall Monday - Friday 11:00a.m. - 1:00 p.m. (202) 544-7077

One of the grandest amusement parks of its time, **Glen Echo Park** (MacArthur Boulevard, MD) now provides a delightful place for a picnic or dreaming of those days gone by while riding the antique, hand-carved, hand-painted, Dentzel carousel for 50 cents! Festivals with folk and ethnic music are held twice during the summer and usually, there is something happening on summer Sunday afternoons. It's always open, but the carousel operates May - September, Wednesday: 10:00 a.m. - 2:00 p.m.; Saturday - Sunday: noon to 5:00 p.m. (301) 492-6229.Recording (301) 492-6282

An ancient teahouse imported from Japan in 1960 commemorates the Treaty of Friendship between the United States and Japan can be found in the **Gardens of the Japanese Embassy** (2520 Massachusetts Ave., N.W.). Open May-October by appointment only. (202) 939-6700.

With a beautiful rooftop view of the Potomac River, the **Kennedy Center** (New Hampshire Ave. and F St., N.W.) features three theaters, a symphony hall and opera house. They offer free guided tours to explain the building's layout and architecture. During the Christmas season there is a program of seasonal music. Throughout the year they provide a free kids' series.

There is an impressive **Marine Sunset Parade** at the Marine Corps Memorial (Rosslyn Metro stop, Between Rosslyn and the Arlington National Cemetery, Meade & Fairfax Dr.) during the summer, Tuesdays at 7:00 p.m. (703) 285-2598.

Very small trees and extremely large goldfish can be found at the **National Arboretum** (3501 New York Ave., N.E.). The 444-acre site features spectacular displays of flowering shrubs and trees, hollies and evergreens, herbs and Japanese Bonsai trees (a Bicentennial gift from the people of Japan). Open Monday - Friday 8:00 a.m. - 5:00 p.m.; weekends 10:00 a.m. - 5:00 p.m. (202) 475-4815.

The Explorers Hall at the National Geographic Society (Farragut North or Dupont Circle Metro stops, 17th and M Sts., N.W.) offers a wide variety of exhibits commemorating over a hundred years of exploration, education, and adventure. **The Grosvenor Auditorium** film lectures require tickets that can be purchased in advance or thirty minutes prior to the presentation. Programs are free Tuesdays at noon. The many free displays and programs depict other world cultures, archaeological finds, space marvels, ocean wonders, and geographical facts. They evoke the same kind of interest and provide the same quality we have come to know and expect of their magazine. Open Monday - Saturday 9:00 a.m. - 5:00 p.m.; Sunday 10:00 a.m. - 5:00 p.m. (202) 857-7588.

National Symphony summer concerts are performed on the West Terrace, the Capitol, and on the Mall.

Lions, tigers, and bears can be found at the **National Zoo** (Woodley Park or Zoo Metro stops, 3000 block of Connecticut Ave., N.W.) along with birds, lizards, hippopotami and giant pandas in the most natural surroundings possible. Over 3,000 animals in a modern 165-acre park setting spark interest and curiosity. The Great Flight Cage gives the impression of observing from the wild. Children have a lot to learn at the Zoolab where they participate in hands-on activity. Zoo Sunset Serenades June and July Tel: (202) 673-4717 Open daily, April 1 - October 15, 8:00 a.m. - 8:00 p.m. and October 15 - March 31, 8:00 a.m. - 6:00 p.m. All buildings close at 4:30 p.m. year round. (202) 673-4714/4955.

Special music and theater at the **National Theater** (1321 Pennsylvania Ave, N.W.) is free on Monday nights for the National Showcase series in the **Helen Hayes Gallery**. Showtimes are 7:00 p.m. and 8:30 p.m., first come, first seated. You will also find free entertainment for children on Saturday mornings. (202) 783-3370.

The musical bell tower seen from Rt 50 near the Marine Corps Memorial is the **Netherlands Carillion**, given to the United States after World War II by the Netherlands. The 49 bells blend in harmony to make beautiful music for free concerts Saturdays, April - September, and National Holidays throughout the year 2:00 p.m. - 4:00 p.m. NOTE: While in the area, it's an excellent time to visit the Marine Corps Memorial.

The Coast Guard Lightship Chesapeake, now decommissioned, is being used by the National Park Service to present educational programs and provide marine biology, pollution, and navigation displays. There is an aquarium stocked with fish from the Potomac River. Open Tuesday, Thursday, and Saturday 1:00 p.m. - 4:00 p.m. (202) 426-6896.

Observe flour and cornmeal being produced the old-fashion way at **Pierce Mill** (Beach Dr. and Tilden St., N.W.). The overshot water mill was built by Isaac Pierce on Rock Creek in 1820. Production ceased after 70 years of operation, but the mill has been completely restored and is now back in business. Open Wednesday - Sunday 8:00 a.m. - 4:30 p.m. (202) 426-6908.

The Sunset Parade at the old Marine Barracks Quadrangle (8th and I Sts., SE) is pomp and circumstance at its finest. The Marine Corps color guard ceremoniously honors the national flag with the music of the Marine Corps Band Drum and Bugle Corps. The Silent Drill Team carries on a traditional display that is unequalled in the field of drill and ceremony. May - August, 8:45 p.m.. Call for reservations three weeks in advance at (202) 433-6060.

During the warm, summer months of May through September, there are a wide variety of free dramas, puppet shows, concerts and pageants at the **Sylven Theatre** (The grounds of the Washington Monument). (202) 433-4011. A summer military band concert series is also held at the Sylven Theater (S) or the Capitol west steps (C) at 8:00 p.m.

Air Force	Tuesday (C) Friday (S) Tel: (202) 767-5658
Army	Tuesday (S) Friday (C) Tel: (202) 696-3399
Navy	Monday (C) Thursday (S) Tel: (202) 433-2525
Marines	Wednesday (C) Sunday (S) Tel: (202) 433-4011

The "Lone Sailor" is not alone at the **U.S. Navy Memorial** (Between 7th and 9th on Pennsylvania Ave., N.W.). Military bands perform nightly during the months of May through September. (202) 524-0830.

the nation's capital

THE NATION'S CAPITAL BIBLIOGRAPHY

A Guide To Prince Georges County Maryland by Windsor Publications, Inc., Ed. Gerry Price; Lanham, MD: Windsor Publications,

A Window on Williamsburg by John J. Walklet, Jr., Thomas K. Z. Ford and Donna C. Sheppard; New York, NY: Holt, Rinehart, 1983.

The Battle of Ball's Bluff; Small Battle Long Shadow by Byron Farwell; McLean, VA: EPM Publications, 1990.

Battle of Ball's Bluff by Joseph D. Patch; Leesburg, VA: Potomac Press, 1958.

The Best of Washington D.C. by Gault Millau; New York, NY: Prentice Hall, 1988.

Arlington Chamber of Commerce Membership and Business Referral Directory by Jack Bauer; Richmond, VA: Hart Publishers Inc., 1990.

Arlington County in Virginia: A Pictoral History Nan and Ross Netherland; Norfolk, VA: The Donning Company, 1987.

Colonial Williamsburg Its Buildings and Gardens by A. Lawrence Kocher and Howard Dearstyne; New York, NY: Holt

Elephants and Quaker Guns by Jane Chapman Whitt; Arlington, VA: Vandamere Press, 1884.

Exclusively Washington Trivia by Anthony S. Pitch; Potomac, MD: Mino Publications, 1989.

Fodor's 89 Washington, D.C.; ed. Andrew Beresky and Candice Gianette; New York, NY: Fodor's Travel Publications, Inc., 1989.

In Honored Glory by Philip Bigler; Arlington, VA: Vandamere Press, 1987.

Frommer's Washington D.C. by Rena Bulkin and Faye Hammel; New York,NY: Simon & Schuster, 1989.

Frommer's Washington, D.C. and Historic Virginia on $40 a day by Rena Bulkin; New York, NY: Prentice Hall, 1988.

bibliography

Going Places With Children in Washington; Ed. Sally Shannon and Ruth Ann Phang, Rockville, MD: Green Acres School, 1985.

Guide Book of Washington; Fairfax, VA: Prince.

The New Settler's Guide for Washington D.C.; ed. Robert B. Minogue; Potomac, MD: Robert B. Minogue, 1990.

Saturday's Child by Deborah Churchman and Anne H. Oman; Washington, D.C.: Washington Book Co., 1987.

The Smithsonian Experience; Washington D.C.: The Smithsonian Institution,1977.

The Smithsonian Guide to Historic America; Ed. Roger G. Kennedy; New York, NY: Stewart, Tabori & Chang, 1989.

Steeplechasing and Fox Hunting by Michael Seth-Smith; London, England: New English Library Ltd., 1977.

Virginia Spring/Summer Travel Guide; Virginia, 1989.

Washington D.C. Visitor's Guide; ed. Elizabeth M. Tusing; Bethesda, MD: Bell Alantic, 1990,1991.

Washington D.C. Official National Park Guidebook; Washington D.C.: U.S. Department of the Interior, 1989.

Washingtonian Magazine; Ed. John A. Limpert; Washington D.C., July 1990.

Washington In Focus by Philip Bigler; Arlington, VA: Vandamere Press, 1988.

Washington Itself by E.J. Applewhite; Washington, D.C.: Knopf, 1981.

Washington Flyer Magazine; Ed. Brian Cook; Washington, D.C., July/August 1990.

Washington, D.C. The Complete Guide by Judy Duffield, William Kramer & Cynthia Sheppard; New York, NY: Vintage Books, 1989.
Washington The Nation's Capital; Fairfax, VA: L. B. Prince Co.

INDEX

notes notes notes notes notes notes

notes notes notes notes notes notes

notes notes notes notes notes notes

notes notes notes notes notes notes

notes notes notes notes notes notes

* compliments * counsel * complaints *

mail to: Daniel Webster Herlong

P.O. Box 8225

Falls Church, VA 22041